THE LAST FREE MAN IN AMERICA:

MEETS THE SYNTHETIC SUBVERSION

AN AUTOBIOGRAPHY

BY

GATEWOOD GALBRAITH

1/22/11

To Tyler -

Enjoy!

Gatewood Galbraith

August 2, 2004
Mark Perkins Press
Lexington, Kentucky

THE LAST FREE MAN IN AMERICA: Meets the Synthetic Subversion.

www. gatewood .com

Library of Congress Cataloging-in-Publication Data

Gatewood Galbraith 1947-
The Last Free Man in America: Meets the Synthetic Subversion /
Gatewood Galbraith—4th ed.—January, 2009

ISBN 1-59975-670-6

1.Freedom—Politics. 2. Freedom—Marijuana. 3. Guns—Politics
4. Freedom—Militia. 5. Constitution—Freedom. 6. Privacy—Freedom.

10 9 8 7 6 5 4

Mark Perkins Press
Mark Perkins, Publisher

Printed in the United States of America
on acid free recycled paper

TABLE OF CONTENTS

TABLE OF CONTENTS *cont.*

TABLE OF CONTENTS *cont.*

TABLE OF CONTENTS *cont.*

The Book...The Book...Ah yes, The Book! My Book! That as-of-yet non-tangible, that concept-to-be-given-form, that thing which will not just materialize out of thin air without sweat equity on my part, a burden brought on by the expectation on the part of certain people that I possess the ability to actually get it done. It has remained just beyond my vision and grasp for some time now, but other people must see it because they ask me all the time, "Gatewood, why don't you write a book?"

I kind of grin and say, "About what?" and they laugh out loud and offer all kinds of descriptions about what they think I have to offer. "About your politics Gatewood, your life. You've run for Commissioner of Agriculture once, Governor three times, Congress twice and once for Attorney General. You're the most successful Independent candidate in America over the past 50 years and you've set all kinds of voting records for third parties in the Commonwealth of Kentucky. You've practiced law for 23 years. You've traveled the world as a spokesperson for changing the cannabis/hemp/marijuana laws and been befriended by Willie Nelson and others. You've also smoked some the best marijuana in the world over the past 35 years. Write about that stuff, Gatewood. We'd like to hear it."

And deep down, I mean really deep down, I am at once both titillated and horrified by the prospect of examining myself and my actions over the years, the self-discovery that it entails and the willingness and ability to couch it in terms that make it worthwhile to have done; and interesting enough to others who might want to take the time to examine it with me. But just because my perspectives and actions have kept me amused all of these years doesn't mean that others might have the same reaction.

Oh, there is little doubt in my mind that I can make various segments of my life interesting to certain markets. I mean, Sex, Drugs and Rock and Roll will always sell, especially when wrapped around politics. And, let's face it, my history as a "Child of the 60's" allowed me to experience it all. (Well, maybe not all of it. There are some things I haven't done but luckily I'm at that age where I can't remember what I haven't done so I don't feel compelled to run out and fill in any gaps with unconsidered behavior.)

And I understand that those of us who experienced the 60s and early 70s as teenagers and young adults were offered a unique opportunity for experimentation and self-exploration which was unavailable to prior generations and illegal for subsequent ones. Large segments of society were in flux, the streets seemed alive and the love seemed free. It was a scintillating smorgasbord of opportunity for a young man willing to take some chances and I reckon I fit that description. The choices I made weren't always the best, or wisest, but none of them have been fatal, as of yet. So I can't help feeling that I may have gotten away with something somewhere down the line, but don't we all?

Fact is though, while some of the paths that I walk now were discovered and decided upon during those tumultuous times, the older I get, the more I recognize that most of my values and core behaviors were taught me long before I reached my majority. And any later deviations from doing the right thing were solely of my own doing. Let's face it, Mom wouldn't have approved of a lot of it, then or now, and that's what has kept this book in my head and off of paper for all this time. Or, at least, that's my excuse. But of this I have no doubt; if it weren't for an exceptionally good Mom and the threat of Eddyville Maximum Security Prison, I would have gone really bad a long time ago.

Truthfully, the real reason this book hasn't been written yet is that I seem to be overcome by waves of inertia and bouts of ennui whenever I think of the task. Competing head on with that is an unquenchable desire to count for something in this life, to believe that my experiences and observations are worthwhile to record and offer for consideration by others for their merit or folly. But believing it ought to be written and doing it are obviously two different things.

The task of remembering the events, judging their "newsworthiness", discriminating as to what I should leave out, hedging my bets so as not to uncover anything that ought to remain covered and transferring all of those mental impulses simultaneously from my brain to my fingertips to the keyboard in a cogent form seems to be an almost impossible chore; and then I watch it done by others and I hear deep down that old standard rallying cry that has aroused me from comfortable inaction in the past, "If they can do it, I can too!" And that generally is enough to activate me and I'm off to the races.

Then I hear my mother saying to me in that mother's tone of voice, which is meant to tell their child that only a pure idiot would disagree with them. "Well, if 'They' jumped off a cliff, would you do it too?"

And she's right of course. Just because other people have written books, exposing their private thoughts and behaviors, doesn't mean I should and that's the real key to it. How much am I willing to reveal about my past to the reader? Or to myself?

An examination of my own life in detail minute enough to try and explain my past actions, intimate and otherwise, has, until recently, been discomforting to me. The Good Lord knows that I've made more than my share of mistakes. In fact, if trial and error is the best teacher, I ought to be the smartest guy around.

But my biggest fear of writing about myself has been the necessity of revealing just how much I haven't gotten done in this life, probably because of my fascination with women. I've spent more time than I can ever admit to in this small a book thinking about women and I always felt a little guilty about it.

Shouldn't I be spending my life's time by reading classical literature, studying medicine, taking taekwondo, pondering quantum physics or actually improving my mind or body in some manner instead of thinking about how to please a particular woman in my life, whenever it's not otherwise occupied by the practical affairs of staying alive? You would think so.

However, the truth be known, a recent study about men has altered my point of view about how guilty I should be feeling about my lifelong libidinous nature.

According to this survey, the average man thinks about sex every 5.6 seconds. What a relief! I'm not even worried that, for me, it's every 3.1 seconds.

In fact, it's a double relief.

For some time now, I've been asked the question, "Gatewood, don't you ever freak out?" And my truthful answer has been, "Every 3 seconds." Now I see that I've probably been freaking out about sex all this time because it's a male hormonal thing and I could not bring myself to admit the basis of it. And all this time I thought it was because I was raised Catholic.

Now that I see how that works, I think I can get this Baby off the ground.

First, I'm going to try to follow certain guidelines.

For instance I'm only going to use descriptions like jackasses, and more colorful euphemisms, on those politicians and assorted newspaper editors who really deserve it. I mean, I've met a lot of people who partially fit into one of these categories, but this book is too small, so I'm only going to name the ones who truly deserve inclusion. The Best of the Worst. The rest of you know who you are.

Second, I'm not going to name names of those ladies who have treated me with kindness. This book is not small enough. You know who you are. (I hope you remember.)

Third, I'm going to have to leave out mentioning a lot of intelligent, artistic, beautiful, sensitive people who have made my life worthwhile by sharing their time and intelligence with me. Some of you know who you are and others of you will never know what you might have taught me by an offhand remark or by my observation of you in any number of circumstances. I have witnessed ten thousand acts of courage and cowardice and learned a little about myself with each one. That's the blessing and the curse of a sentient human being.

Fourth, I am not going to try and meet anyone's expectation of this being great literature. I am, after all, a product of the University of Kentucky's Open Admission Policy so I'll only try to meet the standard of a description crafted by one of America's great poets, John Prine. "It is what it is and it ain't what it ain't."

Fifth, Kids, don't try some of these things at home without adult supervision. Some of the things I did weren't very smart and the way I see it, this society is in a hell of a shape if I'm a candidate to be a hero.

Sixth, I'm not going to write about the really bad stuff I've been into or had happen to me. This is not one of those tell-alls and I sure as hell ain't looking for any sympathy. Going through two bankruptcies, sleeping in the back of my car and feeling my heart shatter in a million, cajillion pieces was bad enough while I was going through it. I don't plan on revisiting it, especially in front of all you folks. This is my book, after all, and I always tell my clients to get over the human Compulsion to Confess. Good advice for everyone.

Seventh, I reserve the right to ignore all of the above guidelines. Hell, it's my book and I have a pretty good idea of who I am. Sometimes. And I expect to find out a lot more as I go along. Thanks for coming with me.

❖ *Childhood*

I was born in Carlisle, Kentucky (pop. 1520) on January 23, 1947, the fourth of seven children born to Henry Clay (H.C.) and Dollie Galbraith. This was pure luck for me because less forgiving parents would have arranged for my disappearance a long time ago. I won't come right out and say that I was a difficult child, but when Mom and Dad went out for the evening, they hired two baby-sitters. One for me and one for the other six kids.

In retrospect, I can only conclude that it was as close to an idyllic upbringing as any child could want. Dad was an inveterate worker with a large family to support and he wore several hats while Mom worked 24/7 at home to keep us bathed, fed and civilized. This was not, however, an easy task and the things we got into, and by with, simply because there were so many of us would horrify even the most hardened Social Service case worker today.

The trees we climbed, the holes we dug, the animals we hunted, the shots we fired, the arrows we aimed, the fires we started, the dares we issued, the fights we had and the chances we took were the stuff of Huck Finn.

Carlisle, Kentucky, the Little Town With a Big Heart, sits on the rocky ridges west of the Appalachians, on the fringes of the Bluegrass Region of Central Kentucky. Like hundreds of other communities throughout the Commonwealth, it depended on farming in general and tobacco in particular for its economy during the early 1900's. Likewise, it secured several small textile factories for its manufacturing base and therefore could offer its citizens an opportunity to be born there, grow up there, get a job, fall in love, raise a family, live and die there because the modest economy could support them if they worked hard.

H.C. Galbraith was born in rural Nicholas County in 1910, the fourth of five children born to Ma (Edna) and Pa (Henry) Galbraith. Pa was a "Raleigh" man who traveled the county in a horse drawn wagon peddling Raleigh products ranging from scissors and twine to pots and pans. He made a decent living and everyone in the family worked hard. A formal education didn't seem to be a necessity if you worked hard enough.

Dad quit school after 10th grade and went to work for the highway department running heavy equipment and building roads. While Pa had a reputation for being a teetotaler (that's a non-drinker to you young'uns) Dad had developed a taste for alcohol, dancing and new automobiles and had somewhat of a reputation for being a ladies man because of it. (I once asked Dad how he could drink so much and he told me that, after Prohibition, it all tasted like soda pop.)

H.C. was handsome, energetic, outgoing and quite the eligible bachelor when he had the great fortune to meet, woo and marry an equally eligible young woman, who subsequently would give him seven children and do her damnedest to put up with him, through thick and thin.

Dollie Elizabeth Gatewood was born to Quince Tilford and Agatina Gatewood in Georgetown, Kentucky on April 26, 1913. She was the oldest of three girls and, after moving between Carlisle and Frankfort during the early stretch, the family settled in Carlisle where Quince operated a drug store and soda fountain on Main Street. They say that he was so tight with money that he used to turn the lights off until a customer actually came into the place to shop. Mom's parents put a high value on education and after graduating from Carlisle High School, she went off to college and got her teaching degree from Peabody College in Knoxville, Tennessee in 1934.

Returning to Carlisle, she helped her family run the store which became the gathering place for the younger set in the town and it was there that H.C. met Dollie and began the romance that resulted in, among other things, yours truly.

The Depression was in full swing at this time but H. always had spending money in his pocket because he worked from sun up to way past sun down. There was no doubt in Mom's mind that he loved her and would be a good provider. When he proposed, she accepted and they were married on May 5th, 1937. Her parents approved and had only one admonition to their new son-in-law. Quince took H. aside. "Just don't interfere with her religion," he said.

At the time they got married, Dad had a job as a gasoline truck driver with a route between Lexington and Carlisle. He earned $125 a month and out of that they bought a house, a car and all of their groceries. My oldest sister Judy arrived in 1939, followed by Elizabeth in '42, Henry Clay Jr. in '45 and Louis Gatewood on January 23, 1947. Soon thereafter came Edna ('50), Michael ('52) and Timothy ('55). Mom was actually pregnant 11 times with seven survivors. I guess Dad took his father-in-law's advice not to interfere with her religion. Catholic, to be sure.

Mom was a devout Catholic and Dad supported her as such in every way but was not a church-goer himself. Mom never missed a Mass and I'm sure that every priest who came to the parish during those years could count on Dollie for whatever the church needed, whether it was support for a project or a meal for the priest or a parishioner, of whom there were few.

I remember being an altar boy along with my brother from the time I was 7 years old. This basically means that we would assist the priest in the Mass and, as we turned toward the audience, I would count the house. On most Sundays there would be 25 to 30 folks there with most of them related to me. The priests themselves were fairly non-descript and they must have been straight or else my brother and I were the ugliest altar boys in the universe.

In fact, the biggest scandal to hit the church came when I learned the priest's part of the Mass also and said it along with him in a deeper voice which drowned out his. It was not the only time in my life when I was told to quit being so fervent but at that age I persisted under my breath, sure that I was headed for priesthood and all the blessings that came with it. Of course, the words priest and Indictment were hardly ever mentioned in the same breath in those days.

Things sure were different back then. The 1950s in many small towns in America were not far different from their portrayal as Mayberry, the slow-moving, laid back community immortalized by Andy Griffith. We had our village idiots, town drunks and the two-cell jail where the jailer's wife would fix you biscuits, gravy and extra sausage if you looked a little down on your luck.

There were many thriving storefronts on Main Street and only a few vacant ones. There were three variety stores, three drug stores, two pool halls, several clothing stores for both men and women, three banks and a weekly newspaper.

Carlisle is the county seat of Nicholas County and the Courthouse sits on a hill on its own block in the middle of town. Back then it was the center of the towns commerce and social life. When the weather was decent, the old men would gather on the Courthouse lawn, sitting on benches or squatting on their haunches, chewing tobacco and swapping lies. Everybody knew everybody and nobody got away with much. Lord help us if the Galbraith children misbehaved because the news of it would reach home before we did.

By the early 50's Dad had made his mark in the town. He owned a little 10 vehicle Buick agency, a garage and a small farm where it was rumored that a still could be found if a person knew where to look. We had one of the larger houses in town with a couple of acres and a barn out back, where we kept a goat named George, a pony named Surprise, a standard-bred named Midnight and a zillion unnamed earthworms just waiting to be dug up by hand, put in a can and drowned in the reservoir two miles from our house. I could be found there on almost any summer day and most school days after class.

Nowadays, I guess, any parent who let a 9 year old take a fishing pole, walk two miles along a highway and spend the afternoon by himself, exploring a large body of water, would be cited for neglect. Back then, no one seemed too concerned about it unless I didn't show up for supper and then they came looking for me.

The person who went looking for me the most was my best buddy and the family housekeeper, Lucille Williams. "Lou" was one of the sweetest people that ever was. She loved the seven of us kids just like she loved her own five.

Lucille was short and round and black with a smile of sunshine and a voice sweet as syrup except when she absolutely instructed me to do something and I rebelled. Then she had the authority to treat me just like her own and I recall having to cut my own "switch" more times than all of my brothers and sisters combined. She also had the patience of Job and it was impossible to outwait her in a test of wills. I sat at the dinner table for three hours one afternoon trying to get out of drinking my milk and she just sat there reading the paper. I finally gave in, drank the stuff and was allowed to leave the table. That was one of my first clues that I would have a lifelong penchant for giving in to strong women.

We Galbraith kids pretty much had the run of the town. My big brother Henry Clay, now known as Hank, and I, were the exact stuff from which the character of Opie Taylor, also of Mayberry, was compiled. We knew everyone in town and roamed for miles in outlying areas, hiking, camping, fishing and chasing every possum and rabbit that we came across. We had fishing rods and bb guns by the time we were 7 and received our own .22 caliber rifle by the time we were 8.

We were taught gun safety and how to hunt by Dad. We could bag our game, prepare and cook it in the field by the age of 9 and many Saturdays during the various seasons were spent walking in the woods listening for the chatter of squirrels or flushing rabbits from thickets in the fields. I could walk down Main Street with that .22 rifle and buy 100 bullets at the hardware store without any ruckus being raised. It was this simple…if I had mishandled that rifle in front of any adult in that town, they had carte blanche to take it away from me, give me a lickin' and then send me home for another one. Things were real simple then. Kids that I knew were taught that guns are not toys and that they must be handled with care. They were familiar objects to us, not taboo and therefore held no mystique for us. They were dangerous and we treated them with respect.

We were allowed these adult type responsibilities despite the fact that Hank and I had displayed some of our more childlike qualities by burning down the old coalhouse in the backyard after a "secret club meeting," (For a week thereafter I wore 6 pairs of underpants cause I knew for sure that we were going to get spanked for that one) and replacing the shampoo in Dad's shower with our own pee, on a mutual dare. "Dollie," he called from the bathroom, "how come this shampoo doesn't lather so well?" To this day, Mom can't repeat what he had to say when he found out the answer.

Many of the flashbacks I conjure up about my earliest days are straight out of scenes from the holiday classic movie "It's a Wonderful Life". Dinnertime with the whole family gathered around the table, talking and laughing. Mom and Dad at each end of the table with we kids jostling each other for the last potato. Christmas trees darn near hidden by the stacks of presents in front of them and we kids jostling for position to be the first to get to theirs. The whole family gathered in front of the first TV set in Nicholas County, jostling for the best seat, to eat popcorn and watch Saturday night wrestling with Chief Don Eagle and Gorgeous George. Come to think of it, there was a hell of a lot of jostling going on in that family and I believe it just made us closer knit.

It has taken me several decades to fully understand how that primitive television set, that could only get two channels, would be so instrumental in shaping my view of history and therefore my actions in life. Back then, 1954 and '55, each Saturday morning, Hank and I would awaken early and go downstairs to watch TV. Just like millions of children do each Saturday mornings now days.

Except Hank and I did not watch cartoons like present day kids. What we watched was the liberation of Auschwitz and vintage D-day footage, American troops and tanks rolling into Berlin. The United States of America putting a 55-gallon can of "whup ass" on those nasty Nazi fascists who wanted us all to have to pee in a cup to prove our genetic worthiness. To this day I hate Nazis, tyrants and fascists of all ilk and there is no doubt that herein lies the basis for my opposition to the "New World Order" and its subsequent global economy.

I remember sitting there, watching the piles of bodies being moved around by bulldozers and thinking, "Who would sit by and let this happen? Who could treat their fellow man with such disregard?" And I made a promise to myself that if I ever caught the Nazis or anyone else visiting unnecessary harm on innocent folks, I would fight them tooth and nail. And that is what I hope I have been doing with my life.

But I'm getting too far ahead of myself. Suffice it to say, that in my child's view of the world, America's might had been used for right. I played soldier everyday with the rest of the neighborhood gang and read all the Sgt. Rock comic books I could find.

I was either going to be a priest or a soldier, I decided, but as the first called for pureness of thought, word and deed, which even then I suspected I might possess in short supply, the second called for a certain level of physical fitness which I simply couldn't meet.

In and among the various accidents and ailments which befall a family with 7 children, I was the one with the most serious physical problems. While the basis was chronic asthma, it didn't help that I was also accident prone to the point of collecting three "ectomies" by the time I was 10 years old. (Appendectomy, splenectomy and tonsillectomy). Add to that the requisite broken arms and various other traumas and it would be fair to say that I was a regular sight at the Nicholas County Hospital.

However, the main basis for my sickliness as a child was that I was subject, at any time, anywhere, to suddenly have my lungs close up on me and be instantly unable to breathe. It was then and remains now one of the most frightening things you can imagine have happen to you. Standing out in open air and being unable to draw it into your lungs. The more you stress about it the harder it is to overcome. It is impossible to relax under these circumstances but that is exactly the thing to do if you can.

In my case, a wide range of factors would trigger my asthmatic "attacks". Dust in the air, cats in closed places, egg whites and goldenrod were included as villainous substances and sometime it just seemed to happen from nowhere. When it did, depending upon its severity, Mom would try a home remedy for a while and if it didn't do the trick, I went to the hospital where an IV and oxygen would be administered. I can tell you from experience that there is no sweeter feeling on earth than to have air sweep back into your lungs just as you feel that you are about to die from lack thereof.

Adding to the fear generated by this condition was the suddenness of its onset. In my childhood, it could happen anywhere, anytime. And, by it's nature, it is custom-designed to breed free-floating anxieties into the character of anyone affected by it. Simply put, even when it isn't happening, you are always worried that it's going to happen.

The home treatments were damn near worse than the asthma. These were the early Fifties and little was known about the disease. At the onset of symptoms Mom would tell me to sit down and rest but the anxiety over being unable to breathe was/is overwhelming. Close your mouth, hold your nose and then try to breathe for 10 seconds. That's how it feels, only there is nothing blocking your mouth and nose. Your lungs simply shut down.

The last home treatment before the hospital run was a ritual where I would go into the bathroom, lie in the tub, put towels underneath the door and Mom would burn this horrible, stinky incense-type substance touted to treat lung problems. From what I allow myself to remember, it smelled like hell and it's a wonder it didn't kill me.

There were several other things that almost did.

I was basically a scrawny and oft-times puny young fellow given to breathing problems and hyperactivity. I would do most anything to fit in with my older brother Hank and his gang of older friends, so I was always the one that they made to go first in some dangerous activity so that I could be in "The Club."

I actually shudder now when I revisit the picket fences I jumped over from the neighbor's roofs or the tree limbs I hung from, upside down, by my knees without a safety net. Thinking of what might have happened to us during those days and realizing my own three daughters are now grown women, I realize that parents whose children actually survive the process of growing up are very lucky people indeed. It's easy to forget sometimes how lucky we all are.

On Christmas morning of 1953 while the rest of the family was streaming down the stairs to open their presents around the family tree, I stayed upstairs because I didn't feel well. That was a sure sign to my parents and they rushed me to the hospital where the diagnosis was a ruptured appendix. Things were tight for a while but the emergency surgery was successful and I recovered within a few days. I recollect that incident because I believe it was the first time I felt like I was really going to die and that there were "otherworldly" spirits who had an interest in the matter.

Today I firmly believe that we all have guardian angels that look after us and help us when they can. I was not fully cognizant of it then, at age 6, under sedation on the operating table, but I can distinctly remember being comforted by voices that came from within me rather than from the doctors and nurses. In recovery, I was visited by spirits who would likely be quaintly described by today's adults as "imaginary" friends. All I can say for sure is that I became convinced that there is a spiritual side to our existence and that nothing goes unnoticed.

It certainly wasn't and won't be the last time I have been able to depend on assistance from my "guardian' spirits.

I recovered from the appendectomy and went about the serious business of being a 7-year-old boy. The high point of those days in Carlisle was when the carnival came to town on the 2nd, 3rd and 4th of July for the Blackberry Festival. The carnival set up on the courthouse lawn, the Main Street block was closed and filled with booths and kiosks, and a young man was liable to find anything there. What I most remember finding there was my first real incentive to enter politics as a lifestyle.

Each year, as part of the Festival, a platform is built in front of the courthouse and its walls are festooned with red, white and blue bunting. The stage faces Main Street and various announcements are made therefrom during the three-day event. But sometimes a candidate for one of Kentucky's various offices would visit our town on the Fourth and address the crowd.

The first political speech I ever remember was watching the Hon. Bert Combs speak to the townsfolk on the 4th of July, 1954, when he was running for the Democrat's nomination for Governor against A. B. "Happy" Chandler. I was standing in the street among the crowd, tired and dirty from a day of running around the carnival and I watched this man speak to me. With his silver white hair, impeccable dress and while being outlined by the spotlight, he appeared to have a halo around him. He looked so clean and neat, so polished. And everybody was listening to him and applauding him so I decided that I wanted to be just like him some day. Being a politician looked just fine with me.

(Years later, when I did run for the Democrats' nomination for Governor, in 1991 and 1995 and, as the Reform Party's candidate in 1999, I gave speeches from that very same platform, literally unchanged in 40 years. But it seems so much smaller to me now then when I stood in the streets before it as a star-struck, 7 year old, political neophyte.)

The summer of my eighth year Dad took me aside. "Son," he said, "you're eight years old now. It's time you got a job. Here is a red wagon loaded with quarts of strawberries for a quarter and Grit newspapers for a dime. Go house to house and sell them until the wagon is empty and then come back with the money."

"Dad," I asked, "what if I can't sell them all?"

"Gatewood, if you knock on enough doors, you'll sell them all," he said.

And he was right. Later in the afternoon I came back with an empty wagon and a pocket full of coins. "Look Dad," I said excitedly. "I've sold them all!"

Dad looked at me approvingly. "That's fine Gatewood. Now fill the wagon back up and go do it again."

We had a big house with a large barn out back, an acre garden and a two-acre strawberry plot. Hank and I learned the business end of a hoe early on and blisters were commonplace. Lord help any of us who dared speak out that we were bored or didn't have anything to do. That meant we had to cut the neighbor's lawn if ours didn't need it, or sweep the sidewalk of the old lady down the street.

We kids all went to Carlisle City School where all 12 grades were housed. We walked about half a mile each morning and afternoon in all weather. Good grades were mandatory and since Mom had a teacher's degree, homework could never be sloppy or incomplete.

At the beginning of the school year in my 3rd grade, I was playing tag on the schoolyard when I fell while running up some bleachers. My stomach hit sharply against the edge of one of the seats and the pain was immediate and intense. Teachers were summoned and, after some conferring among them, I resumed my class. Within an hour my discomfort was quite obvious. I was instructed to walk home because my parents couldn't be contacted. So I walked the half-mile home, stopping when the pain got too intense and arrived about the same time as Mom. We immediately went to the hospital where I was observed overnight and released the next morning.

I took it easy at home, remaining bedridden for the next three days, until one afternoon when I began to throw up immense volumes of blood. I was rushed again to the hospital and Dr. Maurice Royalty, a surgeon from Lexington, 35 miles away, was summoned to open me up and find out what was wrong.

He found that the edge of the step had ruptured my spleen and I had been bleeding internally for the past three days. The blood had surrounded my diaphragm, filling up my chest cavity. It was touch and go for hours on the table while they removed my spleen and no one was entirely certain of the outcome for days to come. I spent thirty days in the hospital in recovery, the first several of them in a drug-induced haze, drifting in and out of consciousness. It was at least ten days before I could sit up and I'll never forget the way the world spun out of control as I fought to remain sitting upright. It was intense.

I often wonder if those two early brushes with death introduced me to life on the edge and a certain devil-may-care attitude. (And maybe an appreciation of good drugs.) I also seemed to develop a certain argumentative nature which lent itself to schoolyard scuffling on a relatively epic scale, so I guess I need to take this time to finally thank my older brother Hank for all the times he had to take up for me when I ticked off some older boy with my fighting words and wiseacre attitude. Mom told him he had to keep a watch out for me and he was burdened, like so many older brothers, with a younger brother who had a fighting spirit and few physical skills to back it up. I must have gotten Hank in a fight every week or so but he never backed down and I probably owe my life to him more times than I owe it to Dr. Royalty. Thanks Hank.

The splenectomy only served to sideline me even more from the rough-and-tumble lifestyle of the healthy youngsters in the town. They could run and play and rough house each other while I couldn't join in because I was the kid with asthma and stitches all the way up his front. So I read, developed my imagination and learned to amuse myself as only those on the disabled list are capable of doing.

I had always been a prodigious reader but now I picked up the pace considerably. By this time I was reading Edgar Rice Burroughs, James Fenimore Cooper, H.G. Wells and Ray Bradbury. Their imagination lent fuel to mine and I decided that I wanted to be a writer along with being a priest and a soldier and a politician. Life was getting more complicated. And crowded with ambition.

Words became fascinating to me and I began a lifelong pursuit of their mastery, interrupted by life in general. Between age 9 to 11, I became lost in books, reading two or three a day, of all sorts, and began to develop a Daydreamer's habit of looking out the window, thinking of all the places I would rather be at any given time.

It got to the point where Dad, walking in on me sitting among books and lost in my own thoughts, shook his head and said, "Gatewood, I believe they could lock you in the outhouse and you'd have a ball."

Later in the 50s, our family had grown. The last child, Tim, was born in 1956 and all 7 of us were at home. Dad's businesses were sufficient to maintain a certain status quo but getting us all a college education was a formidable task.

My oldest sister Judy moved to Lexington and began attending a business college. But her heart was not into it. She wanted to begin working in the real world and rebelled against dedicating herself to study. This led Mom and Dad to a very serious discussion. Mom insisted that their top priority was making sure the rest of us got a college education and that living in Carlisle, with its limited economic opportunities, was going to make that extremely difficult. As usual, Dad agreed with Mom. We would have to move.

THE SYNTHETIC SUBVERSION

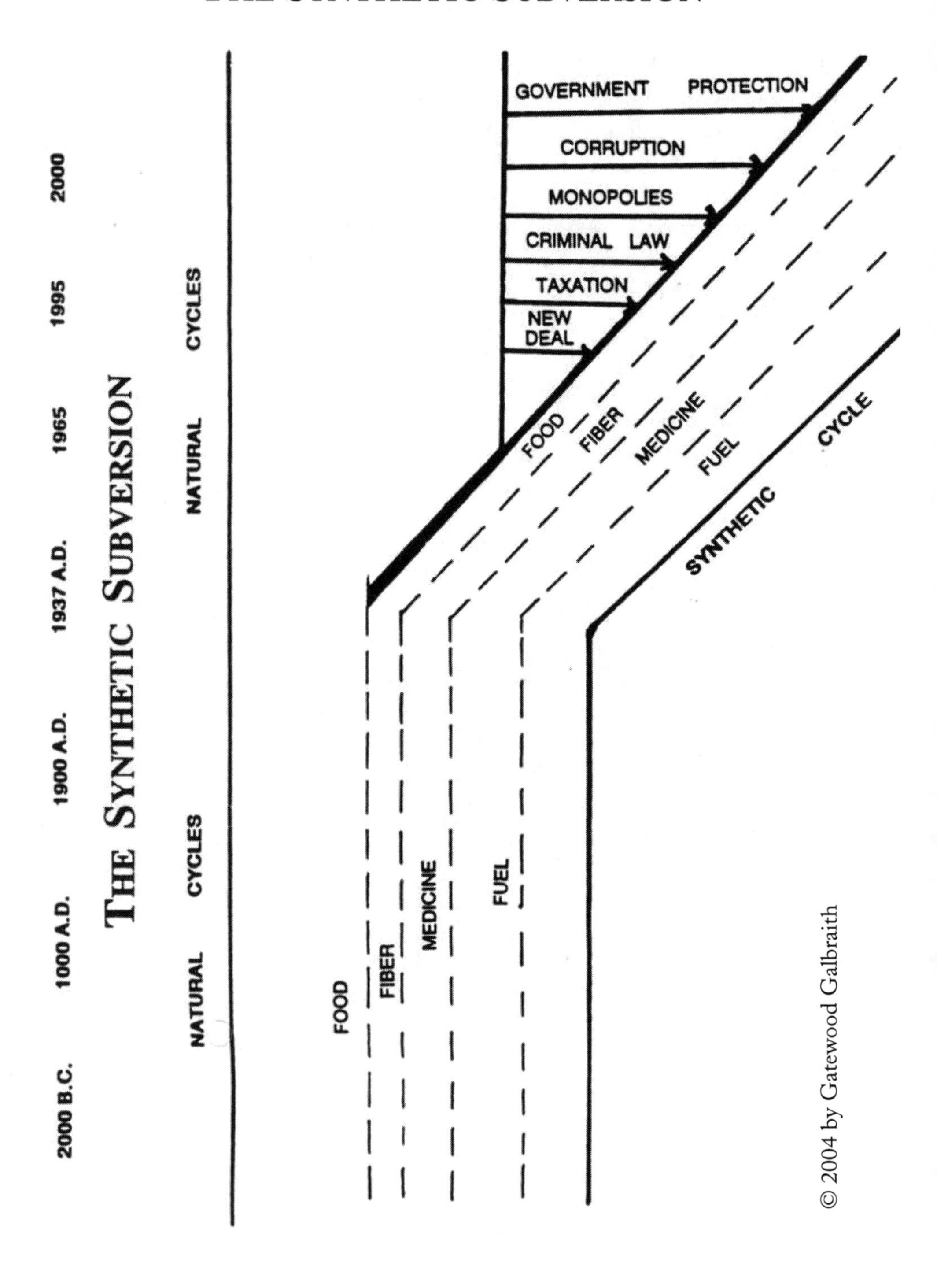

entities allowed the pooling of capital on an unprecedented scale and, more, trust agreements between corporations stifled competition from other markets and gave monopolies to a favored few.

Congress enacted the 1890 Sherman Anti-Trust act in opposition to America's economy being hijacked by a small group of capitalists and it was used to break up the larger trusts, including Standard Oil of New York in 1892. Otherwise, Mr. John D. Rockefeller would have ended up owning everything.

America's economy fluctuated wildly throughout the 1920s and 30s and the Depression took a lot of steam out of America's boast that a free-market was a Divine Mandate. Talk began in earnest among the big players on a plan to enact a controlled economy in the United States and it was to be sure that they were the ones in control.

The institution of a formally recognizable controlled economy in the United States came in the form of what is known as Roosevelt's New Deal legislation. Until this time, there was a Constitutional separation between business and government that resembled that of the wall between Church and State. Government could not/should not favor one corporation or business over another and, ideally, all government work should be competitively bid. Further, government lacked the authority to regulate the actions of the corporations.

But the New Deal changed all of that and there were three major motives that dictated its implementation, its forms and its functions. These included the necessity of responding to the Depression, preparing for World War II and a desire to usurp America's agrarian economy, commandeer its natural products and replace them with synthetically-derived products from a factory economy. The Synthetic Subversion.

These plans were not discussed with the population in general nor put to a popular vote. It was believed, correctly I assume, that consumer preference could be swayed by advertising campaigns. But I wonder if that is what the Chairman of the E.I. DuPont Denemours and Company meant in his 1937 shareholder's report when, after discussing his company's extensive investment in synthetic processes, and one of its new product discoveries, nylon, he wrote that the ability to realize a profit from these investments was directly related to how "the revenue-raising power of government may be converted into an instrument for forcing acceptance of sudden new ideas of industrial and social reorganization."

If there ever was a smoking gun as evidence of the demise of the United States as a Free Market economy, and as a free country, this statement is it.

In other words, a corporation now saw itself in the position of using the government's power of taxation to force the reorganization of society to insure a profit from its investments, no matter the impact on the Constitutional guarantees of We, the People.

At first, President Roosevelt and his corporate buddies had some difficulty in getting the Supreme Court to go along by re-interpreting the Constitution to allow such shenanigans. The Court consistently ruled that this new relationship between Government and business was unconstitutional and lots of legislation got log-jammed at the top. It wasn't until Roosevelt threatened to add six new members to the Court that one of the Justices changed his vote and Congress enacted a torrent of new legislation, on an emergency basis, without the normal legislative debates and outside the spotlight of crucial public examination.

Up until this point in time, the United States Government never had the Constitutional power to outlaw individual behavior beyond that of insuring its own express powers. Obviously an individual could not coin their own money or declare war. These were specifically given to specific arms of government.

Otherwise, there were few federal criminal laws in existence. The government had no Constitutional empowerment to outlaw individual behavior but the strategy of the New Deal legislation was to tax it into oblivion.

Once the "New Deal" was accepted as Constitutional by the Supreme Court, this new combination of players in business and government moved quickly to define, expand and protect its newfound powers.

The first bill to pass Constitutional muster after the Supreme Court reversed its philosophies was the 1937 Machine Gun Tax. The logic was simple. The government couldn't tell you that you couldn't own a machine gun, but they sure as hell could tax it. And if you didn't alert them that you possessed one by filing taxes on it, then you were a tax evader and they could prosecute you on a criminal basis for it. The 1937 Machine Gun Tax Act allowed them to locate and register the automatic weapons of the day held by the public. This was the first step in federal gun control.

The second New Deal piece of legislation to be Okayed by the Court was the 1937 Marijuana Tax Act. Excuse me, was marijuana a big problem back in 1937? Why hell no! Then why did our government decide that this was such an important piece of legislation, to be passed at the earliest possible time?

Essentially, it was this piece of legislation that gave the New Dealers an almost complete control of the country and its means of producing wealth. Here's how it worked.

The 1937 Marijuana Tax Act did not outlaw marijuana. It placed a prohibitive tax on it of $200 per ounce and put its cultivation under a taxed permit scheme which stopped its growth because they simply didn't issue any permits.

Why was this act so important to them? Because, under this legislation, for the first time, the United States Government took unto itself the power to tell its citizens what seeds they could, and couldn't, plant in God's green earth.

From this point on, the corporate moneychangers in the government's temples, the synthetic industrialists, had control of America's land even though they didn't own it. They could tax their competition, the farmers, into oblivion by utilizing "the revenue-raising power of government" as an instrument "for forcing acceptance of sudden new ideas of industrial and social reorganization."

And each of America's succeeding generations lost the basic moral compasses you have instilled when you grow up amid the Natural Cycle. Lessons learned like, If you don't work, you don't eat. You reap what you sow. There is a time and season for all things, including death. You know, the basic stuff everybody should know by the 6th grade. And how's a kid ever going to learn it without ever having to hoe a garden?

❖ *Lexington*

Of course I didn't realize all of this when our family moved from Carlisle to Lexington in 1959. I was 12 years old and the small town atmosphere seemed perfect to me. I was too young to appreciate the forces behind the decision to move and so I felt forcibly uprooted when the time came and we headed to Lexington.

Dad bought a restaurant in downtown Lexington and we moved into a big house on Nicholasville Road. He didn't realize that the bottom was about to be pulled out from under the downtown business owners by a new phenomenon called shopping centers. Like so many other cities, Lexington was on the verge of shifting its population and its centers of commerce away from the heart of the city and into the suburbs.

The restaurant was all right for a year or so, then it began to suffer. Old-line businesses and companies began to move to newer locations on the outskirts of town and with them went their workers who had patronized Dad's establishment. Things got tight and all of us kids went to work.

I began the 7th grade at Saint Peter's School on Barr Street, two blocks from our restaurant on Main Street. After school each day for the next two years I would get out at around 3 p.m. then go to the restaurant to wash dishes until suppertime when I would catch the bus home. I remember the strain on Dad's face as he watched his and Mom's life-savings go slowly down the tubes. There was nothing he could do about it, no matter how much harder he worked.

After our first year in Lexington, we had to forego the big house and move into a much smaller one a block away. It was a damn good thing we were such a close-knit family because the two girls shared a bedroom and I had to start sharing the "boys" bedroom with my three brothers. That's close, Folks.

My own three daughters listen unbelievingly when I tell them about those circumstances. They each had their own bedroom growing up and cannot comprehend having to share a regular-sized room with anyone else, much less three other siblings with only room for two beds and one dresser drawers. My youngest brother Tim and I shared one double bed and Hank and Mike got the other. Things got really crowded when other neighborhood boys got kicked out of their homes and came to stay with the Galbraiths for a while. It was not unusual to roll out of bed in the morning and land on someone sleeping on the floor, or to see several other faces at the supper table. We may have been broke, but nobody ever got turned away at our house.

Some of us bore a higher price to pay than the others, however, and one of these was my youngest brother, Tim. It so happened that our house had a full bath on the ground floor and a half bath on the second floor. We had to put a small dresser drawers in the half bath because there was simply not enough room where we boys slept.

Because Tim was the youngest, we guys made him keep his underwear in the bathroom; and because we guys were constantly running out of towels, we made it a habit of using his clean underwear to dry our hands, then returned them to his drawers. He's 48 years old now and still remembers having to go to school with wet undershorts. I guess it was just brotherly love that we did it even more every time he complained to Mom about it.

As times got leaner, Mom took a job as a teaching assistant in a local parochial elementary school while Liz, Hank and I went to work too. They got jobs at a neighborhood drug store and I got the first of my several paper routes, rising at 5 every morning to deliver the Courier Journal to about 150 homes over an eight block area. I had a bike with a big basket on the front and I would tear down the deserted, early morning streets in the dark, folding papers as I rolled between houses and hitting the porches from the sidewalk more often than I missed.

After a year with the Courier, I switched to delivering the Lexington Herald in the morning, and soon after, the Lexington Leader in the afternoon. Many days in high school, I hand-delivered over 500 papers to front porches over a 10 block area, so I speak from experience when I tell you, the reader, "Appreciate your paper carrier!" You can't imagine the resolve it takes to get up at 5 on a winter morning, with the temperature at 0 and go to place 350 papers on the front porch of homeowners who take it for granted.

In addition to developing character, folding that many papers by hand each day also develops forearm and hand strength, which came in handy at age 15 when I began to hang out in the campus bars and arm wrestle for pitchers of beer.

Despite my childhood physical misadventures, or perhaps because of them, I grew to 6 feet 4 by the age of 14. That is 5 inches taller than any of my siblings so one of my theories for this is that I experienced growth spurts triggered by the life-boosting drugs fed me during my emergency surgeries.

I must have looked older than my age too, because I remember quite well when I bought my first beer, at 15, at the then already-infamous Two Keys Bar on Limestone Street near the University of Kentucky campus. I walked through the front door on a hot summer afternoon, passed by two pay pinball machines on the left and came face-to-face with Jim the bartender, a stocky man in his forties with a gray flattop, beer belly and what I realize now was an all knowing smile.

Who wouldn't smile? I must have been hilarious, trying to get just the right amount of grownup swagger to my gait as I walked over, leaned on the bar, looked at the sign above it and said in a deep voice, "Give me a drought."

That's right. I didn't know that the word draught on the sign is pronounced "draft" and I guess he knew right away that I was not the man of the world I was pretending to be. But he said, "Sure pal," and handed me a frosty mug filled with cold beer. It tasted great and, at 25 cents each, I could afford a second one so I did. When I left to go home, I felt like I had just graduated to another level somehow but I didn't invite my parents to the ceremony.

(One night when I was 16, and drinking at the Two Keys, the police parked a paddy wagon at the back door and came through the front door in a sweep to catch under-age drinkers. They found me all right; after I had gone into the kitchen, put on an apron and began flipping a hamburger. They never gave me a second look as they went by.)

Overall however, I didn't take well to the move from Carlisle to Lexington. After being raised in a village-type atmosphere, where there were no strangers, Lexington seemed so big and impersonal. Everyone was a stranger and there were a hell of a lot of them.

My own self-image didn't help matters any. My asthma attacks contributed to my feeling of physical inferiority, and throughout childhood, I had a chronic problem with my teeth, which were discolored and brittle. I was very self-conscious of my smile and it became more of a snarl which tended to complicate my attempts at forming social relationships. I compensated by becoming a loner, keeping to myself and arming myself with an attitude of defiance and aggression.

From grades 9 through 11 I bet I averaged a fight a month and sometimes two or three a week. It didn't take much to get me started; a comment on my teeth, the "wrong" look. And I didn't just say, "Hey you, step outside with me." Lots of times I said, "Hey, you'all step outside with me."

I fought in grade school and high school, on the streets and in the bars. I just would not back down from any one guy or any groups of them. The combination of my discontentment and overuse of alcohol was volatile and it's a wonder that I didn't get seriously hurt or hurt someone else. Most of the time someone with more sense than me came along and broke it up, so black eyes and bloody lips were the most prevalent signs of my internal turmoil, along with C's and D's on my school work.

I was still an avid reader but of things interesting to me and that wasn't necessarily school work. I went from St. Peter's Grade school to high school at Lexington Catholic in 1961 and I must have been pretty uncoachable and unmanageable. My grade average at the 9th, 10th and 11th levels was C- and I was simply not a good fit in the classroom setting. I was a hyperactive, self-centered, aggressive butthead and I'm not sure how they put up with me as long as they did. It must have been because of Mom and her work with, and dedication to, the Church.

The folks who ran Lexington Catholic however, the priests, nuns and lay teachers finally ran out of patience with a week left to go in my junior year and they handed me my walking papers. I only got credit for a half year and had to transfer to a local public school to finish my last year and take an extra summer class to graduate.

Mom and Dad were busting their butts every day to furnish our family with the necessities and we kids worked also and were left to our own devices in our free time. They were not blind however to my life on the edge of self-destruction and we had a long talk in the summer of 1964 about what could be done for me.

I believe I remember revealing to them just how ugly I felt, with my teeth being in such rotten shape, and Mom suggested I get them pulled and get a set of dentures. I was pretty well desperate to try anything, so in that summer, I had all my teeth pulled, 6 at a time on each Saturday for 4 straight Saturdays.

I had to wait several weeks for my gums to shrink before I could get fitted with my dentures and in the meantime my first days began at my new high school. I don't know if I can describe for you the feelings generated by starting a new school in your senior year with no teeth in your head.

I know I got into 10 fights the first week and developed such an immediate reputation, by whipping the 4 biggest bullies there (one at a time), that soon after, if someone had something to say about my strangeness, they did it out of my earshot.

Then a veritable miracle happened. I was fitted with my new dentures and suddenly I had a smile that I didn't have to hide.

It was like lifting a mask from my face because it was such an immediate transformation. But my underlying aggression was still there and it manifested itself in the way I treated my own body, drinking too much and taking up tobacco.

I started smoking cigarettes at 14, prompted by seeing an older teen looking so cool about it. My parents had warned me about it, but we all know that only made it more fascinating. I was always the trouble-making kid in high school, sneaking a smoke in the john or bringing alcohol to the school gym. I know that Mom and Dad were at their wit's end and they sure were glad to see me graduate from high school in 1965, after passing a summer school class in chemistry with a D. (Thanks Mr. Brown). No doubt about it, I was a mess.

It was anticipated that all of us kids would go on to college and the University of Kentucky was the obvious choice. The location of this traditional land grant college in Lexington was the primary reason we had moved here and Liz and Hank had immediately enrolled upon graduating high school.

Thank God UK had an open-admissions policy in place which meant that anyone with a high school diploma could get in and give it a try, no matter what their grade average. That was the only reason a person like me could get in. I had gone from a straight A student in grade school to a C- student for the next 6 years and things didn't get better in my first two semesters at UK.

I got so far behind in my classes during the Fall semester of 1965 that I dropped out. I had never developed any real study skills in my previous school career so I have no idea why I thought they would suddenly spring upon me. I began again the following semester with the same baggage and the results were predictably the same. I dropped out again mid semester and did what any other socially, sexually and academically frustrated 19-year-old male would do. I tried to go to war.

❖ *The War*

The Viet Nam war was going strong in 1966 and they had just instituted the draft. Anti-war efforts were beginning on campus and the subject was on everyone's mind. I was typically gung ho about it and threatened the first draft-resisters that set up tables at the Student Center. I couldn't believe that good citizens would debunk our own government's policies on "containing communism" and my opposition to them further inflamed my own warlike tendencies. I decided that becoming a soldier in this war could be the answer to lots of my problems if I approached it with the right attitude. I would be John Wayne, by God.

The way I figured it, if I killed enough people, I would be a hero and if I got killed myself, well, if I did it right, I would still be a hero. It seemed so simple back then. (Much later on, I was speaking to one of Kentucky's most powerful people and he said with great sincerity, "Gatewood, you have so much going for you but you're about 3% 'off'." I said, "T… that's a great compliment. You should have seen me when I was about 80% 'off'.")

There was only one problem. Because of my asthma, I was classified as 4F. Unfit for military service and therefore un-draftable. Talk about self-esteem problems. I flunked college and my basic physical.

But I was resilient and went to several doctors, finally convincing two of them that I had "outgrown" my asthma, telling them that my last attack had come several years earlier when, in fact, it had been less than a year. They obviously brought it and I got cleared for the service branch I wanted, the United States Marines Corp. Semper Fidelis.

Let's face it. I was a misfit in many ways but the Marines promised to make a man out of me and I figured that the Corps, like the war, would either kill me or cure me.

So in the spring of 1966, Gatewood Galbraith went off to become a Marine. I'll never forget the bus ride to the base at Paris Island, South Carolina. The bus was filled with grunts-to-be, of any and all descriptions. Everyone was nervous and excited on the way but that gave way to sheer panic when we hit the Island at 2:30 in the morning.

We came to a stop and that's when I saw my first Marine Drill Instructor. He came through the front door like a madman, calling us all maggots and telling us to get our asses out the door and onto the asphalt, lining up by height. His demeanor was designed to put the fear of God and Drill Instructors into us maggots and it sure worked on me, and everyone else who was on the bus.

We double-timed to where we picked up our gear and then we were taken to our barracks where we were introduced to the head DI. He was about 5 feet six inches tall, weighed about 200 pounds and had big, thick arms that reached to the ground. He completed the picture by chewing on the biggest, blackest, baddest cigar I had ever seen.

We were kept up and moving for the first 36 hours on the Island. The Marine program is designed to break down the recruit and then rebuild him into their idea of what it takes to be one of a few good men. It is extremely effective, both physically and psychologically. It takes everyone to their breaking points then teaches you how to go further.

The month I hit the Island, the Corps had reduced the program for basic recruits from 14 weeks to 9 weeks. The war in Viet Nam had been escalated and they needed more grist for the cannon. That's the role of a Marine.

They increased the pace of basic training and I had a hard time keeping up. While I had certain physical strengths, I had never had any sports or conditioning regimen so my breathing and stamina were my weaknesses. Try as I might, I couldn't finish the 5 mile runs with the rest of the platoon and I paid the price by toothbrushing the grout in the showers on several occasions. Only once was I ever paid any compliment during the time I was there. We were running the obstacle course and I was one of the last to finish. After falling in, the platoon was given hell by the DI who then turned to me and said in a different tone of voice, "Son, you're trying too hard." I don't know why he did it, but that comment made the whole experience worthwhile.

About 4 weeks into the program I was assigned barracks duty which meant getting it ready for inspection. Another recruit picked up a broom and as I came around the corner he began sweeping the floor dust in my direction.

Bam! It was like going into a vacuum. Suddenly there was absolutely no air available for my lungs. I went limp and fell across a bunk, trying desperately to breathe. My anxiety level went through the roof and panic prevailed. The other recruits called the DI who had them half carry me to the medical staff.

The doctor put his stethoscope to my chest for less than a second then looked me in the eye. "You're out of here Galbraith." And that was that. An Honorable Discharge under Medical Conditions. I couldn't even qualify for cannon fodder.

(Years later, it dawned on me that this was one of my life's greatest ironies. At the time of my discharge, I was 19 years old and had no idea that marijuana cured asthma. If I had known that then, I might have been a pot smoking Marine.)

❖ Life on the Edge

My return to the civilian realm did little to clear my vision about what I should do with myself. I lapsed into a lifestyle of partying around the campus and drinking as much beer as I could. I held a succession of jobs and enrolled several times at UK but couldn't bring myself to go to classes or finish a semester. I was totally adrift on a sea of chaos.

Despite my proximity to the university party scene I was still a virgin when my 20th birthday came and went. All the mechanisms I had constructed to avoid rejection when I was ashamed of my smile were still in operation and women simply left me tongue-tied. (They still do.)

Sure, even then I was a good speaker in certain situations but they did not include intimate conversations with the opposite sex. Between my small town Catholic upbringing, my feelings of physical inferiorities and a lack of confidence in my appearance, I was a walking basket case, expecting, and therefore receiving rejections in my fumbling attempts to progress beyond fantasy and into the world of real sex.

Not surprisingly then, my first time happened in the only way it could. Quick, unexpectedly and briefly, during a party where the girl I had brought left with another guy and I was left in a deep blue funk. Suddenly there appeared before me a woman of great mercy who took me by the hand and led me into a nearby bedroom where she kindly erased my self-styled label of the "World's Oldest Virgin Guy Who Will Probably Stay That Way Forever" with the briefest of acts. God Bless Her.

Well, what can I tell you? It may have been an act of mercy but it sure was a liberating act of mercy and I could now think of myself as an adult. James Bond and I had more in common then ever before and we could share a world-weary wink if ever we met. Yes 007, isn't it true what they say about women?

Well, how are you going to get a kid back on the farm once he's seen Pareeee? The first time was enough to convince me that I wanted, and needed more sex, so my main focus became the pursuit of much of my efforts. This was undertaken by frequenting the bars, drinking way too much and getting to every party I could find.

I began hanging out with those men who I perceived were successful with women in ways that I wanted to be. Smooth talkers, suave operators and totally opportunistic, they led the wild, shallow lifestyle of Playboys whose main goal was to bed as many woman as they could. It didn't help then and it doesn't help now that so much of our consumer advertising breeds that attitude in each male generation and for a long while I brought the concept hook, line and sinker.

The most successful of these carnal cowboys was a man who I met while we were working for the same company. He seemed to have it all. Looks, the smoothest lines I ever heard and a confidence around the most beautiful of women that was devastatingly effective for his ultimate goal of loving them and leaving them. I watched again and again as he would go into a bar or party an hour before closing and leave with the most attractive woman there who had been pursued all evening by the rest of the men around.

J. exuded the persona of being a man's man. An ex-athlete, he hunted and fished, drank and pursued women nonstop. He would offer to fight at the drop of a hat and many's the time that an evening of bar hopping would end with fisticuffs in the back alleyway. For many reasons he seemed to be what I wanted to be then; successful yet non-committal, pursued but uncatchable and an inveterate risk-taker that always seemed to beat the odds.

We hit the bars every evening and frequented the bootleggers after hours and each Sunday. Things kept getting a little wilder and I kept getting further along my path of self-destruction. I remember awakening from a particularly dangerous drinking contest where I had turned up a fifth of whiskey and tried to kill it, passing out mid-swallow as my body rejected the sudden onset of such powerful toxins. As I came to, I realized that I was lucky to be alive and I wondered how those two shotgun holes in the ceiling of my apartment had come about. J told me that he was convinced I was going to die after I had lain on the floor for 12 hours and he had tried to awaken me from my stupor by several means, including firing both barrels of his shotgun over my head as I lay on the floor. That, dear readers, is what too much whiskey can do to the human mind.

Within days after that near-death experience, something occurred which turned my life around and helped define who I would become for its remainder.

A flesh and blood high school friend turned guardian angel reappeared in my life and his advice influenced my decisions from that day in the Fall of 1968 until now. Even though he died in an auto accident in 1978, I still look heavenward when I occasionally do something right and ask, "How 'bout them apples Teddy?"

❖ Teddy & Marijuana

In September of 1968, I was working at W.T. Grant's variety store in Turfland Mall, managing the men's wear and children's toy departments. One day there came a phone call for me and it took me a second to recognize the voice on the other end. It was a fellow who I had gone to Lexington Catholic High School with who probably qualified as the closest thing I had to a friend in those days. I hadn't seen him for more than two years.

"Gatewood, it's Teddy. I just got out of the Air Force where I was stationed as an airplane mechanic in Bangkok, Thailand. I have something which I think will help you a great deal and you ought to try it."

"What's that Teddy?" I asked.

"I'll show you when we get together Gatewood. How about tonight?"

Teddy Mertens showed up at my apartment at 6 that evening. He had always been different from most of the other guys I knew. He was big and, let's face it, ugly. In fact, he had some of the same feeling of inferiorities that I had experienced in high school and he manifested them in some of the same ways, so it was no surprise that we ended up fighting each other on several occasions. We were pretty evenly matched however and eventually garnered a mutual respect and an insight into each other's psyche. I told him that the reason I hung around with him was that we were both so ugly that we made the other one look good. He could only grin and agree. That was good enough for him. I also knew he was smart, for sure, but I didn't know then just how smart until much later on.

Teddy came into my apartment carrying a loaded Air Force duffel bag. He reached down into it and came up with a brown grocery sack which he opened to reveal hundreds of little cigar shaped sticks, around which had been wrapped tiny, brown, flower-like buds, the like of which I had never seen before.

"What the hell is that Teddy," I asked.

"It's marijuana Gatewood. More specifically, these are called Thai sticks and it is about the best marijuana in the world. I ran across it while I was in Bangkok and all the service men there smoke it. I brought back six grocery bags full in that duffel bag."

"Gee Teddy," I said, "isn't that stuff supposed to be dangerous?"

"Hell no Gatewood," he replied. "In fact, I think it will help you a great deal. It helps you breathe and settles your head and you need all of that you can get."

I watched, fascinated, as he began to prepare the marijuana. He took a Chesterfield cigarette and squeezed about half of the tobacco out of it, leaving the paper tube itself intact. Then he un-wrapped the tiny string that held the flowers to the stick and laid several of the buds on the table.

"Do you have a razor and some aspirin?" he asked. I quickly furnished the materials and he went about dicing the flowers and the aspirin together into a fine mixture that he stuffed into the empty part of the cigarette paper.

"What's the aspirin for Teddy," I asked?

"That's so you won't get a headache," he replied knowingly.

He handed me the first marijuana cigarette I had ever held and said, "Give that a try, Gatewood." And I did.

"Thai stick" was then, and is now, among the most potent marijuana in the world. All of the modern day "Drug War" propaganda that says that present day pot is much stronger than in the earlier days is pure poppycock. You can't get any better marijuana than I held in my hand that evening. I know because I've tried time and again and again and again...

I distinctly remember my first "hit" of the herb. As a cigarette smoker, I had no trouble drawing the smoke deep into my lungs and trying to hold it in as instructed by Teddy. The smoke itself seemed to expand and forced my lungs to expand with it. When I could hold it no longer I exhaled with a coughing fit that took several seconds to subside and during that time I had the most amazing physical sensation of feeling blood rush into my lungs and my brain in a fashion that reminded me of water rushing into parched earth, filling theretofore arid irrigation ditches with life-giving liquid.

The expectorant quality of marijuana was immediately apparent as I coughed up fluid from my lungs and spit it out. Immediately thereafter I took several deep breaths and filled my lungs with fresh air in volumes that I had only known after hospital treatments following my childhood asthma attacks.

Simultaneously my hearing became more acute and the music on the stereo took on new tones and resonance. I could feel its vibrations in an almost magical fashion and they merged with my own internal vibes to produce a feeling of well-being that seemed to cast aside all of the free-floating anxieties dwelling deep within me that had made every breath a potential challenge over all of the past years.

I took several more "hits" from the "joint" along with Teddy and the sense of floating along the musical highway grew even more intense. I became aware that my sensation of touch had magnified and the texture of things around me became fascinating. I had the distinct realization that my prior perceptions of the physical world around me were shallow and undeveloped. I had never truly appreciated color, sound and texture. That all changed in the course of the next 24 hours.

Teddy was already a veteran of this first-time experience and had a hoot watching me become initiated to it. Though we had no idea of the exact physical reactions that were occurring at the time, his intuition that this was medicine that would help me was right on point. (Years later we learned that smoking marijuana expands a person's lung capacity by an average of 17%.) He was aware of my history of breathing problems and attacks of anxiety and his experience of watching servicemen in and around battle treat their anxieties by smoking marijuana was fresh in his mind. My friend was one smart cookie.

I became aware of being hungry and Teddy suggested I move to the couch while he went out and got us something to eat. As a first timer, whose initiation included the best pot in the world, I was in no shape to fend for myself in public and I agreed to let him handle the matter. I went to the couch and he went to Colonel Sander's.

I stayed on the couch for 24 hours, eating, talking with Teddy, sleeping and listening to music. Each person has their own unique experience when they ingest cannabis (a.k.a. hemp/pot/marijuana/weed/ganja/smoke/bud/kind bud etc.) for the first time. An athlete may seek exercise, a swimmer the water, a hiker the forest trail. I was none of these. The landscapes on which I yearned to frolic, in the exercise of my new-found lightness, were almost completely the internal ones, psychological gardens of peace, free from what I later learned to call my free-floating anxieties. The value of ridding oneself of this baggage cannot be overstated, especially for asthmatics, whose life experiences in suddenly becoming helplessly deprived of oxygen dictate that they will forever possess the anxiety that it may happen again, anytime, anywhere.

After a while, this specific anxiety becomes subliminal and attaches itself to most of your considerations in life, even the most simple ones. "Can I take a ride in the country today or will the hayfields or ragweed/goldenrod trigger an attack? Can I stay in the house while Mom fixes an angel food cake or will the egg whites she uses cause me to choke and gasp?"

Many severe asthmatics withdraw from what most people consider as normal everyday activities. Running, cycling, swimming, walking, sports, shopping or just visiting with others might, just might, contain a trigger for the onset. The more you try not to think about it, the more anxious you become of it. It' s like the big green monster standing in your living room corner. You just can't ignore it.

So when I smoked marijuana for the first time and felt my lungs bloom like desert plants in the first rainfall of the season and felt the rush of new blood to the parched regions of my brain, I could also actually feel the demise of whole edifices of anxiety within me, free floating and specific.

I kept taking deep breaths and marveling at the ease in which this basic act was achieved, without hesitation, without doubt that it was going to happen, time and again. It was almost like a runner catching his/her second breath during a race, only this was me, learning to breathe for the very first time in my memory.

Add to this my simultaneous newfound appreciation of the 3rd and 4th dimensions available to we humans on planet earth and you could say I had a truly "religious" experience. I didn't actually meet God but I gained a much deeper appreciation of his handiwork, including his miracle medicine marijuana.

From that time forward, for the next 34 years, throughout all my travels in search of the true "meaning of life" and all of the perilous positions I have put myself in, I have never had another attack of asthma. I have had bronchitis, pneumonia, flu and colds but I have never had the sudden onset of that awful feeling of suffocation and I am positive that I never will. I have since faced many of the triggers that used to send me into intense paroxysms, gasping for air and, today, they are without consequence.

I can't speak for any other asthmatic, or for that matter, any other person about what impact their use of marijuana may, or may not, have had on them. But make no doubt about my own conclusion. Marijuana Saved My Life! Period.

Its impact on me was so vivid that I have spent those 34 years, since my first use of it, investigating just what this herb is and why the laws are so harsh against it and why they exist at all. I am unapologetic about my association with it and have met literally tens of thousands of people, including asthmatics, whose "healing" experiences were similar to mine, and who believe they have been cured by its use.

During this time I have traveled tens of thousands of miles and read tens of thousands of pages of scientific studies to learn more about this plant. I've also smoked marijuana approximately 25,000 times to investigate whether it is possible to kill one's self by its use. I am happy to report that it is not.

So what is the "real skinny" (truth) about this simple green plant that grows from a seed from the earth and which has sustained mankind throughout the ages in all manners beneficial but which today is vilified at every turn by the petrochemical-pharmaceutical-military-industrial-transnational-corporate-fascist-elite-sonofabitches (the proverbial "THEM") as in "Screw 'THEM' S.O.B.s."

These present day detractors are the very folks who have been conspiring "to force acceptance of (their) sudden social and industrial reorganization" upon us by outlawing any and all naturally produced competition to their synthetic monopolies. They have termed this attack on the people and the natural cycle as a "War on Drugs."

In this "War on Drugs", everything from the natural cycle is evil and everything produced synthetically under monopolies is "good." There can be no doubt as to whose agenda is being satisfied by this arrangement. The evidence is that the financial support received by the "War on Drugs" comes exclusively from members of the Chemical Manufacturers Association who control the synthetic monopolies. You can always tell the agenda by who furnishes the money.

This Synthetic Subversion has sabotaged the American Revolution itself, whereby a system of governing was finally devised that recognized the individual human citizen as their own sovereign and the rightful recipients of the processes, benefits and surpluses of the governing process rather than the local king, queen, strongman, warlord or any other " baddest sonofabitch" in the valley who traditionally called all the shots.

The American Revolution was possible because it took place in an agrarian society where the wealth of the nation was spread among the people through utilization of the land as the means of producing it. Where this occurs, the wealth is spread because the ownership of the means of producing it is spread among so many people. Where the means of producing wealth is widely spread, so is the actual political power within that society. In essence, individuals are most powerful when they are self-sufficient and the ownership and access to land gives that power of self-sufficiency.

When the people are deprived of this means of self-sufficiency, and made dependent upon the necessities of life as produced and distributed by synthetic manufacturers through their control of the factories and corporations, they become subject to the dictates of these corporate masters. The very sovereignty of each individual, that most precious gift given to us by our Founding Fathers, is compromised and lost forever.

This recognition of individual sovereignty is immortalized in the Declaration of Independence's phraseology that individuals are endowed by their Creator with the inalienable rights of Life, Liberty and the Pursuit of Happiness. These rights exist outside the dictates of whatever form of government a person lives under. The American Revolution was unique in the history of the world in that it created the Constitution, an actual blueprint for the operation of a form of government that insures that these rights are recognized and protected.

Because it represents the very most commercially valuable product available from nature, and is best suited to make land profitable, cannabis is the main target of the synthetic industrialists. They will spare no expense, and will waste the lives of millions of people, to keep the agrarian cycle and the farmer from competing with them by rediscovering this crop.

How is this possible? Can a plant be that valuable? How can a simple plant represent a threat to the economic well-being of today's largest corporations?

Three words capture the essence of the matter. Hemp IS Petroleum!

That's right. Every one of the thousands of products currently made from petroleum can be produced from the hemp plant, including plastics, cellophane, explosives and a myriad of other items. Henry Ford himself built an entire automobile from hemp except for the motor and rubber tires. There is a famous picture of him hitting the body of it with a sledgehammer to show that such a vehicle was impervious to dents.

Everything that is made from petroleum today can be made from the annual crop of hemp. The petroleum that we use in our cars today is simply liquefied vegetative matter that naturally grew eons ago, and it utilized, trapped and stored the sun's energy during its growth cycle. The process is called photosynthesis. It is the basic energy source for our entire way of life and the petroleum-based oil companies have gained a monopoly on its ownership and production. They generate hundreds of billions of dollars for themselves while criminalizing any farmer who wants to compete with them by growing their own little "oil wells."

❖ Cannabis

The substance that is today most often called marijuana is scientifically classified as Cannabis Sativa, an extremely hardy and tenacious plant that can grow almost anywhere on earth. It is probably the first plant actually domesticated as a crop by early man as they settled into agriculture because it was then, and is now, the most useful plant on earth. It not only furnishes fuel, heat, clothing, shelter, food and medicine, it furnishes the very best of all these things within the natural cycle.

Over time, man discovered that the plant could be bred in different directions to furnish his widest range of needs. He found that he could make it more potent as a medicine if he treated its cultivation in one manner and more useful as a source of clothing, heat and shelter if he directed its pattern of growth in another manner. No other plant acted as such a single source for so many needs.

Though many of its properties seem almost "magical", this plant has unique botanical characteristics that explain its diverse and potent powers.

Foremost, cannabis is an extremely "energetic" creature. By that I mean it more readily traps, converts, utilizes and stores the sun's energy during its growth cycle than any other growing plant on earth. It may be the most effective photosynthetic processor on the planet. This lets the plant grow faster, and in more places, than any other plant. Planted side-by-side with other crops, cannabis will outgrow them in every respect.

This ability to attain heights of 16 to 20 feet furnished early man with fibers stripped from the stalks, which were longer and stronger than any other plant fiber available for weaving cloth and making rope. As an illustration, the cannabis fiber is three to five times stronger that cotton, a highly specialized and later-developed crop. All of the early ships had sails and rigging made from cannabis because of its superior strength and durability. The word canvas is derived from the word cannabis.

Through trial-and-error experimentation over thousands of years, our ancestors discovered that this energy within the plant made it suitable for "industrial" uses including fuel for light and heat if it was grown one way over generations. If grown in another manner, it produced the most widely useful therapeutic, non-lethal medicine on earth.

Today, we call cannabis grown for its industrial uses (heat, energy, lubrication, textiles, paper and food) "hemp," and for its medicinal counterpart, we have accepted the originally Spanish term, "marijuana". They are both cannabis.

It always helps me to think of it this way. Hemp and marijuana are both cannabis in the same way that Danny Devito and Dennis Rodman are both adult males. They are the same basic species of being even though strikingly different in appearance and utility. (That is why a present-day police officer who says that he cannot differentiate between a hemp field and a marijuana patch ought to get the hell out of law enforcement.)

Early in their investigation of the plant, our forebearers discovered that hemp seed was the premier source of nutrition available from the plant kingdom. By modern means we find that this is because these seeds contain the 8 essential amino acids necessary for human growth and development, in proportions that maximizes its nutritional value. It is also the prime natural source of edestin, combined with albumin, which boosts the immune system and of linoleic and linolenic acids (which reduce cholesterol and plaque). In past centuries, during times of famine, many folks have survived by eating gruel, a mixture of hemp seed and water.

Each hemp seed, no matter how small, is a little container of oil, from which many of its nutritious components are derived. Thirty to forty percent of the weight of each seed is comprised of this oil, which means that if I have a 100-pound bag of hemp seeds, I can derive 30 to 40 pounds of pure oil from it. In the preparation of these seeds for food, early man collected this oil and found he could burn it for light and heat, or use it as a basis for lotions and balms. It was used in religious ceremonies during annointments and for the medical treatment for burns, bites and other wounds.

The modern industrial age discovered that this oil was actually the premier, naturally-occurring lubricating oil in the entire world due to its characteristic of constant viscosity. It won't break down as readily in high heat or constant-friction uses as other natural oils so our own government used it to lubricate the engines in our high altitude aircraft during World War II. (During which time the hemp farmers in Kentucky and 5 other states were exempt from the draft because of the importance of this crop to the war effort).

Hemp oil is also a prime source of fuel energy. This was recognized by many people including a Mr. Rudolph Diesel, who, in 1892, patented his new-fangled diesel engine to run off such basic seed oil so that each individual farmer could grow his own fuel and be independent of the big oil companies. (Willie Nelson and I put this to a public demonstration when we poured hemp oil into the gas tank of my Mercedes diesel during my 1991 campaign for the Democrats' nomination for Governor and drove it across the Commonwealth. As far as I know, we were the first folks to operate a motor vehicle on hemp oil in America for at least 50 years. It was an experience that neither Willie nor I will ever forget.)

So this same hemp seed oil that we can pour into your car's crankcase for lubrication or into its fuel tank for motivation can also be poured into a wok to stir-fry your vegetables That's pretty damn impressive seed by any standards.

The hemp plant's biomass produces a second form of fuel, methanol. President George H. Bush said in 1989 that methanol is the fuel of the future and why not? The necessity of developing our energy sources from a program of "sustainable development" dictates that we take our fuels from crops which manufacture their carbon-based energy on an annual basis, so that, in their use, the carbons are redistributed and recaptured by the next year's crop. This is highly preferable to fossil fuel carbons, which were set aside by natural processes long ago and whose reintroduction into the system today causes an overload on the balance of give and take.

Remember, hemp is petroleum. All of our cars are running on the energy of the sun that was trapped and stored by plant materials eons ago. Today's annual crops perform the same function and that energy is readily available by harvesting the biomass and putting it through a process known as pyrolysis.

This is the process whereby ethanol (fuel from corn) is derived and it has already secured a niche in this country's energy market and is sold through gasoline station pumps even as we speak. Hemp is superior in that it has a higher energy content than corn and it does not need pesticides and herbicides to assist its cultivation. It is, without question, the premier bio fuel on the planet.

Our calculations are that if we planted 6% of this nation's farmland in hemp, (and we have more than that already set aside in soil banks), it would produce all of our country's energy needs. We would not have to import another drop of oil from any other country! This would also completely rehabilitate our agrarian economy and farmers. Is there any wonder that the big oil companies are spending billions of your tax dollars trying to convince us that this plant is evil and anyone associating with it belongs in jail? They will do anything to protect their current monopoly on energy production and distribution in America including lie through their teeth and the teeth of the legislative "ho's" they purchase by contributing inordinate amounts of money to political campaigns.

The same is true of the corporate fascists who have a monopoly on the production of paper which is currently derived from wood pulp through a process that is heavily dependent on caustic chemicals and acids, patented and distributed by the DuPonts and their co-conspirators. The side effects of this method include the unnecessary deforestation of our planet and the creation and release of deadly chemicals into our environment. These include dioxin, which, next to plutonium, is the most carcinogenic matter known to man. The paper itself, being acid-based, turns brittle and yellow and has a useful life of only ten to twenty years.

(I find it instructive that our elected "leaders" in Kentucky discontinued the monitoring system for the release of dioxin into the Ohio river simultaneously with their offering incentive packages to paper plants to locate here.)

Hemp, on the other hand, is the best papermaking material on earth. The "hurds" of the plant, i.e. the outside bark remaining after its fibers are stripped, produce paper materials that are not acid-based and therefore have a useful life of thousands of years. The Vatican has never stopped printing its important works on hemp paper. Indeed, our Constitution and Declaration of Independence themselves are written on hemp paper. Because no acid is used in its processing, and because hydrogen peroxide is used to bleach it instead of sulfuric acid, 90% of the dioxin created in its manufacture is recovered before it is released into our air or water. Finally, utilizing hemp for making paper removes the necessity of indiscriminately cutting our forests for this mundane purpose.

Is it any wonder then that those corporations who own the forests, and the patents on the chemicals and processes used in converting them to paper, are willing to jail and murder our sons and daughters who associate with cannabis, to protect their monopolies?

Is it also any wonder that environmentalists everywhere are getting on the hemp bandwagon because it represents THE alternative to the deforestation of our planet?

When cannabis/hemp is bred in this direction, for the production of these industrial/ textile items, it obviously represents such a threat to the petrochemical monopolies that they will literally go to war, against other countries and even against their own citizens, to protect their economic interests.

When cannabis/marijuana is bred in the direction of medicine, the pharmaceutical giants, who already know that it is the safest, most widely usable therapeutic substance known to man, will go as far or further to make sure that anyone associating with it is criminalized or killed.

Because of its pervasive use throughout history, cannabis was the essential basis for more than 50% of the earth's medicines, prior to its illegalization in 1937. Modern research shows that there were good reasons why its many medical uses were recognized early on. Thousands of studies, many paid for by our own government, before it became completely co-opted by the big special interests, prove its medical utility beyond a doubt, in cases of cancer, nausea, stress relief, asthma, emphysema, migraines and dozens of other ailments.

The fact is that this plant is one of mankind's greatest gifts from God and it is being repressed by special corporate interests who don't give a rat's ass about you or me or our children or grandchildren, or how we may suffer and die in this lifetime, as long as we are limited to purchasing possible remedies from their monopolies.

Their purported synthetic remedies are limited and deadly as evidenced by the 200,000+ people who die in our hospitals yearly from adverse drug reactions (ADRs) as reported in the Journal of American Medical Association, January 1998. This should come as no surprise because all of their patented medicines are synthetically derived and humans have no history of their use nor are their bodies prepared to benignly accept such strong foreign materials into its system.

Please don't get me wrong. I realize there are synthetic medicines, which have great utility in the treatment of the diseases and injuries, which befall human beings. As described in the discussion of my own early misfortunes leading to an appendectomy and splenectomy, I have been the grateful recipient of the benefits of modern medicine. But I also recognize that it is vastly over-prescribed by the doctors and abused intentionally and unintentionally by the masses and that God has given us His own natural medicine, which is more therapeutic in many cases, far safer in all cases. It simply will not kill you; it's less caustic to our system, non-addictive and far cheaper.

But don't take my word for it. Look in your Bible. Start with Genesis (always a good place to start) Chapter one, verse 29. " And God said, Behold, I have given you every herb bearing seed, which is upon the face of all the earth, ..." Move on over to Ezekiel 47:12. "And by the river upon the bank thereof, on this side and on that side, shall grow all trees for meat, whose leaf shall not fade, neither shall the fruit thereof be consumed: it shall bring forth new fruit according to his months, because their waters they issued out of the sanctuary: and the fruit thereof shall be for meat, and the leaf thereof for medicine." [13] Thus saith the Lord GOD; ...

There are more than a hundred references to the presence of God's medicines within the leaves and bushes of His earthly handiwork. Nowhere does it say that He gave us Prozac or Doan's Little Back Pills for mankind's use.

If you believe the Bible is the word of God, literally or through the eyes of his disciples, than you must wonder, as I do, who are the corporate whores who trample His words, His gifts and His intentions for we, His creations?

Wouldn't you know it? They are the very same people who promised their shareholders a return on their investments in the Synthetic Subversion by using our own tax system to force "acceptance of a sudden new ideas of industrial and social reorganization." "Them" again.

And they have been very successful in their mission, as evidenced by the hordes of ministers and preachers purportedly representing the word and will of God by preaching from their pulpits against this green natural plant. You reckon they have any church funds invested in the pharmaceutical stocks? I bet they do.

As part and parcel of this intentional subversion, society's knowledge of the history of this plant and its uses has been systematically diminished by removing all references of it from our historical and popular literature. Our very libraries have been stripped of books and articles, which referred to its valuable uses. As an example, even though our nation's sailing ships were useless without hemp sails and riggings, and our pioneers and western settlers were dependent on the material for their clothing and to cover the Conestoga wagons used in their expansion westward, the Smithsonian Institute no longer uses the word hemp, because "it just confuses the kids."

Because of this planned obfuscation of history, it has taken other activists and me over 3 decades to unearth the foregoing information about this plant. It didn't come all at once and may never have happened at all were it not for one of the true geniuses of this generation, named Jack Herer, whose seminal work, *The Emperor Wears No Clothes*, first published in 1985, broke the silence and spotlighted the conspiracy. But I'm jumping ahead of myself here. I knew none of this information when I smoked marijuana for the first time in 1968. I simply knew that it cured me of asthma and that I was going to associate with it for that purpose as long as I continued to live. My friend Teddy was absolutely right. Marijuana has been velly, velly good for me.

❖ *Role Models & Women*

Though my newfound herbal medicine relieved me of asthma and its inherent production of anxieties, it didn't necessarily give me insight into what I wanted to do with the rest of my days. Teddy and I proceeded to smoke up his stash over the Fall and Winter months, until he left to go west and work on his uncle's ranch in California. I continued to work at W.T. Grants and drink incessantly. With no particular purpose in life, it was easy to say okay the following Spring when my buddy J. asked if I wanted to go to Myrtle Beach with him where he had a job as a lifeguard. I was not very good in the water myself but he assured me his boss could find me a job hanging around the beach. That was good enough for me so, at 21, I hit the road and, for the next 7 months, it hit me right back.

J. had been a lifeguard at Myrtle Beach for several summers during his youth and his reputation as a drinker and womanizer was still intact, as was his ability for water rescue. He took his seat on the beach the day after we got there and I assisted his employer in the rental of chairs and umbrellas.

The next two months were a blur of spending days on the sand and nights of drinking and carousing among the nightclubs. I have since met a lot of men who had a way with women but none of them even came close to J's talent for getting anything and everything he wanted from the women he met. He was charming and ruthless, amoral and asocial. He would cajole them and strong arm them, lie to them and rough them up if they resisted him. Whatever it took for him to get exactly what he wanted from them and Myrtle Beach was his smorgasbord. Thousands of women come there for one or two weeks of the year to party in anonymity, far from the restraints of reason cast by their hometown lifestyles.

One particular day, I was asked by J to occupy his guard seat five times while he and a different woman went to have sex in the float house where all of the chairs and umbrellas were stored during the night. Over a two-month period of time, I saw him "score" with at least 100 women, many with whom he mated within hours of meeting them. I was in awe. I had never seen anything like it, before or since. (Because of this experience however, I can appreciate the possibility that Wilt Chamberlain was telling the truth, years later, when he said he had made love to over 20,000 women in his lifetime.)

Try as I might however, I was a complete failure at emulating the success of J with women. I couldn't bring myself to lie to them and I certainly would not strong-arm them. I was still inherently very shy and my upbringing was one where women were to be respected and treated with dignity, not misled and debased.

I guess you could say that while the basis of his approach was, "You WILL do as I say," mine was the more typical "please, please, please."

As much as I liked observing J to learn what it took to be an alpha male, I was equally put off by his increasing predatory behavior toward women. Finally, one night when I came to our apartment and found him with a woman who was obviously being abused, I reached my breaking point.

I challenged his treatment of her and offered her the opportunity to leave but she refused. It was all her fault she said and she would do anything to work it out with him. I flashed on the reality that what J. actually had was a genius for finding the weak point in every woman's persona and appealing to it in whatever way was necessary to overcome their resistance to his advances. What I had mistaken for strength and abilities on his part was actually the result of his weakness for preying on the weakness of others. Truly strong and capable women terrified him and if he could not destroy the self-reliance they might possess, he wanted nothing to do with them.

He informed me that if I didn't like his style, I could get the hell out. It was 2:30 in the morning and he reckoned I had no place else to go. He was wrong. I picked a pair of jeans and a sweatshirt from my belongings, went out the front door to the two-lane highway, stuck out my thumb and hitchhiked to California.

❖ The Road

It's a hell of a long way from South Carolina to California. And there are very few ways to romanticize the process of hitchhiking from there to there when you start with $40 in your pocket and one change of clothes in a brown paper bag.

I had some experience in hitching rides because I had twice traveled from Lexington to New Orleans for Mardi Gras by such a method. After a while, the thinking hitchhiker realizes that there is an art to standing along side the road asking for a ride. Some folks stand in one spot in the classic pose of their thumb out and pointing in the direction in which they wish to travel. Others walk with a seeming sense of purpose, trusting the passer-bys to deduce that they would accept a ride if it was offered. But the basic lesson that is learned, if you stay on the road long enough, is that the success of hitchhiking is much like the secret to the success of owning a restaurant. Location, location, location.

If you stand in a spot where folks can't see you in time to stop or if there is no place for them to pull over, then you will likely stay there for a very long time. Sure, it definitely helps if you look clean cut or, for that matter, if you just look clean. It also helps to wear a friendly smile while you watch them drive by. And it increases your chances dramatically if you are holding a sign with some specific destination written on it because it tends to show that you have a purpose in your travels rather than just leaving from where you started.

Like most of the other things I've learned, these realizations came to me through the result of trial and error. (In fact, if trial and error is truly the best teacher, I ought to be the smartest guy who ever lived).

Because I started out in the middle of the night on a poorly lit highway with minimal traffic, I walked several miles before I reached the outskirts of town and the sun began to rise. I stopped at a service station and bought a map of the U.S. to plot my route and fix a cardboard sign that simply read California.

During these times, the Viet Nam war was having various effects on the youth of the nation, coloring their basic outlook with a certain devil-may-care attitude. Relative to being drafted against your will and forced into a foreign war where you could expect to kill or be killed, standing along your own nation's roads asking strangers for a ride seemed a fairly benign undertaking.

At this point, the beginning, I was fairly presentable and looked like a typical college-age student type on a summertime lark. This was 1969 and there were lots of young folks on the road. Many of them, like me, had read Jack Kerouac's classic On The Road and there was a certain romanticism about striking out toward the horizon, relying on one's wits and subject to the vicissitudes of whatever fate had in store for you. But the romantic part is only viewable in retrospect, because there is very little "in the moment" appreciation for it when you have stood for 8 hours in one place, cold or hot and hungry, thirsty and tired, without a cent in your pockets or the immediate prospect for relief.

In those years there were no major highways leading west out of Myrtle Beach so I took a series of smaller roads. I had formed a general plan to get to St. Louis, Missouri where I could pick up the fabled Route 66 and take it "down to St. Louie, down through Missouri, to Oklahoma City, looking oh so pretty...." To get there, I had to get through and/or around some other metropolitan obstacles such as Atlanta, Birmingham, Memphis and Little Rock. It took me 4 days and innumerable rides with a group of characters "straight out of central casting."

Men, women, blacks, whites, young and old, driving expensive Cadillacs and wheezing heaps. What most of my benefactors had in common was that they were mostly local folks who were unanimously amused that I had set out on such an ambitious undertaking. "Why are you going to California," they inquired and I had no ready answer. I was still trying to figure it out myself.

Most of the time I just stood there so I had plenty of time to consider the matter between rides. The internal dialogues I engaged in ran the gauntlet from pure reason to naive hopes, firm resolve to sheer panic. I discovered that if you are not careful, it is possible to view each car that passes you as a rejection, not only of the offer of a ride, but of you as a human being. If you let it, these become cumulative and grow until you begin questioning your own dignity as a person. It is difficult to stand with pride, straight and tall, when you are hungry and in need of help.

Hitchhiking is certainly designed to strip away any social pretensions a person has of being special, no matter what their mama told them. And the value of an item becomes a very relative matter. Now days, a hamburger doesn't seem to be a rare or valuable possession, but when you haven't eaten for 36 hours, it's a pretty big deal.

I spent a lot of effort finding something to eat. One of the ways I survived was to approach the managers or owners of roadside restaurants and cafes and offer to wash dishes or clean up the parking lot for a meal. I can't imagine what I must have looked like to them since I spent more than a few nights sleeping along side the roadways or under bridges. On countless occasions they would find something for me to do and then offer me an extra $5 or $10 and a place to clean up before I struck out again. Lots of times I got the offer of an actual job, but the drive within me was too strong and I had to leave.

Years later, I came to recognize this process, and its applicability to the human condition, when I read Fydor Dostoyevski's observation that "Originality and the feeling of one's own dignity are achieved only through work and struggle." No one can hand you your own individual character or give you the feeling of self-worth. You can only gain them by following your own path and finding it on your own. Only you can recognize and exercise your capacity for passion and how to spend it. A person who never discovers what they would be willing to fight and die for in this lifetime has certainly not explored the full 360 degrees of potential they possess as humans.

Life is a journey and unless you map out that journey for yourself, the odds are much greater of falling into Thoreau's "mass of men leading lives of quiet desperation."

I didn't realize the analogy at the time but going on the road for me was a modern age version of that rite of passage where young Indians left their villages and took to the wilderness to experience deprivation, hunger and thirst so that they might achieve that Originality and Dignity, become closer to a basic communion with their Creator, and rise through adolescence into adulthood.

I have also come to understand that some people don't need to hit the road to learn these lessons. Some people can travel completely around the world and never learn a damn thing while someone else can sit still along side a pond and see the entire universe.

Hitchhiking as a mode of traveling is one way of learning to appreciate the nature and character of roads in general. America's interstate highway system today is one of mankind's Seven Wonders of the World. It boggles my mind that just 100 years earlier, a traveler in a wagon might cover 10 miles or less in a day while we think nothing of driving 60 to 100 miles to meet a friend for dinner.

The basic plan for this interstate system was initially devised by a certain young Army Captain Dwight David Eisenhower, who appreciated its necessity after being ordered to conduct the Army's first cross-country automobile caravan from Washington D.C to San Francisco, California in 1919. It took him 62 days at an average of 5 miles per hour. This demonstrated a major flaw in any military plans for our national defense. So when he became President in 1952, he insisted that a system of smooth, level highways be built throughout the nation to interlock and allow the rapid transport of military hardware and necessities of war to anywhere within our borders.

These roads were meant to span canyons and rivers, tunnel through hills and rise above swamps and wetlands. Also, in every five miles of highway built, there must be a one mile stretch which is as straight as an airport runway in case a military plane has to land in that area.

Even in the late 60s, traveling by auto over long distances was different than today. The system was not yet integrated, seamless. There were fragments of 4 lane highways throughout the country which might run for 10 to 20 miles, then intersperse with two lanes for the next 70 miles. It would be another 25 years before all 42,000 mile of it would come together.

There were also no bypasses around the major cities, so if you did not have a plan on where you wanted to be let out on the road, you stood the chance of being stranded in the heart of a metropolis, where the nature and character of sticking out your thumb was viewed in a different manner.

The police were much more likely to inquire about your circumstances if you were on the streets in their city. Sometimes their suggestion that you get the hell out of their particular Dodge City was leveraged with the alternative of spending some extra days in the hoosegow. Undoubtedly, I hiked more miles getting from the centers of the cities to the outskirts then I ever did walking on rural highways.

There were several times however when the offer of 7 days-to-serve had a certain attraction to it. The chance to take a shower, rest and eat didn't come often and, like I said, everything is relative, especially suffering.

By the time I made it to Oklahoma City, I was on the third version of my California sign, the letters growing much larger in each instance.

That one word seemed to convey different meanings to the people who watched me hold it. Resoluteness, determination, and at least the semblance of a plan, with an ultimate destination so far away, it disguised the reality of just how clueless I was about my future.

The sign also seemed to help with the length of the rides I got. Some folks who stopped had a lot of miles to cover and needed someone to talk to or even to help with the driving. The average rides that used to take me 10 to 20 miles soon became good for 100 miles or more.

After 7 or 8 days on the road (these circumstances will definitely alter your perception of time) I found myself standing outside Flagstaff, Arizona in some pretty chilly May weather. I had spent most of the previous night holed up in a café in Winslow, where I tried to doze without attracting too much attention from the owner. Finally I got to my feet and out the front door when I got an offer for a ride to Flagstaff. I slept the whole way.

He let me out on the highway in the early dawn and I was on the road for about an hour when a man that I judged to be about 30 pulled up beside me in a new, dark green Dodge Charger. He looked at the sign I held and said, "Hey, I'm going to California too but I want to stop in Vegas for a couple of days. Will you work for a living?"

"What do you mean?" I asked, trying to delay my getting in his car until I figured out what he had in mind.

He laughed and replied, "Don't worry, it's honest work. But there's a lot of people who won't give an honest hour's work for an honest dollar." He went on to explain that he was working his way around the country by stopping in various cities, going to the business districts and offering to detail the cars of people while they worked. He had all the tools in his trunk and, alone, he could handle 2 cars but the both of us could earn even more. Our only other requirement was access to an outside faucet.

It sounded like a hell of a deal to me and I had certainly never been to Vegas. I readily accepted his offer and hopped in.

I don't remember Rick's last name but he was one hell of a nice guy. He had done some "hitching" of his own and knew what it could be like, especially being underdressed for the weather like I obviously was. We found a lot to talk about and the ride went pretty quick. It couldn't possibly have had anything to do with the fact that he opened that big Charger motor to full steam ahead every chance he got. We rocketed across the desert and hit 120 mph regularly all the way to Boulder City.

While I found the geography between Oklahoma City and Albuquerque to be of some interest because it was the first time I had seen it, I was truly impressed by the desert territory throughout the Southwest. From Flagstaff to Las Vegas, the desert landscape is sparse but filled with a distinct presence as if unseen energies occupy the air while the mountains that interrupt the flat desert floor offer cooler air, more greenery and sometimes even snow. Everyone should explore the magic of the Southwest territory if they get the chance. I recommend you have your own transportation.

We got to Las Vegas in the early afternoon and went straight to work. We pulled up to a little strip shopping center, with a back parking lot with outside faucets. Then he approached the shop owners about giving them a heck of a deal on detailing their car while they worked. I looked more than a little road weary so he did the selling and I started to work.

To his credit Rick joined in as soon as he lined up the third car which was all we could hope to do that day. He had two hand polishers, a sweeper, soap, buckets, rags and wax. We ran a line to the nearest outlet in the store/shop and we busted our butts for the next 6 hours.

All of the customers seemed satisfied and willing to pay the $15 each we charged them. Rick took $5 for the supplies and we split the remaining $40.

It seems like to me that you could get a decent motel room with two beds in Vegas back then for about $16-$18 so we split the cost, cleaned up and went out to dine in Vegas where you could eat like a king for $5.

Life on the road looked a hell of a lot better from here than any other place I had occupied thus far. A full belly and a place to sleep was all that I could ever hope for so I opted out of exploring the strip and retired to the motel while Rick went on his own frolic and detour.

Rick woke me at dawn the next morning. We ate breakfast (Vegas never sleeps) and started working early. We got a referral from one of our previous customers and then another. By the end of the day we had finished another 6 gleaming testaments to the power of the proverbial "elbow grease." And we split over $100 because several tips came our way.

I splurged on a new shirt and light windbreaker before we walked around several casinos for entertainment that night, dining well once again. The city of Las Vegas wanted your gambling dollar and went out of their way to provide food and entertainment at reduced prices to get you there. It worked for me but I wasn't going to gamble away my last dollar so again I retired early because we were leaving the next morning.

Rick and I started driving down the main Vegas strip on our way out of town at about 9 a.m. He was describing his winning streak the night before which had netted him another $200. An impulse overcame me. "Let's pull in here for a minute Rick," I pointed to the parking lot of the Golden Horseshoe casino, famous for having 100 $10,000 bills in their lobby, encased in glass and surrounded by a gold frame shaped like, what else, a horseshoe.

"Man, I can't come to Vegas and not gamble at least once," I explained.

The rest of what happened is as clear to me now as if it happened yesterday. I had exactly $20 to my name and I bought two $10 chips. I went directly to the roulette table, which was empty, except for the croupier who was talking to another employee.

Without really thinking about it, I laid both chips on the number 21 and stepped back. It was the only bet on the board. The croupier smiled, turned the wheel and let the ball go. Round and round it went and, when it stopped, there rested that blessed little ball in the 21 slot.

The two guys looked at each other in amazement. Rick was stunned too. But no one was more stunned than I was when they handed me $720 worth of chips and invited me to play more.

"I've been here 20 years," said one of them, "and I never saw a single bet on the board win like that. Son, you're on a roll."

Man sometimes I'm glad that guy said that and sometimes I wish he hadn't. It struck me clear as a bell that this was my opportunity to hit it big, get something for nothing and live like a king, cause I was "On A Roll". I believed it was obvious to everyone, so I went back to the blackjack tables where I thought I knew the game and would parlay my new found status of "anointed one" into some real cash.

I never even saw the dealer's hands move he was so quick. Beaten at blackjack in 16 straight hands. What are the odds? In 10 minutes they had it all back except for one $20 chip. I was stunned again. And this time a little queasy.

In the 10 minutes I possessed the money I imagined arriving in California with a pocket full of money, establishing a base of operations and living "large" as they say. $700 was significant and the lack of $700 became even more significant. I cashed in my remaining chip and we headed out toward Los Angeles. It would have helped my mood greatly if

I had already learned from Rudyard Kipling's fabulous poem IF, to "treat triumph and disaster as the twin imposters they are." I know my mood arced from one end of the emotional spectrum to the other in a very short period. I was pretty glum for the last 200 miles.

Coming upon Los Angeles from the east was unforgettable because the first thing you saw from 50 miles away was a big cloud hovering over the ground. The city couldn't be seen for another 40 miles but the smog sure as hell could.

I had decided to go to San Francisco because I had been reading about the upcoming "Summer of Love" expected there. Rick and I examined a map and decided the best way to get to San Francisco was through Bakersfield and Fresno. He and I parted company on a freeway outside Los Angeles.

It took me less than a day to get to Frisco. Four hours of it was spent waiting while the three people hitchhiking in front of me on that particular entrance onto the freeway caught their ride. I had never had competition for a ride from other hitchers before and there were certain unwritten rules. Don't butt in line. If you don't have a sign expressing some unique destination that sets you apart from the others (Frisco didn't qualify) and they got there first, they get to go first. Just go sit down and wait.

Waiting, waiting and waiting some more are all art forms a person can mold if they wait long enough and often enough. Like everything else, time, just like time spent waiting, is relative. (I know Einstein told you that but as it is, we tend to rediscover it for ourselves every time we have to think about it.)

The time spent watching another hitchhiker trying to catch a ride is particularly excruciating. You tend to become critical of their style and judgmental of them as human beings so I waited with a measurable angst as the three others caught rides and my turn came around.

I got lucky again. My next ride was going right into San Francisco and we drove through the increasing darkness at a steady pace. This guy was driving a black Lincoln and relished telling me that he was a bodyguard for some union brass. From his appearance and demeanor, I could believe him.

He let me out at 3:30 in the morning in downtown San Francisco. It was cold and windy and the streets were deserted. I felt more alone there in that major city then at any other time before on the road.

I ducked into an all night pool hall and saw all the street people trying to sleep with their eyes open and pretending to watch the games so they wouldn't get thrown back into the darkness. I felt the urge to do the same but decided against it. I wasn't going to find the "Summer of Love" there, or anywhere in the city, in the mood I had arrived in.

I had spent 10 days on the road hitchhiking from coast to coast to find my destiny. But where was the Love, Man?

After 45 minutes on the streets of San Francisco, I turned around and hitchhiked back to South Carolina.

It should be against the law to describe an 8-day period of time in which you hitchhike 3000 miles, and face possible peril with each decision you make, as "uneventful." That must have been the case however, because nothing stands out in my mind about this leg of my journey. In reality, each time a person decided to stop and offer me a ride was an act of considerable kindness and a renewal of my sometimes-flagging faith in human nature.

I must have experienced the discomfort of hot days, cold nights, rain and wind, hunger and thirst but they seemed more the norm than the unusual. At least I had the more formal plan now of having an exact destination, which was to recover my belongings in Myrtle Beach and hit the road again. The thought of having a ready change of clothes and basic toiletries brought me great comfort. It wouldn't be much but at least it would be mine.

It really came as no big surprise however when I got to the motel in Myrtle Beach where we had been staying and found it occupied by other people. J. had moved and my stuff had been left by the curb long ago. Luckily I remembered that the fellow I had been working for still owed me for several days so I stopped by to see "Badger" and he came through with $50. He told me that J. had been arrested for assault several days earlier and nobody wanted to go his bail. That included me.

I spent a day at the beach and decided that I might not have given the West Coast much of a chance. I made up my mind to try it again but this time I would travel the northern routes and aim for Alaska. It still had the lure of being on the "frontier" and a guy's manhood would definitely be tested if he got there and tried to stay. Off I went to find out.

The most vivid memory I have of this particular undertaking occurred soon after I got started. I planned to go from Columbia, South Carolina through Augusta and then to Atlanta. From there I would bear north to Nashville, St. Louis and then Kansas City.

I struck out in the early morning and again things were slow getting away from the coast. "Badger" had given me a small suitcase and a couple of shirts to which I added new underwear and a shaving/shampoo kit. Hell, I felt ready for anything.

The rides however were sparse. It seemed like everyone was only going a few miles and by the time I reached the outskirts of Augusta, Georgia it was about midnight and hot and humid as hell.

My ride insisted that he knew the best spot to let me out. He said it was a bypass, where I was likely to get the longest rides. I took his word for it but when I got out of the car and he pulled off, I immediately sensed that I might be in trouble.

I stood beside the road and waited in vain for some traffic to come by. Any traffic. It was pitch dark and all I could hear were the critters of the night doing their thing. Clouds obscured the moon and stars and I felt very lonely and vulnerable. Remembering the old adage about "whistling past the graveyard" I picked up my suitcase and began walking.

I walked for about three hours during which two cars drove by, neither stopping nor even slowing down. The humidity was oppressive and I began developing a king-sized thirst, which only worsened the more I thought about it. I couldn't see through the underbrush along the road but I got the impression that I was in a swampy area and it didn't seem like a good idea to lay down to rest.

About the time when I became convinced I had been let out in the middle of hell I saw headlights coming my way. I knew that all they could see of me was a large dark shape standing beside the road and the chances of them stopping were slim and none. When they slowed down and then came to a halt in the middle of the road I could scarcely believe my luck.

It was a decades old pickup truck and I could make out two people, a male driver in a beat up hat and a woman sitting right next to him.

"Hop in fella," the man said and I didn't ask any questions. I don't think I was ever so grateful for company in my life. "Where you headed?"

When I said Alaska they both laughed out loud. They didn't seem concerned at all about the danger of picking up a stranger out of nowhere in the middle of the night. The next thing they did was offer me a warm beer which I accepted and drained. They had been dancing in town and were polishing off a six pack on the way home.

Bob and Mary. Husband and wife for 25 years and they sat next to each other in the truck like they were still in love.

As we started down the road again, I noticed that Mary shifted the gears in the truck with her left hand while Bob drove with his own left hand. It struck me as a little strange but I didn't mention anything about it.

Bob and Mary had a farm "up the road" where they raised "some pigs." They informed me that the "bypass" I was on actually went nowhere and had very little traffic. They thought it would be a good idea for me to come home with them and get some sleep and they would take me to a better spot in the morning.

A little while later we got on a gravel road and thirty minutes later we pulled up to a small unlit farmhouse surrounded by the unmistakable ambience of nearby pigs. It wasn't until we got inside and Bob turned on the lights that I realized why Mary had shifted his truck gears for him. He didn't have a right arm or a right eye.

His wife went immediately to the kitchen and began fixing some food. She wouldn't take no for an answer and, at 5 in the morning, she made me sit down to pounds and pounds of ham, bacon, pork chops, biscuits, gravy and eggs. Neither of them ever quit smiling while I ate until I almost fell asleep, face first, into my plate. They fixed me a cot in their living room and I don't even remember my head hitting the pillow. I was out like the proverbial light.

It was noon before I awoke on my own. Mary made over me some more and they both insisted I spend the next night with them again to rest and get ready for the long trip ahead. I couldn't say no.

Bob and Mary were totally in love even after 24 years of marriage. Bob had lost both his right arm and right eye on the beaches of Normandy on D-Day, 1944. He had come back to his childhood home and Mary, his childhood sweetheart and they had not spent a night apart since that time.

They married and bought the fifty acres we were sitting on shortly after. They had built everything that stood on the land with their own three hands, including the house, a small barn, fencing and the pig sties.

The house had four rooms and stairs leading to an attic. They had measured and cut every board and Mary would hand them up to Bob on the ladder where he would lean against them with his right shoulder and nail them into place with his left hand. I was blown away.

They made over me like I was the son they never had. I helped them slop the 50 or so hogs they had and wondered how long a person had to hang around pigs to get used to the smell. It obviously didn't bother Bob and Mary because they never stopped laughing with each other the whole time I was there.

In the 34 years since I met them, I still haven't found two happier people than Bob and Mary. There was not a thing in the world they wanted that they didn't have. If they wanted it, they made it.

There was not a pretentious bone in either of their bodies nor was there any remorse about what difficulties life had handed them. Bob was proud to have served his country and simply glad to be alive. The most valuable treasure that they had found was each other, and it was palpable in every glance they shared.

I've met many people since Bob and Mary, rich and poor, under any and all conditions, and at every level of education, but I have never seen anyone more satisfied with each other and with life than this one-eyed, one-armed pig farmer and his wife living in the woods outside Augusta, Georgia. It must be true that happiness is not getting what you want, but wanting what you have.

The next day they gave me a ride to another highway and handed me a $20 bill as I got out. They wouldn't take no for an answer. I couldn't thank them enough so I made up my mind to pass it on when I got the chance to perform a kind act for another. That, I concluded, was the way it is supposed to work.

For the next several days I made my way west, through Nashville, St. Louis, Kansas City and on to Denver. Three rides later I was in Sacramento, California and headed north on highway 5. Three days later I was in a small town in Washington just inside the Canadian border. I think its name was Blaine.

I knew that customs would not let me cross the border as a hitchhiker so I bought a Greyhound bus ticket to Vancouver and took my seat. I had never crossed a border before and didn't know the procedure but I learned quickly enough when agents boarded the bus to check tickets and i.d.s.

My bag and I were pulled from the bus and taken to the Customs station where I was interrogated as to my plans. They soon let me know that my $18 and the best of intentions on finding a job in Alaska were not sufficient wherewithal to allow me to cross into Canada. Honestly, I was a little relieved because the weather was colder already than I had imagined it would be.

I went to the nearest bar I could find and drank several beers. I decided to call some people I knew from Lexington. I knew Teddy wasn't around so the next guy who came to mind was a mutual friend who had married and moved to Florida. I called his family in Lexington and they gave me his number.

He was still friendly as ever and his wife was just as receptive. Come to Cape Kennedy, Florida and stay with us a while they offered. That was good enough for me and so, once more, I set out across the country.

Cape Kennedy was originally named Cape Canaveral and is the center of America's space program. Our first rockets were launched from there and our space shuttle still is. By the time I got there I was pretty spaced myself. I had been on the road for almost 40 days solid now and coast to coast twice. I was worn to a frazzle and eager to stay in one place for a while. The welcome I received from my friends made me think this might be the spot.

B.J. and C.C. had known me in high school and nothing I did ever really surprised them. They acted as if it was the most natural thing in the world for me to take over a back bedroom of their trailer and look for a job. They both worked and they helped me find a spot pumping gas at a nearby service station.

For the first few days I did little but eat, sleep and work. I had a lot of catching up to do in all three areas. One evening, after about a week, we were sitting around listening to music when B.J. said, "Gatewood, do you like LSD?"

I didn't know what to say. I had heard about it, of course, but had never met anyone who admitted to ever doing it. I confessed that I had never seen it before.

"I have some 'orange barrel'", B.J. informed me. "I think we should do it tonight and go to the beach in the morning. Is that okay with you CC?" he asked.

"I don't want to," she replied, "but you'all go ahead."

❖ *LSD*

LSD, (lysergic acid diethylamide), was accidentally discovered in a lab in 1938 by chemist Albert Hoffman. He got some on his skin and, on his way home from work, he began hallucinating. In the first experiments that followed, it was thought that it mimicked schizophrenia and could give insight into the treatment of same. Many chemists and scientists studied it, perhaps the most famous being Dr. Timothy Leary, who popularized it by encouraging its use and for the users to "turn on, tune in and drop out." This obviously scared the hell out of the authorities who illegalized it in the late 60s. But too late. The genie was out of the bottle and word had gotten around, especially the "hippie" crowd. If you wanted to "take a trip and never leave the farm", this was the drug of choice.

People who used LSD related that what they experienced depended a great deal on how much "acid" they consumed. Doses ranging from 20 to 80 micrograms caused minor physical sensations where the senses of touch and hearing became more acute as did colors. Folks who did a lot more of it, such as 100 to 200 micrograms ("mikes") reported more vivid experiences including visual hallucinations and feelings that time might not move in a uniformly linear manner. Also, it was believed to redirect impulses along the body's neural passageways so that what started as sound might be ultimately experienced by the brain as a visual color. Therefore some folks said they could see sound and hear color. (A little like Walt Disney if you ask me).

On the negative side, emotions and internal feelings might be magnified so those folks with underlying psychiatric problems reported feelings of anxiety and sometimes panic attacks. The authorities exacerbated these reports in their usual manner so it was difficult for anyone to actually know the truth about it second- hand. As it was with me and others oriented towards experimentation, if it was available and a friend recommended it, I was likely to try it.

B.J had "tripped" several times and offered to guide me through the experience. There were two different mindsets about this. Leary proposed the "set and setting" method where the person about to embark on the journey arranged to be in familiar and comfortable surroundings so that surprises would be minimized and unpleasant interruptions unlikely. He also suggested a "guide," (someone who had experienced a trip) help with the initiation.

Another proponent of the LSD experience, Ken Kesey, author of *One Flew Over the Cuckoo's Nest* and *Sometimes a Great Notion*, was much more experientially oriented. He and his group, called the Merry Pranksters, preferred to get out and interact with the world while under the influence. They had, indeed, traveled the U.S. in the mid-sixties, in a bus painted in psychedelic colors, in a tour de force of early performance art captured in Tom Wolfe's best-selling book *The Electric Cool Aid Acid Test.*

B.J. was an experienced tripper under both conditions and suggested that I try it first in his living room with pre-prepared food and drink nearby and then on the early morning beach if I felt comfortable with it.

About 8 p.m. that evening he handed me a teensy speck of paper and told me to put it on my tongue and let it dissolve there. I followed his instructions and sat back to await the results. After about an hour I reported that I didn't feel anything yet so he gave me another one. Within a half-hour the first one kicked in and the second one followed a while afterward.

There was no sudden onrush of intoxication or hallucination but I became increasingly aware of my surroundings and their influence on me. I sensed that the wall between my spiritual and physical being was dissolving and I could feel the essentially arbitrary nature of many of the rationales furnished me by society about my relationship as a human creature with the physical world around me. Basically, everything came into question. Who am I? What am I doing here? What is my purpose? Is yellow the best color for a banana?

B.J. and I had intense discussions on all of these matters over the next 10 hours and then he decided that I was "good to go" and we headed for the beach. When we arrived and began walking along the natural path, instead of being cooped up in the man-made environment of his living room, I became aware of the palpable life force emanating from all living creatures. Everything that had washed up on the shore during the night, the sea urchins, the crabs and the seaweed itself had a life aura that I had never noticed before. I felt the vibrations of the light from the rising sun and my heart and the sands themselves pulsated with the rhythm of the ocean waters. I felt more at home with the physical world then ever before. I realized that I was an integral part of it rather than just a temporary visitor. I was a part of every one of the invisible and still visible stars and of every one of the many grains of sand beneath my feet.

In the introduction to his biography, Willie Nelson acknowledges that he believes we are all stardust, made from the same material that makes up the rest of all of creation. A universal building block of matter. Willie laughed when he told me that Buddha's order at Burger King was "Make me one with everything."

Now I had some insight into what Buddha was talking about. My initial experience with LSD showed me the truth of that by lowering the defensiveness of my manufactured ego and allowing me to feel "as one" with "everything."

After several hours on the beach B.J. drove us back to his trailer and we slept for the next twelve hours. I awoke amid the usual surroundings, thoroughly grateful for the experience but relieved that it was over. I had "returned" with a hell of a lot to think about. Life itself, for example.

For the next week or so, B.J. and I discussed the episode and I worked as many hours as I could pumping gas. I felt a growing urge to hit the road again with my newfound perspectives. I definitely wanted to see Teddy again. His initiating me to the use of cannabis was a milder form of my initiation to LSD and I wanted to share the experience with him. He had been my "guide" before and now, perhaps, I could return the favor.

I called his family in Lexington and found that Teddy was working on his uncle's almond orchard in Northern California. I didn't bother to call him and let him know I was coming. I just cashed my paycheck and asked B.J. and CC for a ride to the nearest Interstate. They obliged and I found myself again standing on an entrance ramp on the East Coast holding a sign that said California. As it turned out, that sign was worth far more than its weight in gold.

❖ *Teddy & Me*

I got my first ride within two minutes of beginning my trip. It was with several students in a station wagon who were headed north to Jacksonville. Just after we reached Daytona Beach, we were passed by a late model Chevrolet, with California tags, and a service man's uniform hanging in the back window. At my request, the fellow driving the station wagon pulled along side the Chevy and I got the driver's attention and held my sign up for him to see. He nodded and pulled over to the shoulder.

He was, indeed, in the Air Force and lived in California. He was driving coast to coast but planned to spend a week with his parents in Oklahoma City. He was glad for the company and with help driving. Me too. I thanked the students and got on board with Mike. What a break!

I remember this trip quite clearly because of my incredible luck. We turned north when we reached Tallahassee and headed to Montgomery, Alabama, then on to Birmingham, then Memphis, Little Rock and finally Oklahoma City. Driving in 8-hour shifts, we stopped only for gas and reached the west side of the city in less than 28 hours. He let me out on the bypass and I stuck out my thumb once again. Within 5 minutes I caught my next ride and another big break. He was headed to Los Angeles. We arrived there 48 hours later.

I've often wondered if that could be a record time in hitchhiking from one coast to the other. Three rides in three days. If that isn't a record it's missing a hell of a chance to be one.

It took me another day and a half to get from L.A. to the town of Chico, about 150 miles north of San Francisco in a valley situated between 5 different National Forests. Teddy's uncle's almond orchard was located several miles outside the city. It was the early part of August and the heat was stifling. I got directions to his ranch and walked the last several miles along a two-lane road.

He wasn't hard to find. Wherever the most smoke and noise was, there would be Teddy. In this case, deep in a tree-lined orchard, he was standing on the back of a tractor on which was mounted a pneumatic air hammer, able to swing horizontally, with a vise-like grip on the end of it.

Attached to the rear of the tractor was a twenty-foot trough on wheels with a tarp rolled up on one side of it.

As the tractor went from tree to tree it stopped so that the Mexican laborers who followed it could grab the ends of the tarp, which had been split down the middle, and run them under both sides of the tree. When Teddy gripped the trunk of an almond tree with the vise and fingered the trigger on the air hammer, the machine shook the tree violently and its nutty fruit dropped like rain onto canvas.

Two of the Mexicans carried long sticks to encourage the more tenacious nuts to join their brethren below and when the tree was clean, the furthermost ends of the tarp were run back to the trough and fastened to an electric roller. The nut-filled cloth was drawn to the trough and emptied onto the bottom where a conveyor belt carried the nuts to a large wooden box at the very end of the line.

Teddy was sweatin' and cussin' which told me he was having a good time. He was thoroughly surprised and happy to see me. He called a break and took me to meet his uncle who looked mighty skeptical when Teddy suggested he hire me to work alongside his migrant troops.

"It's hard work Gatewood and it gets to be 110 to 112 degrees out there. The weeds are waist high and the snakes are afraid because the ticks are so big but if you want to make a fool of yourself in front of the Mexicans then go ahead. We'll see how long you last."

With a send-off like that, I was hot to prove that I could handle any menial job that another guy could do so I busted my butt from the very first day and proved one thing beyond any reasonable doubt. Man, could those little Mexicans work!

Harvesting almonds in 110 degree heat among weeds, snakes and ticks is pretty close to hell on earth if you are an adult gringo who has never done it before. If you are a migrant Mexican laborer who has done it since you were 10, it's pretty well another day at the office. They know how to pace themselves.

Pedro, Juan, Miguel and Jesus are some of the names I remember. They traveled with their families in pickup trucks with campers on the back or vans loaded with everything a family of six or more could want. They were on the road for 9 months of the year, following the harvest north. They would sit around the campfires at night, enjoying their families and the rest. The crews I worked with ranged in age from 12 to 40 or so and everyone was friendly.

They should have been. I gave them lots to laugh about my first several days there. I couldn't keep up with any of the rest of them as they raced the tarps under the trees and got out of the way before Teddy pelted their heads with his "incoming" fire. He was proud that his gang out-harvested the other three crews working in the orchard that early Fall and he reminded me a little too much of my Drill Instructor at Paris Island but we got the work done. Eventually, I resembled someone who could tell his ass from an almond tarp.

I told Teddy about my LDS "trip" and it turns out that Teddy had tried it in Thailand and really enjoyed the experience. We both looked forward to trying it again with each other when we had the time to enjoy it.

We worked twelve hours a day, seven days a week for the next 3 weeks. Time-off was spent drinking beer, smoking marijuana and talking about psychedelics.

When the harvest was done on his uncle's place the Mexicans moved on and Teddy and I discussed our own options. "The Summer of Love" in San Francisco, so close by, had an irresistible charm to men our age so we arranged for his uncle to give us a ride to Berkeley. He was as skeptical of our lack of planning as he was about everything else in life.

"I don't understand it," he said for the tenth time as let us out in the middle of Berkeley's Telegraph Avenue where the national media had assured us we could score whatever illicit substance we had in mind to try. "You don't have a place to stay and don't know anybody. You each have one suitcase and a few hundred dollars and Ted you have a hunting rifle in a rifle case. Don't you want to get a motel room and search for a place…?" he went on.

Ted finally waved him off with a grin. "We'll be all right," he assured him and we both waved as he drove off. "There goes one skeptical man," I observed.

"Yep," replied Teddy. "He sure is."

It was two in the afternoon and the place was teeming with life. Everyone seemed to vibrating, with some sort of noble destination and a purpose in their step. Music was coming from many of the various street-front shops and open windows along the Avenue. Everything seemed brightly colored and the word psychedelic seemed to actually hover in the air until I realized it was the hippie standing on the nearest corner who was actually hawking acid on the streets in a low voice to certain people walking past him. Being naturally drawn to temptation I approached him as Ted stood off to the side with his bag and rifle. The guy didn't miss a beat as he eyed us both.

"Whatch'a got?" I inquired.

"Purple dot and orange barrel," he said.

"How much?"

"Two dollars for heads, four dollars for straights and six dollars for narcs. You can have it for four."

There went my first 8 bucks.

Teddy and I decided to check out the bulletin board at the Student Center where we immediately struck pay dirt. Right in the middle of the board, and less than an hour old, was an invitation from two girls for two roommates, male or female, to share a 4 bedroom, fully furnished house in the middle of everything for the next 12 months. It sounded perfect and, as it turned out, it truly was.

Melanie and Sandy were longtime residents of Frisco who wanted to live where the action was while they went to school. They knew of a professor couple who were going on sabbatical for a year and needed someone to look after their house. It had everything and the rent was cheap. We jumped at the chance.

The girls gave us a break and okayed the deal after we bought them supper. Within 5 hours of being let out on the streets of San Francisco for the third time in my life, I was settled in with a full belly and 2 orange barrels. I was beginning to feel the Love, Man.

Both of us guys went to look for a job the next morning and I got home mid-afternoon. About 3:30 there came a knock at the door and when I opened it up there was a fellow, about 30, with long brown hair and a big smile. I can generally spot a salesman a mile away but he wasn't carrying anything so I was curious.

"You just move in?" he inquired as if he could be of help.

"Sure did."

"Where you from?" he studied me and I knew he had something on his mind.

"Kentucky," I answered. "Can I help you?"

"Maybe I can help you," he said. "Do you need anything? Any drugs? Any Pills? Any pot?"

For one of the few times in my life, I was speechless. I looked up and down the street and saw nothing out of order but all kinds of scenarios played themselves out rapid-fire in my imagination.

He sensed my confusion and asked to step inside. I didn't really feel threatened and soon he was describing his venture as we sat in the living room.

"I used to deal on the street corner like everyone else," he began. "But there was too much competition and always the cops. So I decided to map off six square blocks here in the middle and keep track of who lives where and what they do. Some of them were my customers to begin with but I've added a lot more because they are all tired of buying off the street where you never know what you're getting. Whenever anyone moves, I knock on the door and, if they look straight, I just pretend to have the wrong address. If they look like you, I let them know what the deal is."

"So you're like acid-age Avon, eh?" I opined.

"Exactly," he grinned. "Now what time would you like me to return with my wares?"

"Tonight, tonight. I know another guy who's going to love meeting you."

Teddy got a job the first day as a mechanic and two days later I began work at an employment office in downtown San Francisco. On the fourth day there, a huge anti-war demonstration swept through the streets below our offices. Thousands of people marched and demonstrated at noon and I felt compelled to join them, swept up in the energy and flow of the event. My views on the war were changing and I was beginning to understand that my country's motives for sending young men like me to die in Viet Nam might not be as righteous as I had been led to believe.

The diversity of the people marching in the streets caught my eye. They were young and old, hippie and straight, well dressed and otherwise. Several younger men with bullhorns, including veterans in their uniforms and medals, were in front of the procession and they led the crowd in chanting anti-war slogans. More and more office and white-collar workers on their lunch hour joined the group until at least 5,000 to 6,000 stood in a downtown park and heard speakers decry our government's policy of military expansion of our ground war in Asia.

I believe that this was the first time I really began questioning my country's motives for being in Viet Nam and to recognize that business and corporate interests were calling the shots on our foreign policies. What was good for General Motors might, indeed, be good for our country but it was tearing the hell out of a lot of individuals and families.

I started to realize that true patriotism doesn't mean blindly accepting whatever the country's officeholder de jour tells us is in our best interest. It occurred to me that young lives were being sacrificed to advance economic policies and political careers and not to "contain communism" as we were being told. The vivid righteousness of this particular war began to fade for me that day and I vowed to examine the sources and motives of all future calls-to-arms issued by our politicians and draped in the red, white and blue cloak of patriotism. I began to study the nature and character of the "merchants of death" who sponsor conflict to feed their bottom line.

The people responsible for war knew only too well which buttons to push and which chimes to ring to get young men to volunteer to go to war and, when it becomes a hard-sell because of the sheer number of body bags coming back on the return flights, they institute the draft to continue the unending stream of grist for the mill.

These munitions and chemical makers, these petroleum companies and the investment bankers all have vested interests in maintaining a constant wartime footing someplace in the world. It has been like this since the DuPont family (the "Merchants of Death") got the exclusive right from George Washington to manufacture gunpowder for the United States Army, a right they held for the first 119 years of this country's existence. War is Hell for some people and Profits for others.

War also drops a question into the lap of the generation who is asked to actually fight it. It's a simple question but most folks would rather not have to face it to find the answer. "What is worth fighting and dying for in this lifetime?"

I didn't realize it at the time, but I would ask that question hundreds of times in front of future audiences, who I encourage to find their own answer, because the pursuit of it is what lends true passion to life.

At first, Ted and I planned to get residency in California by living there for a year, then going to school. However, I started getting a little homesick and it was contagious. By the 4th week of paradise, we decided to take a break and attend a music festival south of San Francisco, in Monterey, then hitchhike back to Kentucky. California dreaming was fine for a while but nothing beats family and the old homestead.

But first the music festival. Let me offer an apology to anyone whom I have told in the past that I attended the 1969 Monterey Pop Festival at Esalen Institute in Big Sur, California. That concert was actually at the Monterey Fairgrounds and I wasn't there. I was at a festival at Esalen in the Fall of 1969 but it was under another name.

I found out I was mistaken about which concert I actually attended while doing some present day research on just who played there. I remember Crosby, Stills and Nash, Janis Joplin, Jimi Hendrix and Joan Baez and I know the rest were just as well known but I can't bring them to mind. George Carlin once said, "If you can remember the 60s, you weren't a part of them." I've been working on the 70s, 80s, 90s and 00s too.

What I will always remember is sitting on the most beautiful cliff side on the whole West Coast, overlooking the Pacific Ocean with several thousand other kindred souls and listening to the best music of the decade played by the original artist, thirty feet away. Adding to the mix of music and psychedelics was a portion of the 10,000 kilos (2.2 pounds) of "Panama Red" which had been smuggled into the San Francisco harbor the day before. It was a categorically righteous smoke that would have made a hobo reading a phone book entertaining and whoever had a stash was taking it out and liberally sharing it with the rest of us. I liked their Karma.

This was a two day festival and as the first day came to an end at sunset, the out-of-town crowd scrambled for places to spend the night. There were no accommodations on the grounds so everyone piled into their cars and headed south to the several campgrounds on the coastline. Ted and I caught a ride to one, thirty miles south, and it was almost filled when we got there. Campfires were everywhere as was music from dozens of guitars and drums being played around them.

Ted and I had sleeping bags and we commandeered ground near one of the fires. We wandered around a bit and came upon one of the bigger fires with several folks around it. One lady, dressed in gypsy finery, had a blanket spread in front of her on which lay at least twenty bags of marijuana. I watched as she exchanged them one at a time for money but I couldn't hear her terms. Finally I worked up the nerve to approach her myself.

"Is that the 'Panama Red' I smoked today at the festival?" I asked.

"It sure is," she answered.

"How much?"

"Seven dollars an ounce and twelve dollars for two."

I stood there for about five minutes trying to decide whether I wanted to spend another five dollars for a second ounce of some of the best marijuana in the world. Ultimately my better judgement kicked in and I got the two-ounce deal. Hell, I saved two bucks and this might be the closest I would ever get to the Summer of Love, Man. Damned if I was going to pass it up.

After the second day of music, sun and fun, Ted and I got a ride back to Berkeley and made our arrangements to come home. We gave everything we had away except for what we could carry in one small suitcase plus Ted's rifle. It never occurred to us that anyone would hesitate to pick up two particularly desperate-looking individuals standing along side the road with a rifle and little else. And, in fact, they didn't.

Melanie gave us a ride to the outskirts of Frisco early in the morning. Our first ride took us to the outside of Bakersfield where we got out in the late afternoon on the two-lane road leading east. With about an hour of sunlight left, we were figuring out where we would spend the night when a pickup stopped beside us. The driver was friendly enough and offered to take us as far as he was going and let us out on a "busy" road with lots of traffic. That sounded good and we hopped in. Things were going splendidly.

For the next 3 hours we headed east and, once beyond Barstow, there were no more little towns. The landscape seemed to grow ever more desolate. At about 11 p.m. the driver took a left turn off the two-lane blacktop onto a gravel road and stopped. I hadn't seen a car in the past hour.

"Well guys, here's where I got to let you off," he said.

I looked around and there wasn't a light to be seen that wasn't coming from his headlights, the stars or the moon. Nothing!

He must have noticed our hesitation. "This is my driveway," he pointed toward the gravel road that led off into the darkness. "My ranch is 12 miles this way and I can't take you no further."

"I thought you said this was a busy road," I groused a little.

"Don't you worry," he replied. "Cars come by here all the time."

Teddy and I got out and I picked the suitcase and the rifle from the truck bed. The pickup started along the "driveway" and as we stood there watching, its taillights got smaller and smaller until they disappeared altogether in the vast and complete darkness.

"Well Teddy," I sighed. "We finally made it to a spot that I've always heard about but never have actually been to. The middle of nowhere."

This was the middle of nowhere all right. We looked for signs of life in every direction but all we could see was the outline of mountains to the north. Gradually, as our eyes became accustomed to the starlight and moonlight we were able to distinguish shapes and figures of bushes and brush growing in the parched earth beside the road.

During the daytime the desert is oppressively hot but when the sun goes down the temperature drops dramatically and this night was no exception. We both had light windbreakers with us but they were barely enough. I suggested we gather some brush to try and light a fire but Teddy flatly stated that he wasn't traipsing off in the underbrush to gather wood because he didn't want to step on a rattlesnake and that logic was good enough for me. He also didn't want to begin walking along the road because the snakes loved to sleep on the asphalt at night to soak up the warmth captured there during the day. My friend made some great points so I stood there with him, shivering, cussing and stomping our feet to let all the snakes know that we were thoroughly dangerous critters and that they had better stay away.

Gradually we both got tired of griping and began to look instead of talk. I don't believe I have ever seen more stars in the heavens then I did that night. There were no man-made lights to compete with nature and no clouds to obscure them, so every twinkle was magnified and there were thousands and thousands of them. The moon itself was huge and bright enough to light up the desert floor around us. Still neither of us wanted to sit or lie down. If we could see the snakes then they could see us.

Another thing that struck me was the overwhelming silence of the desert. There was no wind, thank goodness, so no rustling of the brush and no creature sounds either. With all apologies to Simon and Garfunkel, I really do know the sounds of silence. And when that is all there is, it can be deafening. I was certainly glad to have my best friend there with me.

We must have stood there for a good three hours and not one car came by. We cussed to overcome the silence and then we cussed the guy who let us off there but it didn't help. Well, maybe a little but not much.

About the time we had decided that one of us would lie down in the road and the other would stand guard, the silence was broken by a far-off noise that seemed familiar but we couldn't identify right away. It seemed to be coming from the west and we strained to see its source but everything looked just the same as it had since we got there.

Gradually the sound became louder and we could see a light from its general direction. It was still miles away and we lost sight of it as it negotiated the hills and curves of the desert road. When it reappeared, the lights were closer and the sound more distinct. No doubt about it, there was a Volkswagon headed our way.

I called on all my experience on the road and did some quick calculations. It was the middle of the night and we were two big shadows standing along the road with a rifle and a suitcase in the center of nowhere. Things did not look promising.

A plan occurred to me that was born out of sheer desperation. "Teddy, you need to take the rifle and go hide in the bushes. They might stop for one unarmed person and if they do, I'll explain the circumstances and ask if they have room for us both. If they don't, we just have to stick it out here together."

I got no argument from Ted. He picked up the rifle and disappeared within a few steps off the road. I pondered as to which technique to use to maximize our chances for a ride. I thought of standing in the middle of the road and waving them down but decided that would probably scare them. But I couldn't stand off too far to the side because they might not see me so I split the difference and stood about three feet onto the road so they could see me but not have to swerve to avoid me. It seemed like forever before they got there.

There was about a mile of straight road leading to where I was standing and when the VW came into view I could tell it was a bug and not a van. There goes our one hope I thought. If they are travelers they won't have room even if they wanted to help.

The car wasn't going very fast to begin with but as soon as the headlights picked me out it began to slow down. When it got to me, miracle of miracles, it stopped completely and the passenger side window came rolling down. As I leaned over to speak to the occupants I could see that there was a passenger and driver and that the entire back seat was filled with clothes and bags. There didn't seem to be one square inch of room left. I quietly took cussing back up.

"You guys need a ride?" the driver asked me. It took me completely by surprise because there was no way they could have known I wasn't alone. I 'fessed up immediately.

"We surely do," I said. "My friend had to use the bathroom over there," I gestured in Ted's direction but I couldn't see him myself.

"Is he carrying that rifle in case he sees a snake?" the driver inquired.

I looked again for Ted and still couldn't see him. How the hell did these guys know?

"Yep," I lied. "Is there any possibility that you'all have room for both of us?"

"Sure," replied the driver. "You may have to lay some of our clothes in your lap, but we'll give you a ride. Where are you heading?"

When I told him Lexington, Kentucky, he laughed. "Well, we can probably help you out. We're headed to New Jersey."

I called to Ted and he came out for the underbrush about thirty feet away. I still couldn't believe they had seen him hiding there.

They parked the car right where they had stopped and why not? There was no other traffic anywhere to be avoided. Introductions followed and we met our very own Good Samaritans, S and T. They arranged and rearranged their carefully packed back seat so that Teddy and I fit when we covered ourselves with their clothes that had been hanging before we got in. These were the friendliest guys in the world and they kept on talking as we settled in. They didn't seem worried in the least about any mischief on our part.

Finally my curiosity got the better of me and I had to ask. "Guys, how did you know that Teddy was in the bushes and carrying a rifle? And why didn't that freak you out?"

S, the passenger, turned and looked me squarely in the face for the first time and grinned. He didn't have to speak. The energy coming off of him was electric and his pupils were as big as saucers. The man was maxed on psychedelics and he had the night vision of a hundred owls.

"We saw both of you about ten minutes ago, before Ted went behind the bushes. The moon is about as bright as the sun, don't you think?"

I laughed. "Well it looks to me like you have some internal illumination going on yourself. Watcha' got going on?"

"Mr. Natural blotter," he confided. "The best. Made by Augustus Stanley Owsley himself. You want some?"

"Sure thing," Teddy answered for us and S reached into his pocket and pulled out a little mint tin. He took a small sheet of paper from it and tore off four little squares, giving two of them to each to us. "Bon Voyage," he said.

It is a fact that you can get a "contact buzz" from other people doing psychedelic drugs. Their natural energy field, or aura, becomes much more intense and, if you are in their vicinity, they can actually alter your consciousness. Sitting in a small Volkswagon with so much energy already bouncing off the walls was itself "electric" and when the acid we took kicked in a little later, Ted and I were soon on the same astrophysical plane as our benefactors. Was this a great country or what?

For the next three days the little VW never stopped except for gas and food as S and T took turns driving, never over 50 miles an hour. Each day we replenished our internal supply of Mr. Natural and I could see why Mr. Augustus Stanley Owsley, originally of Eastern Kentucky, then of Berkeley, California, then of the underground, had earned such an exquisite reputation as the world's best "acid" maker. This was pure LSD. It contained no additives, no strychnine and no speed. It didn't make you grind your teeth or put you on edge like much of the acid you bought on the streets. This was the real thing.

We studied the map every day as we putt-putted across the Southwest on Route 66, passing through Albuquerque, then Amarillo and on to Oklahoma City. During our conversations we learned that S and T were from New Jersey and had been in California for the past two weeks. They both went to school but if they were any more specific than that, I can't remember it. What I do remember is just how nice they were.

From Oklahoma City they decided to go north through Springfield, St. Louis and then onto Indianapolis and Dayton. Teddy and I asked to be let out in Dayton so we would have a straight shot south to Lexington. S and T were only too happy to oblige. When we finally got there and they let us out it was like parting company with someone you had known all of your life.

"Men," I began. "I can't tell you how much we appreciate your vast generosity. First of all, you save our lives by giving us this ride and then you share your wonderful stash with us. I've got to tell you that is the best acid I've ever done. And it's the strongest. I don't believe I've come down for a minute since you gave us the first hits."

"Well Gatewood, you probably shouldn't have," said T, pointing to the back seat Ted and I had occupied the last three days. "After all, you and Teddy have been sitting on 20,000 hits for the entire ride. Well, we're off to turn on New Jersey. Bye."

❖ *Choices*

It may be true that you can never go home again, but sometimes the old Homeplace you do come back to looks a hell of a lot better than you remember it. Especially after you get out and see some other places for a while, including the middle of nowhere.

We caught a ride out of Dayton going all the way to Lexington. I felt an overwhelming relief that I had caught my last ride on this mad rush to find myself and became convinced that, if I were going to leave a mark in this life, it would be in Kentucky.

Lots of folks brag about their birth state but there is something about the Commonwealth of Kentucky that really brings it out in its native sons and daughters. It's a relatively small state and it consistently ranks in the mid-40s in standard of living indexes. However, it is the birthplace of bourbon whiskey, the best thoroughbred horses and tobacco in the world and the premiere college basketball program in America. More recently, it has attained worldwide fame for producing some of the best marijuana on earth. (A development of the 70s and 80s).

The point is that this Commonwealth has always been on the cutting edge of the vice industry because there is a certain pioneer consciousness that its citizens carry around with them. After all, the original settlers of the Commonwealth were fugitives from the Whiskey Tax enacted by the Federal Government in 1791. Rather than pay it, they moved west, over the Alleghenies/Appalachias to escape Government regulation and they've had that attitude ever since. My kind of folks all right!

I hadn't done a very good job of keeping in touch with my family so they were relieved that I was home and healthy. They did the first thing any responsible parents would do and told me to get a job. I didn't need much encouragement and landed what I still think was one of my favorite jobs, a milkman.

The old Dixie Bell Dairy stood on the corner of North Limestone and Third Street where now stands the Transylvania Soccer Field. It was a rambling complex that held twenty home delivery trucks, refrigerated rooms for milk and dairy storage, offices and a little grill/restaurant. I'd wake up at 4:30 every morning and be at the plant at 5:15. If that sounds early, it was. It did, however, beat the hell out of waking up under a bridge after 3 hours of fitful sleep with traffic rolling over you and rainwater seeping down your collar.

I began hanging around the campus again, becoming more and more involved in the antiwar movement. There was a growing activism and revolution in the air. The bars were filled with students and the war and the draft were the main topics of discussion. I resumed my prodigious drinking and carousing, many times going from an all-night party to my milk route, finishing work and sleeping most of the day.

And here I guess is as appropriate a place, as any, to offer my most sincere apologies to all you folks whom I offended in my days of alcohol abuse. I can think of several instances, that you won't read about here, that still embarrass me so I can imagine how you might feel. Sorry Guys!.

Well, wait a minute. I know that isn't good enough. Hell, I've got so much to apologize for, that one paragraph isn't going to do it. Let me be a little more specific.

I apologize for being a loud-mouthed, insensitive clod to each and every one of you who had to endure me during this time. Between the alcohol and the angst, I must have been insufferable. All I can say is that I came to realize this at a later time and I'm still trying to make up for it. I ask your forgiveness and your patience.

Because I liked being where the action was, I gravitated toward the political activists who seemed to be able to get the most done on a grass-roots level. They were the ones who knew the value of a mimeograph machine, ink, three reams of paper and a bullhorn. Several of them formed an organization named the Grosvenor Street Zoological Gardens which acted as an information and referral center for all activist groups and efforts. Naturally it attracted the attention of the police.

Empowered by the success of Woodstock, the Zoo threw a three-day concert, called Woodstick, at the farm of a local physician. The police arrived early on the morning of the third day, a Sunday, and according to the account of the local newspaper, had to disperse the crowd with "a machine gun mounted on the hood" of a patrol car. In reality, at 7 in the morning, about 20 people were rousted from their sleeping bags by uniformed and "undercover" cops who arrested two of them for being naked underneath all those blankets and the physician landowner for disturbing the peace. (And the police)

The Zoo organized a big march on downtown Lexington on behalf of the doctor during his trial and I think everyone was surprised when about a thousand people showed up. We were getting pretty good at this organizing thing. The procession stretched for several blocks and ended in front of the Courthouse on Main Street where all the speeches were made but to no avail. The doctor was convicted of six misdemeanors and fined about $1000. I felt bad about that but I also learned that I felt good about leading a march with a bullhorn in my hand.

About this time, almost simultaneously, two events occurred which changed my life dramatically.

By 1971 the psychedelic wave had drenched all of America. Just about anything a person wanted could be had and good LSD was no exception. My friends B and his wife, and Teddy, got together one afternoon and tried some out. As with most other things I did during this time in my life, I tried to outdo everyone else around me, the result being my ingestion of about 4000 "mikes" of pure LSD 25. (About 20 "hits.")

Looking back, I can only surmise that my chronic over-the-top attitude finally managed to irk my friends and they began critiquing me as only real friends who know you can do. They wouldn't let me make an excuse for any of my failings, and the bigger question in my life was: What wasn't a failing?

It seems I could actually feel them stripping away layers of pretensions and armor, defensiveness and arrogance, from my body until I had no protective layers left. None that had been inculcated into me by society or any that I had made in response to my experiences. I felt totally naked and when I looked down at my body during the height of the sensation I was further amazed to find that I had achieved X-ray vision.

I know it sounds strange and believe me it was. I only had on shorts but the fact is that I was looking at my body and all I could see was my skeleton. I couldn't see the skin or muscle, the blood or the tendons. I could only see the bone.

It seems that my friends had stripped away everything except my skeletal framework and what I could only visualize as a piano-wire thin cord that stretched from the top of my spine to the bottom along which ran all the mechanisms of my self-awareness. I was at the very essence of being, peeled to the core, without a crutch and tired of listening to myself explain why I just couldn't seem to get it all together.

At this point an inner voice came to my realization and gave direction to my thoughts. I couldn't identify whether it originated from my own inner self (Freud's super ego) or whether it was a guardian angel or even God. I only know that this voice spoke to me in this way.

"Well Gatewood, here you are finally at the bottom of things. Even your friends don't want to put up with you any more because you are such a wastrel and scoundrel. You come from such a great family Gatewood and they are all distressed to see you waste yourself like this, drinking and carousing, going from job to job with no plans for the future. Let's face it Gatewood, you're a loser. Now let me show you something."

I felt myself being led to the edge of nothingness. I looked out before me and it was totally dark forever. The voice continued. "Gatewood, Benjamin Franklin said that nine out of ten deaths are suicides, and that was before they invented pre-rolled cigarettes. So most people seem to pick their own forms of suicides. Some people do it quick and others stretch it out like you seem wont to do. You're drinking too much and you're smoking too much and you are way too experimental with the drug de jour. You are throwing away your life right in front of everyone and your family deserves better than that. They shouldn't be made to fret over your extended self-destruction, so I'll tell you what. I challenge you to be a man about it. If you don't feel like life is worth living in a positive, upbeat manner and you want to continue on the suicidal path you're on, then jump off right here and get it over quick for those who might care. That's right, put up or shut up. Was it Sartre or Camus who said that the only true intellectual choice that mankind made was whether to commit suicide or not? And this is your most essential of choices right here and right now Gatewood. Either make something of your life or give it up.

The first thing you must know, Gatewood, is that you are, indeed, expendable, just like the government thought you were when they had you convinced to go half-way around the world and kill men, women and children or be killed yourself. Only now, since you have survived that impulse, you have the unobstructed choice of how you, and only you, want to spend your life and the karma attached to it. Right here, right now, you are stripped down to your most essential expression of worthwhile life, which is lucid self-awareness. (An unexamined life being not worth living, according to Socrates.) From this moment on, if you choose life, you get to reassemble your whole being, physical, mental and spiritual and decide how you want to spend your life to make it worthwhile.

But with this opportunity, and the choice to remake yourself, comes the burden of being totally responsible for all of your actions and their consequences to yourself. You can no longer blame your shortcomings on anybody or anything else from here on out.

I suggest Gatewood that if you choose life, as others before you have done, you will find that you get the most joy out of helping those who need help and can't do for themselves. Look at your assets. You know you're expendable so you never have to think you are above the fray. You've been to the middle of nothingness and you're not afraid to go there again. You are well suited to stand on the bottom and give other people a leg up when they need it. You're one lucky guy."

Of course I was. I had come face to face with the "grim reaper" who was actually a pretty matter-of-fact kinda guy. He told me that most of his appointments are by invitation from people who are glad to see him come. People who are worn out with sickness, disease, despair and oppression or just plain worn out. Unlike a lot of those people, I still had a choice.

An overwhelming desire to live washed over me and I felt like a diver who is out of air and breaks through the surface of the water into the oxygen-filled sky for which he is so grateful. And the sheer appreciation, for the ability to appreciate the opportunity to have such a choice, compelled me to take an Oath on the spot to make this life one of passion and activism, finding a great principal to fight and perhaps die for, to give real other meaning to my choice to live. I vowed to make something of myself.

The second major event that changed my life occurred shortly thereafter. Unrest on campus over the war was growing. More and larger demonstrations were taking place all over the country and, for once, Kentucky was abreast of the times. UK students occupied the Student Center to protest the war and another group outside the Center was pepper-gassed in the "free speech" area. This only served to solidify the student body from which more and more demonstrators were willing to join the ranks.

During the demonstrations that followed the gassing of the students it came to pass that "the old ROTC building" (as it will be forever known) burned down and it became great sport among the students, the administration, the local police, the state police and the feds to speculate as to whether it was arson and who might have done it.

(I was sure I saw Mitch McConnell running from the building with a gasoline can in his hand.) Rumors ran rampant and so did the official response.

The Governor, Hon. Louie Nunn, the only Republican governor among the last 18 Governors of the Commonwealth, called in the National Guard to the University of Kentucky campus. And while this was not a unique occurrence in America's colleges during those days, it is notable that, except for Kent State and Jackson State where students were killed by Guardsmen, Kentucky was the only other school where the Guard arrived with live ammunition in the chambers of their rifles.

The day following the "old ROTC building's" demise, the inevitable confrontation between the students and the Guardsmen played itself out. The Governor was determined to keep the University open and the students had vowed to close it. The Guard formed ranks and herded the main body of demonstrators away from the Administration Offices and off the main campus, across Limestone Street and onto the lawn of what was then the College of the Bible, a Seminary that sits across from the UK Law School.

As the circumstances had it, I found myself in the middle of South Limestone Street, standing between 5,000 riotous students and 500 armed and nervous National Guardsmen at a time of great unrest. Since I was one of four folks who had a bullhorn in my hand I figured I made a pretty target. I was unarmed and nervous.

It was one of the clearest moments of my life when it came to me. "You know," I told myself, "you could turn into Superman and go over there and kick butt on everyone of those Guardsmen if your current wishes came true, but that wouldn't solve anything. They would just send 500 more. You don't even know who sent them or what rules they used to do it with. Or how they got the power to do it. You are one dumb bunny.

You don't know how the system works and that makes you grist for the mill. With what you do and how you do it, you are going to end up dead or underneath the jail at an early age. You're just another loudmouth punk who will fight a running buzz saw and they are going to eat you up. You're just a pawn in their game when you don't know the rules.

If you want to survive Gatewood, you had better learn the rules and, along the way, the actual language with which they will put you away if they get the chance. It appears that your only hope to stay out of jail in this lifetime is to go to college and become an attorney. And while you're at it, become Governor so that you will be in charge of the National Guard. And, oh yes, also while you're at it, change the marijuana laws. They are such a vivid illustration on how the government has overstepped its bounds in policing private behavior and besides, I'm damned tired of paying $12 an ounce for it!"

And that was it. Right then and there I decided to make my way to the inner sanctum of the little man behind the curtain and run the machine myself because I figured that I could do a better job for the people than the guys who were running it then. (Or now). I didn't know how long it would take or the sacrifices involved or what else I would have to do without but I did know one thing beyond a single doubt. It was my only hope for survival.

(Years later I tell my audience that there are only 4 places for an aggressive young man like me from Kentucky to go: Jail, Law, Politics or Tennessee. I've been to the first three and I'm sure as hell not going to Tennessee.)

For the ensuing 32 years I followed that dream. Thank God for UK's open admission policy. Despite 6 years of on-again, off-again registration and class attendance wherein I had earned 0 credits, I was allowed back in and I started my formal education in the Fall of 1971. I was 24 years old and a milkman. Is this a wonderful country or what?

❖ College/Drugs/History & Politics

Taking college seriously was no easy task. I had virtually no study skills and little self-discipline so I knew I had to get to work on several levels. I made up my mind that this was like anything else in life; if I wanted it bad enough, I would do whatever work it took to get there. And I wanted to get there as soon as possible.

One obstacle was having to earn a living. I would have to work full-time while going to school. That necessitated a nighttime job, which I landed at The Paddock, a local beer hall located on the corner of Euclid and Rose Streets. I worked 6 nights a week from 4 p.m. until well after midnight for $1.60 an hour plus all the beer I could drink. It was a hell of a deal, especially since I averaged 12-15 beers per shift. Of course I weighed about 230 pounds and had the beginnings of a major beer belly but my basic needs were met and I soon fell into a routine of study, work and drinking.

The Paddock Bar had a well-deserved reputation as Revolution Central in those days. The longhairs, hippies and leaders of the growing anti-war movement gathered there each evening to plot strategy, drink beer, play foosball, pursue sexual liaisons, score some good pot, mescaline, LSD, speed or mushrooms and raise hell in general.

The campus was alive with activists for many causes including the anti-war effort, women's rights and a small but growing group that called themselves environmentalists. It was an exciting time to be young and curious and mine was a very curious generation.

God Bless human curiosity. It is the natural precursor to experimentation and the desire to try different things is a natural drive within the human animal. It is innately human to experiment with different substances to achieve different perspectives at any given time. This is called altering one's consciousness.

Thankfully I am a curious guy and have always considered the ability to alter my consciousness as a God-given blessing, which I must treat with great respect. Therefore I tried most of the drugs available at the time including LSD, mescaline (from the peyote plant of the Southwest U.S.), psilocybin (from psilocybe mexicana mushroom), pills (mostly "speed") and I once tried a Quaalude, which I didn't like. It made me feel too "out of control" of my physical body. And, you guessed it; I tried every brand of marijuana that made it into this part of the country.

The lesson I learned from these experiments upon myself is that you can trust the stuff from the natural cycle far more than the stuff from the synthetic cycle. The big lesson is that there is nothing from the natural cycle which is physically addictive. You cannot become dependent on green, natural substances but it is an entirely different story with synthetically produced powders, pills, serums and potions.

This lesson is not one taught by the establishment. They have an economic and political agenda, which groups substances by their own ability to monopolize the production and distribution of the substance. Medicines in their natural form cannot be patented or monopolized and therefore they must be eliminated from competition by vilifying and illegalizing them. This is accomplished by exposing the population to a massive propaganda campaign, which has little regard for the science and truth of the matter.

The central aim of this campaign is to vilify both the natural substance and the people who desire to associate with it. For instance, people who ingest Cannabis are derisively referred to as "potheads" or "druggies" whose use of the substance to "alter their consciousness" is portrayed as sick or out of the ordinary.

Nothing can be further from the truth.

For human beings, the desire to alter their consciousness is as basic as sex, hunger and thirst. It is the human being's ability to alter their consciousness that sets them apart from the rest of the animal kingdom. The act of thinking itself is the most basic alteration and if we didn't possess it, we would still be single-cell amoebae swimming around in the chemical soup of the planet.

In his landmark book, *Intoxication*, Dr. Ron Siegle, a psycho-pharmacological anthropologist at UCLA, shows that the drive to alter consciousness cuts across time and species. His observations of other animals reveal that they have an inborn instinct for locating and ingesting natural substances that alter their behavior. The better-known instances include elephants dining on fermented bananas and cats playing with catnip. In fact, all animals, including humans, alter their consciousness with everything that they ingest.

Think about it. Your outlook at 8 in the evening after you have eaten a spicy pizza will be different than if you had eaten a plate of steamed vegetables. The recognition of this innate human drive is essential to formulating its appropriate accommodation in society. To deny its presence is an invitation to construct an imbalanced and unnatural paradigm on the human condition. This describes the reason for the miserable failure of the so-called War on Drugs. Any attempt to force a population to conform to an inhuman and alien form of lifestyle must fail and that is the fate of the WOD.

The so-called War on Drugs has stated that its ultimate goal is a "drug-free" society. This is pure bunk. There has never been a "drug-free" society and there never will be. It is a totally artificial and unnatural concept, invented by those forces who are currently constructing a totally artificial lifestyle for us, where they continue their monopoly on the production and distribution of all of life's necessities, including powerful synthetic substances which are far more harmful to the body than any natural substances that humans voluntarily ingest.

The War on Drugs is, in fact, a War on the People, conceived and implemented by the petrochemical pharmaceutical ghouls to overcome the individual rights of self-direction inherent in our Constitution and Bill of Rights.

It is the method by which they have illegalized competition and managed to subvert human rights in the name of protecting We, the People, from ourselves.

All of this is easily proven by the fact that the Partnership For a Drug Free Society is entirely funded by the Chemical Manufacturer's Association, the inordinately powerful lobbying arm of the synthetic industries.

This abdication of our Constitutional and human rights has been systematically achieved through the complicity of Congress, which is the willing puppet of the special interests. The checks and balances which were carefully constructed to spread the power of government among the many have been demolished by the expenditure of extraordinary amounts of special interest money which has purchased the White House and both Parties from the top down.

Lots of this money is international in origin, coming from those I previously identified as the "petrochemical-pharmaceutical-military-industrial-transnational-corporate-fascist-elite-sons-of-bitches" who have never said the Pledge of Allegiance to the Flag of the United States of America, or to the Republic for which it stands. And they are not warm and fuzzy about us or our children or grandchildren.

As a matter of fact, these international forces see the Constitution of the United States and the Bill of Rights as impediments to the implementation of the New World Order and their grand scheme of a global economy. So they buy the votes of our elected officials and continue their dismantling of the Republic.

They do this because the American idea of an individual having the power of choice does not coincide with their drive to monopolize the markets in all of the basic necessities of life. An individual who has the choice of being self-sufficient is a direct threat to their drive to create a controlled economy and achieve a monopoly over it.

They have sought control over the individuals in America's modern society by creating arbitrary laws which criminalize basic human behavior and make criminals of citizens who present no threat to any other individual, or to the health, safety and welfare of society in general.

In addition to purchasing special interest laws from Congress, these same forces have constructed a perverted and pervasive campaign of vilification of all who oppose them. These propaganda campaigns, paid for with taxpayer dollars, are studies in deceit and double speak. They ignore and misstate the science and truth of the matter and no workable solution to the real drug problem in America will ever be formulated unless it has truth as its basis.

So, in essence, the officials now in power cannot be trusted to tell the truth or do the right thing to solve America's addictions to the synthetic medicines, which their corporate masters produce. Their credibility is completely shot and that is why so many of us ignore their self-pious bleatings over the War on Drugs. They are failures as elected officials and even more so as human beings. They give me no confidence in their leadership so I'll make up my own mind on these matters.

While sorting all of this out, one thing became apparent to me. My own alcohol use was getting in the way of my education. I was downing 50 to 70 beers a week at the Paddock, where I spent off-hours in addition to my work schedule. Something had to give, so I swore off drinking and decided to smoke cannabis for my "social lubrication." It was one of the two or three most important decisions I ever made regarding my health and my future. Long Live Choice!

Stopping drinking was easier then I thought. Actually sitting down and studying was harder than I imagined. The first Friday night of my first semester back in school was a memorable one. I distinctly remember standing in my apartment and reaching for my textbook on Psychology instead of heading out the door to any one of several parties I knew about. The actual award of a Law Degree was 6 to 7 years off but the commitment to getting there began that Friday night when I sat down and opened that book. Some long journeys don't begin with the first step but with having a seat.

The thing I missed most was the crowd that inhabited the bars. I had become much more of a social animal over the last five years and I just knew that lots of folks were out there having fun, while I sat there reading material which I felt I could never put to use. Overcoming the urge to go join them was a major hurdle and a prime lesson in my life. If I wanted something bad enough, even if it's far off, I'm capable of doing whatever it takes to get there.

The necessity of some isolation, and that curious nature of mine, also led me to experimenting with non-drug methods of physical and psychological exploration. My most valuable discovery along these lines was the benefit of practicing Yoga.

❖ *Yoga*

Like a lot of my fellow "children of the 60s", I had a tiny glimpse of Eastern meditation and thought when the Beatles went to India and met Ravi Shankar. Gradually, I read books on the subject including Ram Dass's *Be Here Now* which describes his passage to enlightenment, and all of the Carlos Castanada series on Don Juan, the Yaqi Indian Sorcerer.

These books left me no doubt that there was a vast internal journey yet to be taken and that drugs offered only transitory windows and doorways to the path. The mind and body were themselves enough to find and stay on the path, if they could be coordinated to function on an informed and disciplined basis.

That's not the way I was thinking of it, I'm sure. I was probably smoking cigarettes at the time and wondering how I could stay in shape without having to work up a sweat. These people I saw doing this Yoga stuff stood in one place, seemed to be fit and they looked happy. Or at least serene.

So one day I bought a book on the subject. It was Richard Hittlemann's *28-Day Yoga Plan*. It had nice pictures and only lasted 28 days. Hell, I can do anything for 28 days. I made up my mind I would follow it religiously.

Like most of us I reckon, I was amused when I first saw yoga practitioners bending and stretching in such awkward-looking poses. And if you think it's amusing to watch, you ought to try to do it sometime. You'll learn a lot about yourself. Right Away.

That's right. It doesn't take 28 days to find out just how stiff and tight you are. 28 seconds is more like it.

That was my experience. When I tried to imitate the postures of the book's model, I was humiliated. And she wasn't even really trying. She was doing it for beginners and I must have been a beginner's beginner. I could feel the tightness in my legs and back, the knotted muscles and stiff joints. I was only 25 and I already felt stiff and brittle.

But Damnit, I stuck with it, no matter how ridiculous I felt trying to touch my toes and not even getting to my knees. And I'm glad to say that, not only did I complete the 28-day plan, I continued the workout I developed to fit my own needs, every day, for two years.

The results were fantastic. After the first month I quit cigarettes (for the first time). It also lowered my body's center of gravity and made me much more conscious of my legs and feet.

Up until then, I had thought of my center of gravity as my chest and I carried my weight around my shoulders. The practice of yoga involves the whole body, and its balance, so it taught me to think more with my feet and legs. I've suffered far less sprained ankles and leg injuries over the past 35 years because of it.

However, the main lesson of Yoga is how to control your breathing. That's right. Breathing is the basis of all life and, if you can control your own breathing, you can handle most of life's circumstances with style and grace.

Life is the processing of energy through our bodies and its vehicle is oxygen. We can live for days without food or water, but only a few seconds without oxygen. Obviously, the more efficiently our bodies process oxygen, the healthier we become.

The postures we see these Yogis (practitioners) attain is possible mainly because they have learned to control their breathing and therefore can relax into the positions. Most of these cannot be reached by exertion. It takes balance, focus and controlled-breathing. It takes the ability to shut out the idle chatter that we all constantly process through our brains, like an internal never-ending soap opera, so that imagined scenarios don't cause us to lose focus on the here and now task at hand.

So through the use of several specific exercises, I gradually gained theretofore-unknown control over my breathing and some flexibility throughout my whole body, especially my spine. I had much more balance and confidence in my movements. And I slept better at night because I wasn't doing tobacco any more.

The explanation of what the practice of Yoga has done for me couldn't fit into this book. After my initial discipline, I have lapsed into an on-again, off-again practice, mostly off. But I utilize what I learned from it everyday, even after 30 years, in many ways. Whether it's being aware of my balance when I reach for something or stretching a particular muscle to relieve a cramp, or just trying to catch my breath after exercising, yoga has extended my life and its quality immensely.

And anyone can do it. Right now. No matter what shape you are in, no matter what body size. The first time you bend over the first little bit has an immediate effect. The same with breathing. The first time you become aware of your breathing on a Yogic level, you are instantaneously benefited.

(I used to lead my radio audience through an exercise where I told them to straighten their spine and lift their heart and sternum toward the sky! You try it. Right now. See. It opens your chest, takes the weight of your shoulders off your lungs and internal organs, and facilitates breathing and the suppleness of your spine.)

You have now practiced Yoga. And you are better off for it. And you can do that one anytime, anywhere.

But I can tell you that is possible to sweat, a hell of a lot, while standing in one spot and simply stretching. Two years ago, I did a session of "hot yoga" at the Lexington Massage Center. It was a 90-minute class in 102-degree heat and led by a merciless, Meg Ryan-type instructor who would have made a hell of a drill sergeant.

I started to quit at least a dozen times, and yell "Medic" several more, but I couldn't catch my breath to muster the effort. But I persevered (still that fear of drill instructors, I reckon) and at the end, I had dropped 6 pounds. So for all you guys and gals who think Yoga is for wimps, I suggest you try that.

I encourage you to try Yoga no matter what shape you are in. Because its practice is actually more mental than physical.

In my on-again, off-again practice of the discipline, I discovered the Yogic concept of Ananda. Essentially, Yoga is a celebration of the here-and-now. Since you are not carrying on conversations with yourself about other things, you can concentrate on this exact moment of your existence, not the second that is coming to you or the second that just passed.

Ananda is the concept that the second that you are in, right now, is totally filled with Bliss. Total Happiness. And most of us can't experience it as such because we are too caught up in yesterday's battle and tomorrow's challenges.

The practice of yoga is the experiencing and appreciation of those instants when we can shut the other stuff out and experience the Ananda.

And you can do that anywhere, anytime. You don't have to do Yoga to experience the Bliss of Being, but it's a healthful reminder of the opportunity.

❖ *Me and Learning the System*

College itself was fairly tough at first so I was relentless about attending and participating in classes. At 24 I was older and more experienced than many of the other students and, with my attitude, I would actually question and/or argue with the professor, much to the chagrin of my peers.

In the first day of my Philosophy class, the instructor asked, "What is a Philosopher?" and I answered, "Anyone who asks 'Why'?"

"Oh no!" he retorted. "It takes much more than that to be a Philosopher."

"No it doesn't," I stuck to my guns. "It doesn't take a diploma or a title or using big words or writing about it. If there is one word that can be used to describe Philosophy, it is the pursuit of the answer to that one word, Why? And furthermore, anyone who asks the question is a Philosopher."

By the reaction of the instructor, an observer would have thought that I had savagely attacked the man and his entire family lineage. He immediately launched into a 15-minute description of who and what a Philosopher was and it sounded pretty autobiographical to me. Apparently he didn't believe that someone without a college degree was Philosopher material and I couldn't believe that simply attaining a degree in it made someone a true Philosopher.

It was an argument that arose in every class and lasted the entire term. Mid-way through the semester, the class took a vote to throw me out. It was me or them they said. I was damn sorry to see half of them go. I got a B in the class.

In my first full year, I had a 3.2 GPA. This was particularly gratifying because, after leaving my steady source of beer at the Paddock, I was working 40-48 hours a week, washing dishes and short order cooking at the Campus Corner, a burger-and-fries place sitting on the corner of Rose Street and Columbia Avenue.

Anyone who has ever done it will tell you it is a real grind to work full-time and go to school full-time. There was no time for a day off or a true social life. I had to fight the jealousy I felt toward those students who didn't have to work. I realized it wasn't their fault and that they were actually missing the opportunity to find out what they were truly capable of doing. And despite their outward signs of success, I knew that they, too, had their own burdens to bear. We all have our own lessons to learn. And we can learn them only when we are ready .

The reason for that is simple enough. Different parts of each individual bloom at different times. Learning by an individual is never on a progressive linear plane and people are motivated by various things and at various times. The desire to learn is the key ingredient and in my case, it caused me to look for knowledge both inside and outside the classroom.

One day I was standing on campus talking to a Department Chairman when a particularly scruffy fellow hurried by, obviously up to sedition and anarchy.

"Now there goes a dangerous man," voiced the Chairman.

I was intrigued. "Why do you say that?" I asked.

"Because he knows the system inside out. He knows how it operates." He looked at me. "If you don't know the system, you don't stand a chance against it. But you know that. That's why you came back here to begin with, right?"

Yes, that was it, I agreed. But it was nice to hear another person recognize it.

I finished my undergraduate degree in three years and a lot of it is now a faded memory, but certain people and things stand out. My Journalism instructor, Dwight Teeter, wrote his own textbook containing a vivid phrase that has stuck with me since first I saw it.

"Every generation must re-win its own freedoms."

Those words still cut right through me these 30 years later. Damn Right Dwight! The sacrifices of our past generations cannot insure our present day freedoms; only the opportunity to fight to preserve what remains of them if we can.

This phrase ought to be the mantra of every student of the American system and its history. The Constitution and the Bill of Rights are only words written on a sheet of paper. They have no life of their own and have force only when they are personified by a human being who gives them voice by insisting on their guarantees. Then they are very formidable documents indeed.

I sought out the classes that explained "the System" itself. History and sociology, psychology and journalism, communications and literature, all contributed to my understanding, as did my re-reading of the Federalist Papers, those documents and letters written by our Founding Fathers to communicate their visions of the makeup of this new nation.

Finally I began to get a grasp of it.

The formation of the United States of America and its method of government is one of the grandest experiments ever devised by man.

Prior to the emergence of this country, all forms of leadership around the world were Fascist in nature. Fascism may be defined as the exercise of arbitrary power by one or more rulers, or the arbitrary exercise of power by those in charge. Therefore, kings and queens and despots and warlords were fascists in nature because anything they commanded got done. There were no sets of rules that inhibited their exercise of power. If they said "Off with their head!", that was it. No one had the right to intercede and there were no checks and balances on that power. It was whatever the ruler said it was and it was unlimited. That is a classical and older form of fascism. The newer form is described by Karl Marx, "Fascism is when government and business combine to keep the people down."

The founders of our country recognized this, especially since they were suffering at the hands of a fascist king, George III. They felt he was violating their basic rights in an arbitrary manner, but these were not rights given by the government itself. These were "inalienable rights given to us by our Creator" which no entity was empowered to take from us. So Adams, Jefferson and the rest set out to devise a form of government which recognized this and institutionalized the protections for it. They aimed to cast off King George and create a limited form of government, with transitory managers and well-defined job-descriptions, beyond which government could not operate. The blueprint for this form of government was a document called the Constitution and the Founders saw this as an antidote to Fascism because it expressly limited the powers of government, whatever its intentions.

The Constitution divided the power of leadership between three branches of government and instituted checks and balances to keep any one of them from gaining despotic control. They had no misconceptions about the inherent tendency of all governments to expand their powers. And they knew that expansion can only be done at the expense of the people.

When asked what kind of government the people had been given, Benjamin Franklin responded, "A Republic my Dear. If you can keep it." He also pointed out that the United States is a Republic, not a democracy. When asked to explain the difference, he replied, "A Democracy is when two wolves and a sheep take a vote on what's for dinner. A Republic is when the sheep is well armed and can beg to differ with the vote."

The inherent predatory nature of government itself raised concerns about the eventual erosion of those "inalienable" freedoms, thought to be possessed by the individual. That led to the formation of the Bill of Rights, which expressed specific rights of the citizens in Amendments 1 through 8, with the 9th and 10th Amendment designed to let everyone know that all the other rights not covered elsewhere, belonged to the people. Not the Government.

Those were fine principals indeed. And they were committed to hemp paper, which meant they would last for several or more centuries. But they were only words on paper. They had to be given life by real people.

"Every generation must re-win its own freedoms," Dwight reminded me over over and over. And I was constantly reassessing my ability to fight that battle.

Education was the key. I read everything I could get my hands on. My friend Les R. loaned me his first 11 volumes of *The Story of Civilization* by Will and Ariel Durant, about 14,000 pages. That took me two years itself. Knowing the System on its day-to-day basis. The language, the sources, the rules. I wanted to be a well-armed sheep, by Golly. Law School was the key. Getting there was still a chore.

❖ *Law School and My Model Plan for Legal Marijuana*

Though I knew I was aiming for Law School, I remained undecided as to what my major might be. I must have switched it several times and despite my commitment to my academic goals, I still had trouble with foreign languages and physical sciences. These were requirements for graduation but I avoided them in the main, hoping to hack my way through when the time came. It was therefore a very exciting development when those requirements changed.

I was walking next to the Administration Building one day when the President of the University, Otis Singletary, opened the window to his office and called to me to come see him. I stepped into his office and he was all smiles.

"Gatewood, good news. We have just developed a degree program which even you can graduate under. It's called the Bachelor of General Studies and it doesn't require any foreign languages or physical sciences. What do you think?"

"Otis," I replied, "that's my ticket out of here, Brother."

As far as I know, I was the first person to graduate with that degree and was the first person with such a degree to be accepted into the UK Law School. There must have been some head scratching over my application. From grades 9 through 12, I had averaged about a C- and over my first 6 or 7 college semesters I had flunked everything. Then came an obvious turnaround with 4 years of undergraduate work completed in 3 years with a pretty hefty GPA and LSAT score.

I reckon they thought I had earned a chance to prove myself further. I would like to believe I had too. If nothing else, it proved to me again that if you want something bad enough, and are willing to pay the price, you just might get it, if you're lucky too. Then came the hard part.

Law School was difficult mainly because it was a lesson in rules and procedures for a guy who consciously avoided rules and procedures at every opportunity. Sometimes I felt like an Indian must feel, dressed in white man's clothes, and having to listen to the ways that mankind has devised to confine one another. Physically and spiritually.

Laws here, rules there, statutes and regulations everywhere. It was enough to make any free-thinker go mad. And several people in my first year class did go over the top, either leaving school or worse, committing suicide.

Truthfully, that first year was difficult. The legal language itself is arcane, especially for a student who hasn't grown up around it. But I was determined to work through it and studied at least 50 hours a week outside the classroom for the first two semesters, making sure I landed on my feet grade-wise.

During Law school, I was living at the Elizabeth Wheatly YWCA on the corner of 4th and Upper Streets near the Transylvania campus. I rented the whole building and sublet several bedrooms to friends and family. It was huge, having served as the Black YWCA for many years. My own bedroom was 25 by 30 with a fifteen-foot ceiling and the living room was a small gymnasium. We threw some hellacious Halloween parties there, which will never be forgotten by those in attendance. And you know who you are. But I can't remember.

In the Fall of 1976 I was beginning my third year and anxious to make my mark in the national debate on marijuana. It had simmered as a legitimate political issue for over 10 years and groups such as the National Organization for the Reform of Marijuana Laws (NORML), centered in Washington, D.C. had emerged to keep it in the public eye, lobbying for a change in the national laws and representing similar-minded folks like me who were looking for a voice.

However, this group's goals were described as effecting "decriminalization", which I felt was very limited and did not provide solutions for the questions of where would people get their herb if they didn't or couldn't grow their own and who would make money off the market as it emerged from under its criminal status.

One day I sat at my desk and pondered this scenario. Okay Gatewood, marijuana has just gone legal. Who gets the market and why?

My first consideration was to recognize that everyone has an inalienable right to plant a seed in God's earth and consume the green natural plant that comes up out of it. So each family or individual would have the right to grow their own. This would not, however, preclude the existence of a huge commercial market for those people unable or unwilling to grow their own. America's farmers should be allowed to grow for that market.

The next thing that occurred to me was to keep the large corporations out of the picture. Any wealth generated by commerce in marijuana should be spread to as many people as possible. I would rather see a million farmers make ten thousand dollars a year from growing it than to see ten thousand farmers making a million dollars a year. Corporate and other large farming concerns should not be allowed to control the market.

My third concern was to structure a system whose principals were already proven in other markets. Therefore I decided to synthesize the production and marketing techniques already at work in the alcohol and tobacco markets.

Farmers would be allowed to grow a certain poundage, under an allotment system, and they would only be able to sell it at a central warehouse, to the government who would label its potency, package it in ounces, tax it, then deliver it to licensees who would market it out of their own homes in their own neighborhoods . The government's only intercession would be in the commercial end of it. Growing one's own plants for individual and personal use would be no business of the government.

I called my plan The Model Plan for Legal Marijuana in Kentucky and it was the first economically based modern argument for re-instituting cannabis as a cash crop in America. It was based on my desire to return land as a means of producing wealth and keeping the family farmers in business. Given Kentucky's heritage of growing thousands of acres of cannabis over hundreds of years, it seemed a natural course to pursue. I just couldn't really figure out why no one else seemed willing to discuss it.

❖ *Happy Chandler, Me and Marijuana*

One warm fall day in my last year, I took the afternoon off and traveled to my favorite sunny rock in Red River Gorge. For those not familiar with central and eastern Kentucky, this is a beautiful spot in the foothills of Appalachia where the Red River has carved out a deep path along a valley floor. It is a part of the Daniel Boone National Forest, the largest National Forest in America and is a favorite hiking and camping spot for many.

The river itself isn't more than two or three feet deep in many places, but its bed is strewn with huge rocks that have broken from the rocky shelves above and tumbled into the water. These create partial dams behind which pools form, pools, which are as close to the "old time" swimming holes as you will find in the mountains.

My favorite rock is right off a major trail about a mile from the road. It's rectangular and sits straight up with one end in the edge of the river-bank and the other standing upright about nine feet to the top. A tree has grown up next to it and if you can grasp the right branch you can pull yourself to the top of the stone monolith and find yourself in the bend of the valley where you can see for hundreds of yards both up and down river.

The space on top was at least 15 by 20 feet and directly under the sun. This was truly an excellent spot to bake and get "baked" (stoned) when you had a lot on your mind and I did.

In less than a year, I was going to have a degree in law, but I didn't have a clear vision as to how best to utilize it to bring about the changes I wanted to precipitate.

The "going to college and becoming an attorney" part of my pledge to myself, made five years earlier, was a reality. Now the "becoming Governor and changing the marijuana laws" part was my next challenge.

The sun was hot, the air was humid and the birds were singing up a storm. My world couldn't have been more serene as I took out a bag of marijuana and began rolling a joint.

Suddenly I had a distinct feeling that I was being watched. It was the most peculiar thing and it made the hair on my neck stand straight. I could feel someone's eyes on me sure as the dickens and the paranoia almost made me physically ill. I stood up and walked around the edges of my perch, eyeing the thousand of trees that met my gaze. I couldn't find another human being anywhere I looked.

"Damn it," I thought to myself, as I struck a match. "I'll just light up this joint anyway and if I'm caught, I'm caught!" And immediately I was struck by the reality of the situation.

I was already caught. Caught up in the paranoia engendered by the government's propaganda campaign against this plant and those people who associate with it. Kept prisoner by myself, in my own mind, I was becoming increasingly guarded about thinking for myself, afraid to step out of line, believing I had something to lose that was more important than being true to myself and my pledges.

I almost shouted my next thought. "Never again," I decided. "Never again will I act to imprison myself over this matter. Never again will I ignore the science and truth of this matter out of the fear of being made criminal or being ostracized by my profession.

Rather than be afraid and paranoid about smoking cannabis, I am going to be fearless and up front about it, spreading news of its benefits at every opportunity. Someone has to take the government on over this issue and counteract their scurrilous, mean-spirited and fascist attack on this plant and its proponents."

I was thinking fast and feeling inspired.

How to do it? How to do it? What was likely to persuade the most people to want to change the laws against this plant? The answer was simple. Money.

That's right.

Money

I had to show the state and the powers-that-be how we could make lots of money off the transition and solve our state's chronic budget shortfalls. Kentucky has long ranked in the bottom 15 % of the states in the standard of living indexes. If we could create a system of taxation on the already-existent black market in marijuana in Kentucky, we could feed our hungry, house our homeless and educate our children. Further, we could redirect our law enforcement dollar toward true criminal acts and all be the safer for it.

My mind was really racing now.

A Plan. A real, honest-to-goodness Plan for eliminating Kentucky's poverty. My God, what could be simpler? Take marijuana out of the criminal category, tax it and fund the budget. An actual, true solution, not some product of mental masturbation where a market must be started from scratch with a product still to be identified as dear to the public. This was already a proven winner and tailor- made for Kentucky, which at one time, was the largest producer of this plant in the world.

It seemed like a hell of an idea. But I knew that I had to check it out with someone who might know something about the issue. Not the marijuana issue, but the issue of bringing an industry to the state which had been illegal at one time but which could now bring in tax revenues due to a change in the laws.

I needed to speak with "Happy" Chandler.

Twice Governor of Kentucky, 1935-39 and 1955-59, Commissioner of Baseball 1945-1951 and United States Senator, 1939 – 1945, Albert Benjamin "Happy" Chandler was a legend in Kentucky politics. Many of Kentucky's famous distilleries had located here during his administration after Prohibition had ended so he knew something about taxing the "sin" industry. And he certainly wasn't afraid of controversy since he was Commissioner of Baseball when Jackie Robinson came into the major leagues. And finally, he didn't toe the party line for purposes of conformity. In fact, in 1967, he had bolted the Democratic Party, which he had twice led, and supported the Republican nominee for Governor who won the seat for that party for the first time in 36 years.

Happy was certainly qualified to have an opinion on these matters and enough of a maverick to give it. I had met him before as a young man and he had a much-deserved reputation for never forgetting a name or a face. Literally, he could meet you once, then see you forty years later and remember your name and where he met you. What a great gift for a political type to possess.

I made my way back to the car at the end of the trail. Stopping at the first pay phone I came to, twenty miles down the road, I called information and got his number. He lived in Versailles, about 15 miles west of Lexington.

A man answered the phone and I asked for the Governor. (Once you have been Governor, that's what people call you from then on.) A few seconds later his distinctive voice came on the line.

"Hello, Governor Chandler?"

"Yes, this is Happy Chandler."

"Governor, this is Gatewood Galbraith. We have met before."

"Yes, I remember you Gatewood. I met you in Carlisle in 1955 when you were just a youngster. What can I do for you?"

Damn he was good! For a second I was tongue-tied.

"Well Sir, I would like a half hour of your time to speak to you about a matter of great importance to the state."

"What is it about," he asked?

Well," I stammered. "I would rather tell you about it in person." I believed I could be more persuasive face to face than over the phone and I was afraid the subject matter would bring a quick end to this conversation.

Happy was insistent. "You'll have to tell me what you want to speak to me about Gatewood. A half hour is a long time when it's something I don't want to talk about."

I stammered again but got it out. "Governor, I would like to talk to you about legalizing marijuana."

Bless his heart, he didn't hesitate for a second.

"Be here at Noon tomorrow, Gatewood. I'll give you an hour."

Governor Chandler's residence was in downtown Versailles and his office was in a cabin in the back. I arrived promptly and was ushered into his study by his constant companion, "Foxy" DeMoisey.

Happy was sitting in a big, well-worn leather chair. He rose and shook my hand with a vise-like grip that may have been the strongest handshake I have ever received before or since.

"How ya' doin' Partner," he inquired through his famous smile. It was the infectious sort and I was immediately caught up in it.

I felt at home even as I resisted the urge to massage my hand after he was through squeezing it.

He invited me to sit in another chair beside him and Foxy sat across the room, never saying a word.

We were just getting over the formalities when Happy's wife of 40 years, his beloved "Mama", came in with three big slices of cake and coffee.

Happy introduced me and handed me my plate. "Baked by Mama and sweet as she is," he smiled.

We made some small talk as we ate the cake then the subject got serious.

I told him that I had come to him with my idea because it was obvious that he was able to set aside personal prejudices he might have about a human's use of a substance to alter their consciousness, if he thought it was in the best interests of the state, economically or otherwise.

I told him of some of the medical properties of the herb, including my own experiences with it as a remedy for asthma. I told him of the government's own studies, including the most recent Shafer Commission, which concluded that marijuana was not a "gateway" drug and was not a threat to the health, safety and welfare of the public. That very same government commission recommended decriminalizing it in 1972.

For over an hour Happy listened to me, nodding occasionally and asking me this and that. Finally, he asked for my best estimates on how large the Black Market in marijuana was, and when I told him at least 20 Billion, he asked me my plan for taxing it.

I described my Model Plan for Legal Marijuana in Kentucky.

"Well young man," Happy said as he stood up and extended his hand to end the meeting. "They always told me that it made you crazy, but if what you are telling me is correct, we ought to be growing the hell out of it. You just need to figure out how Kentucky can tax it."

He didn't need to tell me twice!

On the way back home, my heart and mind were racing. Talk about encouraging words, and from one of the greatest minds in Kentucky politics. Ever. I knew I was on the right track. I might not be as crazy as I thought.

But I needed a plan. I needed an organization. I had business to conduct. And what better way to conduct business than through a corporation, which I was taking a class on that semester.

I drove straight to the Law School after my meeting with Happy. The necessary language to construct a corporation was simple enough. The key was going to be its name. It had to be catchy and forceful but euphemistic enough to pass muster by the Secretary of State.

I finally settled on the Kentucky Marijuana Feasibility Study. Hell, I figured it was feasible to study anything. And generally not illegal.

By 4 o'clock I was standing in the Secretary of State's office handing the forms to a secretary. She read the name and her face blushed. She immediately stood up and said, "I'll have to clear this with our counsel," and walked into another office.

After another minute, I heard a clear voice from the back room cut through the office chatter. "Sure that name is all right. There's nothing that says he can't study the feasibility of marijuana in Kentucky."

The secretary came back to me, took my fee, stamped my papers and handed them to me with a smile. "No problem, " she said.

I remembered her words all the way back to the Law School, where I wrote the charter for the corporation I filed the next day, The Future Marijuana Growers of Kentucky, Inc. The same secretary stamped those with a smile too.

Overall, my three years of Law School were not easy. I worked some and lived on nothing. Eating twice a day was a luxury but for a "True Believer" it was a small price to pay. I was becoming a "well-armed sheep."

❖ *Me and the Kentucky Bar*

When a person applies to take the Kentucky bar exam, they must submit the names of two judges or lawyers and three citizens who endorse their application.

Because I had never curried any favor among the judiciary, and didn't hang out with lawyers, I wondered for some while who I might get to endorse me.

One of my very favorite professors at the Law School was a gentleman named Gene Mooney. Gene looked remarkably like Mark Twain, with flowing white hair and a long, wide mustache. He had an Arkansas twang and a mind like the proverbial steel trap. I took him for four classes because he made everything interesting including the Uniform Commerce Code, an almost impossible task. He did it with humor and style and was much admired by all of us students.

Gene also realized that I was a little different than the others even though we had never talked on a personal basis. I didn't hobnob with any of the professors and very few students. I was a definite outsider, with no legal bloodlines and a penchant for asking that embarrassing question. "Why?"

All in all, Gene had seemed friendly enough to me so I approached him one afternoon in his office in the basement of the Law School.

I can still see him sitting in that chair, observing me as I entered. "Gene, I would like to get your endorsement for the bar exam."

He replied. "Gatewood, I have an iron-clad policy against endorsing any of my students for the Bar, but I'm going to endorse you because you are going to have trouble finding that second person." He did endorse me, God Love Him, and he was right. I did have trouble finding that second person.

But I had lots of faith that I would be able to find the three citizens to say good things about me. Because I had gone public with my desire to change the marijuana laws, I thought that it would make good sense, and help the cause, if three prominent members of the community would back me. So I went to the President of the University, Otis Singletary; the

County Judge Executive of Fayette County, Bob Stephens; and Kentucky's Speaker of the House of Representatives William Kenton.

I found Otis in his office. "Otis, I would like for you to recommend me to the Bar."

"No problem Gatewood. Come back next week and pick up your letter."

I found Bob Stephens at the Courthouse. "Bob, I would like for you to recommend me to the Bar."

"No problem Gatewood. Come back next week and pick up your letter."

I found William Kenton at his office. "Bill, I would like for you to recommend me to the Bar."

"No problem Pal. Come back next week and pick up your letter."

Man, how easy was that, I asked as I left Bill's office. This will for sure get me in because they are such important people. And so friendly.

I went to pick up the letters the following week.

"Otis, is my letter ready?"

"No Gatewood, it isn't. And I can't give you one. You didn't tell me that you had started a national marijuana legalization corporation. I can't endorse that or anyone who is a part of it. " He left out the word sorry.

Only slightly daunted I went to Bob Stephens. "Say Bob, is my letter ready?"

"No Gatewood it isn't. And I can't give you one. You want to change the marijuana laws and that makes you too radical for me to recommend." He didn't say sorry either.

With some trepidation, I went to Bill Kenton's office. "Bill, got my letter?"

"No Pal, I don't and I am not giving you one. What do you mean challenging the marijuana laws? You're too hot for me and I can't help you."

I tried to analyze these turnabouts as I went back onto the street. It was obvious that the institutions and the people who occupied them were scared to death of me. I must be on the right track.

Still I needed three people to recommend me to the Bar. I wondered who might have had the chance to observe me at the Law School so that they might feel confident that I could handle the job. Three names immediately came to mind so I hustled on over to the school and got the three of them in the hallway.

Imogene and Winston were "housekeepers" at the Law School and Charlie Morrow was an electrician with the University. We had spoken to each other almost every day over the last three years and I valued their friendship.

I explained the situation to them and asked, "Do you Folks think I would make a good attorney and would you recommend me to the Bar?"

Charlie replied as the other two nodded. "Gatewood, you're the nicest guy that ever came through here and I think you would make a great attorney. I'll have your letter ready for you tomorrow."

"Me too," said Imogene and Winston. And they did.

During my three years in Law School I guess you could say I developed a reputation for questioning authority. I was open about my marijuana use and let everybody know my opposition to its criminal status. In my third year, after I had written the Model Plan for Legal Marijuana in Kentucky and it garnered me national attention, word was passed to me that there would be repercussions. I wasn't sure of the form they would take but I tried to prepare for any eventuality.

My grades in Law School were nothing to brag about but I thought I had a pretty good handle on the law. I had been a professional student for some time now and knew when and if I understood the material I was supposed to have learned. Nevertheless, I took the Bar Review course in preparation for the exam which would finally let me practice law for a living.

I took the two-day exam in Frankfort, along with several hundred other students. Everyone is assigned a number so that the test is supposed to be administered anonymously. I felt pretty good about it but, like everyone else, I would have to wait several months for the results.

When they were finally published in the newspaper, my name was not listed among those that had passed. It was quite a blow but I didn't believe it then and I don't believe it now.

I hadn't failed a test in six years and I sure as hell hadn't planned to start with the Bar. But there it was. A big fat failure. Oh well, nobody ever said it was going to be easy. I was only sad for a few minutes, then I got mad. I renewed my rallying cry of "Screw the Bastards" and I promised they would never, ever, defeat my efforts to change these laws.

❖ *Susan & Me*

In June of 1978 I was studying for the Bar for a second time and feeling a little tattered around my self-esteem so I probably wasn't the most confident guy at the Jefferson Davis Inn when I smiled at the beautiful, long-haired woman sitting over by the bandstand. My heart perked up considerably when she smiled back.

Susan C. Sears was 24 years old with a degree from UK in Philosophy. I knew her brother but I had never met her before. I guess you could say we hit it off from the very start that night since we got married in her hometown of Owensboro five months later. And Gee Whiz, why not?

Susan was smart and lovely (then and now) and wonder of wonders, she understood most of my obsessions. Her Dad was career military, a Colonel in the Army and her Mom was a teacher. Further, she had begun having episodes of epilepsy when she reached high school and she knew what it was like to be looked at and treated differently by the high school crowd. She wasn't afraid of my being different and that just about put her in a class all by herself. She also treasured her family as much as I did my own which was one of our most valuable mutual core issues.

I was 31 years old and full of dreams about meeting the "right woman" to "complete" my life, whatever that meant. I knew that I was a little crazy and frightened lots of women with my oversized dreams, but Susan was a little crazy too, with her own dreams. We spent lots of time together and finally decided that we weren't going to let being crazy stand in the way getting married and starting a family of our own.

I was selling Encyclopedia Britannica for a living and also studying for the Bar. It was "deja vu all over again" as Yogi Berra would say. I sold some books, collected a paycheck and two days later married Susan Carroll Sears on November 25, 1978.

We both should have been given a medal for bravery.

❖ Jack Herer

For our honeymoon Susan and I went to Key West for several days then headed north to Washington DC to attend a national convention of NORML, The National Organization for the Reform of Marijuana Laws. Begun in the early 70s, this group was the most visible and vocal of the groups calling for a change in the nation's marijuana laws. Their core group consisted of attorney activists who had mapped out a plan for decriminalization, which they were trying to push during President Jimmy Carter's administration and they had made some progress.

They were, however, somewhat dogmatic in their agenda and they were certainly protective of the turf they had laid out for themselves.

Their leaders let me know upon our arrival at their convention that they were not interested in any of my plan for the revival of our agrarian economy and they weren't interested in anything else I had to say. After that, I wasn't much interested in them either until I was asked to join their national Board of Directors, many years later, to clean house on the relics still in charge. It was a labor of love.

The most notable thing about this event was our meeting with two men there who became, and have forever remained, my heroes, Jack Herer and Dana Beal.

After our rebuff by the NORML poobahs, we congregated with several other "outsiders" who had come from around the country only to meet a similar reception. We all had long hair and none of us were dressed in three-piece suits. I guess you could say we were noticeably different from the crowd that surrounded us as we met in the dining room of the Capitol Hilton, less than 500 yards from the White House.

Everybody else there was dressed in furs and silk and the linen on the tables was an inch thick. There were 8 of us at our table in the middle of it all and Susan was the only person I knew. She sat on my right.

We had only been seated for a minute and the waitress came to take our drink orders. While she stood there, the dark-haired bearded man on my left, looking exactly like Phineas T. Freak, of the Fabulous Furry Freak Brothers, took out a bag of marijuana weighing at least two ounces, laid it out on the tablecloth and began rolling a joint the size of a small cigar. He didn't seem the least bit concerned about where we were. He acted like we were at his house.

I looked at Susan and she and I both took stock of the table. No one else looked ready to jump ship and we'd be damned if we would be the first. Even the waitress seemed to make no note of what was going on. She took our orders and left.

The man rolled two joints and put the bag in his pocket. He felt in his pockets then looked at me. "Got a match?" he said.

I gave him a packet of matches. He lit one of the joints and took a deep breath. "Thanks," he sighed as he handed the joint to the guy on his left. (Hippies always pass left).

For a moment I didn't know quite what to do, then I decided to sit and watch. Susan followed suit as did the rest of the folks at the table. When the joint came to them, they took a drag and passed it on. When Susan passed it to me, I took an extra heavy "hit".

I am still not sure how good Jack's marijuana because I was already "blown away" by his actions and demeanor. This man had inner power and strength; Conviction and Courage. I was impressed.

I introduced myself and Susan and he returned the favor.

Jack Herer had traveled to D.C. from California where he owned several "head" shops that sold smoking paraphernalia and counter-culture items. He was also a charter patient in a government-backed study at UCLA of the effects of marijuana smoking on the lungs so he actually had the permission of the government to smoke marijuana. And he certainly wasn't shy about where he did it.

We smoked until our meals came and we smoked another after eating. In a crowd of several hundred diners, I swear to God, nobody paid us one iota of attention. It was a great lesson for me. If you don't act like you know what you are doing is wrong, neither will most other people.

Jack Herer is/was totally committed to changing the cannabis laws around the world. He first tried marijuana when he was in his late twenties and it relieved his anxieties and helped him face the demons he had collected up to that time. He started selling paraphernalia, rolling papers and pipes with his business partner, Captain Ed, and they both took a pledge to devote their lives to ending marijuana prohibition.

Later, Jack was convicted of selling marijuana and spent several months in prison where he began writing a book on the history and uses of the cannabis plant. One discovery led to another and upon his release, he had compiled an extensive and unique collection of studies of the cannabis plant, most of them originating from the government.

Jack had started out investigating the medical and recreational properties of the plant using such references as Dr. Tod Mikuryia's revelatory work, *The Medical Marijuana Papers*, a compilation of historic studies of marijuana's use as a medicine. As he got deeper into its history from other sources, Jack became aware of the plant's history, and value, as an industrial/ textile resource. He was fascinated by this and especially with the fact that none of this was common knowledge. There appeared to have been a concentrated effort by someone to keep this history out of our textbooks and our classrooms. Jack made up his mind to learn it all and write a book about it. He began his quest in 1973 and it remains unfinished to his satisfaction. Boy, are "They" in a world of trouble.

Jack and I hit it off right away. Here was a man with a vision and some idea of how to achieve it. To him, knowledge was power and he had set about acquiring it from all available sources. He had scoured the libraries in all the major cities looking for references on cannabis, marijuana and hemp.

"Yea, hemp," I offered early on. "I'm from Kentucky and we used to make rope and bagging for cotton bales out of it."

"You made a lot more than that out of it," Jack informed me. "It was also used to make fine clothes, cooking and heating oil, lubricating oil, sails and other ship rigging and paper. The Constitution is written on hemp paper. And the Conestoga wagons that carried us westward were covered by hemp canvas. They became the first Levi's jeans when they came to the West Coast."

I looked at him askance. I had never heard any of these things spoken about with the authority he possessed. He noticed my uncertainty.

"That's right. Marijuana is the most useful plant on the planet," he continued. "It just depends on how you cultivate it."

"It's all the same cannabis plant. If you grow it for smoke, you want it to be bushy and resinous and you grow it so that each plant gets plenty of sunshine. If you grow it for fiber and paper you want it to be grown closely together so that you get long stems and almost no leaves."

My mind raced in several different directions. If what this man was saying was true, how come it wasn't common knowledge where I came from, Kentucky. The world's largest producer of hemp for over one hundred years and there was not a word of this spoken in any history class within the state.

When I mentioned this to Jack he explained why. His research showed that the reference books on cannabis, hemp and marijuana had all been removed from the libraries of this nation. He had gone into major library systems and been unable to find one reference on hemp or marijuana.

To further make his point about the conspiracy afoot to dumb us down about the history of this plant and its uses, Jack told me the story of how he came about owning the last public copy of a film produced in 1942 by the United States government entitled "Hemp For Victory."

At some point during his quest, Jack thought that he remembered seeing a film about hemp and the war effort. It seems that during World War II, hemp farmers were exempted from the draft if they were engaged in the production of this crop for the war effort. By law, they were required to watch this film and then sign an affidavit signifying it. (By the way, Kentucky was the leading producer of hemp during this time period. They grew it mostly for seed, both for next year's crop and to secure the seed oil which was used to lubricate the engines of high altitude aircraft. It is well suited for this because of its natural constant viscosity.)

The trouble was that no reference to any such film existed anywhere in the government's catalogues. Jack researched government archives in vain. Finally, he personally went to the Library of Congress and examined all of the catalogues there to find a reference to it. There were none. Jack went back to California.

A week later, it occurred to him that the earliest catalogues he had examined were printed in 1950. The librarian who accompanied him had insisted that all earlier works were incorporated in that printing. Jack couldn't let the possibility go uninvestigated. He flew back to Washington DC and the Library of Congress.

"Isn't it possible," he asked the librarian, "that the 1950 catalogue had not incorporated all of the earlier listings."

That was not possible, he was assured.

Completely unassured, Jack insisted on looking for catalogues printed prior to 1950. After a lengthy search, in a dustbin, they found a catalogue printed in 1944. In that booklet, big as Dallas, was the listing of a 14 minute film titled "Hemp For Victory." The film itself they found on a shelf where the material was scheduled for destruction. Jack had struck pay dirt again.

The film is very instructive as to the value of hemp, both to the war effort and to industry in general. It mainly discusses the rope, fiber and textile uses but the government also utilized its seed oil for diesel fuel and motor lubrication. The hemp crop was seen as a vital domestic source of petroleum and natural fiber. (Jack struck similar pay dirt years later when he discovered a comic book designed and distributed in 1938 by Adolph Hitler encouraging German farmers to grow hemp for their own war effort.)

This man, Jack Herer, has been indefatigable in his efforts to learn the truth about this plant and why so many powers-that-be are spending billions of dollars to vilify, criminalize and punish everyone who associates with it. The result of his work is the seminal underground blockbuster, *The Emperor Wears No Clothes*.

This book is a compilation of all the pertinent government studies, which show the value of cannabis as a medicine and industrial/textile plant. It also traces the politics which resulted in its criminalization at the hands of the DuPonts and their industrial cronies. It is exhaustive in its scope and credible to the nth degree.

At the end of it, Jack issues a challenge to everyone in the world. He offers a $50,000 reward for anyone who can prove this statement wrong.

"If all fossil fuels and their derivatives, as well as trees for paper and construction were banned in order to save the planet, reverse the Greenhouse Effect and stop deforestation;

THEN there is only one known, annually-renewable, natural resource that is capable of providing the overall majority of the world's paper and textiles; meet all of the world's transportation, industrial and home energy needs, while simultaneously reducing pollution, rebuilding the soil, and cleaning the atmosphere at the same time...

And that substance is – the same one that did it all before –
Cannabis... Hemp... Marijuana!

No one has ever challenged Jack on the statement. It's a Winner. It's the Truth! And the "crowd should go wild!"

The "Emperor" has sold over 1.2 million copies worldwide and been translated into 27 languages. It has spawned dozens of other books on the subject by other writers and has precipitated the activism of tens of thousands of citizens in many countries, inducing their involvement in sustainable agriculture, stopping deforestation, protecting the environment and reviving the agrarian economy.

It has alarmed civil libertarians and true conservatives alike with its revelations of Constitutional abuse in the name of corporate profit and monopolies.

And finally, it has sparked such revolutions as the reintroduction of hemp as a viable cash crop in Canada and the passage of Proposition 215 in California in 1996. (Allowing marijuana as a medicine in the state.)

If, as Einstein once said, "Genius is one percent inspiration and ninety-nine percent perspiration," then Jack Herer is truly a genius. He has spent the last thirty years in unrelenting pursuit of the truth about the cannabis plant, in the face of active government repression and at a ruinous financial burden to him.

His efforts have endeared him to millions however and future generations will hold his memory in respect because of his contribution to individual freedom and the American way. It just won't be the Nazi or the corporations who celebrate him.

I am one of the millions whom he has educated and I will celebrate Jack.

❖ *Karma*

After our honeymoon, Susan and I came back to live in Lexington and started to settle in. Several months later we decided to go to New York and visit some friends so we took off in my vintage 1963 Dodge panel truck. Things went very well the first day and we stopped in Pennsylvania to spend the night. Arising early the next day we ventured on toward the big city.

As we entered into New Jersey, we passed two state troopers standing along side the road. They looked at us long and hard and one of them pointed at the van. I knew that we were following the speed limit but something about their demeanor led me to tell Susan to make sure everything was put away and that we were shipshape.

We hadn't gone another two miles before the troopers sped up behind us and turned on their lights. I sat in the truck and watched them approach both sides of the truck, their hands on their weapons. It was obvious that they were both riding some sort of adrenaline rush, but the trooper who approached on the driver's side was easily the more aggressive of the two.

He asked to see my license and papers on the van. As soon as Susan opened the glove compartment he shouted that he suspected drugs in the van and ordered us out. There was nothing in plain view that he could have seen but it was obvious that we were the "hippie type" and fair game for his tyranny.

Within seconds we had handcuffs put on us and they were taking the van apart, emptying everything out of its container. When they got to some clothes they found two big buds of marijuana that had been given to us as a wedding present. The leader of the two yelled triumphantly and held them skyward like a trophy. He pranced around and got close to my face while telling me he just knew I had some marijuana with me when we drove past them earlier. There wasn't much we could do about it. We were "popped."

Susan and I were put into separate cars, which I was not happy about. I was matched with the real excited one.

On the way to the small town jail where we were to be booked, the trooper kept crowing about how he could spot a marijuana smoker anywhere and just how proud he was to be able to put them in jail.

I kept quiet for as long as I could stand him and his attitude, then I had to speak up. "Haven't you ever heard of Karma, man? You know, what goes around comes around."

He sneered at me and chuckled. Then he grasped his crotch with his right hand in the universal sign of contempt and said, "I got your Karma right here."

When we got to the police station in the small town, he handcuffed me to the radiator in the clerk's office and went from desk to desk to show each clerk the best looking marijuana he had ever seen. He kept on bragging about how nothing got by him on the road. I could tell by the reaction of the clerks that they had seen him act this way before and they were not impressed.

We got booked and put into two small cells. Susan made a call to her friends in New York and they got there two hours later to bail us out. As we were leaving through the front door, a deputy jailer took me aside. "Don't feel so bad," he said. " Lamonica's done that to a lot of people. He's a real go-getter."

"By the way, this might help you feel a little better," he said with a wink as he handed me two joints. God Bless that guy, he was right. Later, Susan and I completed a diversion program, paid a fine and had our records cleared.

Eight or nine years later I was running for the Democrat's nomination for Governor and I was driving to Paducah in the Far Western part of the Commonwealth. A news flash broke into the programming.

The public in Kentucky and all police officers were to be on the look-out for a certain type van, thought to be traveling through Kentucky and suspected to be operated by fugitive terrorists, possibly remnants of the Weatherman group who had been sought for years.

This vehicle was believed to be the one pulled over by New Jersey State Trooper Phil Lamonica the day before. As Lamonica approached the van, someone opened the door and blew him away with a shotgun.

I could scarcely believe my ears. Obviously the SOB had pulled over the wrong vehicle this time. Further, if the suspects were long-time fugitives it was unlikely that they were driving in a manner that would normally draw the attention of the police. Therefore he had probably pulled them over arbitrarily, simply because he had the power to do so. So his own arrogance had probably done him in.

There was only one response called for in this situation. I grasped my crotch and looked to the sky. " Hey Lamonica you Bastard. I got your Karma right here!"

❖ *Me and the Kids and Earning a Living*

I was 31 and Susie was 24 and we got started on a family right away. Thirteen months after we were married, on December 24, 1979, we were blessed with the birth of our first daughter Summer.

Simply put, I have never been more proud of anyone then I was of Susan when she elected to have our children by natural childbirth. We went to the Lamaze classes, practiced our breathing and stored breast milk in preparation.

When the day came and her water broke, we were ready for the trip to the hospital. When we got there we had a tape player with the Beatles' "Here Comes The Sun" playing on it. Ten hours later, we were holding the most beautiful child ever born on the planet. Of Course!

Like most other new parents, we doted over our firstborn and named her Summer Sears Galbraith. She was perfect. Of Course!

We, of course, were less perfect as parents, disagreeing ourselves on such things as how long to let her cry before Susan got her out of the crib and rocked her to sleep. We never did come to an agreement about that one. But raising your first child is certainly a learn-as-you-go proposition and we did our imperfect best.

One thing I did learn from Summer, and which was re-taught me by Abby and later Molly, is that no matter how old the parent and the child get to be, their relationship is going to be divided into two very distinct phases: before the child learns to say "no" and after the child learns to say "no!" It happens at about eleven months, folks, and everything is different after that .

There is no perfect time for having children and nobody is completely prepared to be a parent. For one thing, there is nothing that prepares you for the Patience you need to find, to be a good parent. For most of everyone's adult life, they work on being reasonable with other humans so that they can work things out or at least tolerate one another as mutually reasoning humans. Forget it with a baby.

Babies are the most unreasoning creatures alive. They're not at all sympathetic about how tired you are or how you have to work for a living. They cry when they are tired and hungry and sometimes for no reason at all. Except to irritate the hell out of you. You have no idea of your own limits of patience until it is you who has total responsibility for caring for the needs of that unreasoning, dirty, smelly, crying, hungry little critter. That's when you find out just how patient you can be. By necessity.

And let's face it. Necessity is the mother of character. I mean, most people don't develop character until they are put in a position of having to do it. Nobody can hand you character. It's what you put together within yourself when you go through the trials of life. And it's hardly ever fun and most people won't do it unless they absolutely have to. That's why having infant children will expose most people's character just about as quick as anything.

Another thing about children is that they need to be fed (I don't think that ever stops) so I had to earn a decent living somehow. I took the Bar Review course for a second time while selling Encyclopedia Britannica door to door. I made decent money and it allowed me to study on my own schedule. When the Bar results came out and I failed to make it for the second time, it was pretty devastating.

This time it not only effected me. I was now a married man with responsibilities. Also, the Kentucky Bar Association had what they called a three-time rule which meant that if you failed the Bar exam three times, you were forever barred from taking it again.

They already had two strikes on me and I made up my mind to step away from the plate before I got called out on strikes. Some folks, somewhere, didn't want me to practice law. I had to find another way to make a living.

About this time I got a call, from an old friend of mine, about another man who was getting a tractor company off the ground in New England. He was looking for people to introduce his machine in various parts of the United States and my friend wanted to know if I might be interested. My answer was an immediate yes.

The "Quadractor" was/is a four-wheel drive, four-wheel steering machine that looks like a table with a motor and seat on top and same-sized wheels at the bottom of all four legs. It was belt driven, sending power to the legs, which were, in effect, vertical axles. All the gearing, a 42:1 ratio, took place inside the hub of the wheel at the bottom of the leg.

This made it bottom heavy and safer on hillsides, even with its 32-inch clearance. Also, with its skid-steering, it had a zero turning radius which made it ideal for managing small woodlots because it could go through forests, over stumps and around trees just like a horse.

This was an incredibly interesting machine with which a person could not only manage a woodlot, but also farm with any category-one farm implement such as a 14-inch plow, hay rake or manure spreader. Because of its clearance and four wheel drive capabilities, it was perfect for working in flooded fields or cranberry bogs, or rice fields, for that matter. Unfortunately, it was this last matter which undid my tractor/farm implement career.

The inventor of the Quadractor, a Canadian named Bill Spence, began negotiating with Chinese officials to license its construction in China to satisfy what should become a huge demand for light weight machinery to work their extensive rice fields. After a series of stops and starts in their talks, Bill announced to the band of entrepreneurs and visionaries who had assembled around this machine over the three years of its existence, that he no longer controlled the company and that production would cease immediately.

This was devastating to me because I had put more than three years into the project, not to mention every dime I could get my hands on. I had secured the dealerships for Kentucky and Tennessee and demonstrated the machine to hundreds of farmers and landowners who were interested in purchasing a machine when it went into full production. I had hoped this would be the way I could make my living. Now it just vanished into thin air.

During this time, another "most Beautiful Child to have ever been born" arrived, and Abigail was her name. This time I got to cut the cord and the miracle of birth amazed me a second time. You cannot watch this happen and not believe in miracles. I certainly can't.

Susan was a champion once more , insisting on a natural birth.

The financial effect of losing the Quadractor had a severe and long-lasting effect on our family of four. We lost what little we had and I needed to get to work in another field. I went back to work selling Encyclopedia Britannica door to door. Is this a great country or what?

At this time we got some great news. Three and one half years after I failed to pass the Bar for the second time, the three time rule had been suspended because of the threat of legal action by Black students against the Kentucky Bar Association for discrimination. I immediately took the Bar Review again and this time I passed it. I truly hope it had nothing to do with the fact that they had replaced the Chief Bar Examiner who had graded my last two attempts. But I'm pretty sure it did.

❖ *Practicing Law 1981 - 1983*

Well finally. Gatewood Galbraith Attorney. Ten years after my promise to myself, it was a reality. Now I had to make it work. It was time to begin my practice of law.

My first shingle went up in 1981 at 115 Cheapside in downtown Lexington when I rented a little cubbyhole from another lawyer named Jim Early. Jim had been in practice for about 10 years, mostly as a Public Defender dealing with murder and death penalty cases. He was a "trial attorney" in my eyes, meaning he actually went in front of juries where there was big time riding on the line instead of spending his time inside libraries reading law books. That was what I wanted to do. Be where the action was.

After a while, I began to wonder whether the action was going to find me or not. For the first several weeks almost nothing happened. I made several appearances for Jim to get continuances, or for other minor matters, but otherwise things were quite slow.

One morning Jim called me from his house and asked if I could make an appearance for him in District Court where he had an agreement with the County Attorney to get some charges dismissed against a certain lady. I said sure and off I went to get it done.

When I arrived at the Courtroom I was surprised to find a large audience there and they seemed to be waiting for Jim Early. It took me a minute or two to catch on. The judge, Don Paris, helped "splain" it to me.

"Where is Mr. Early?", the Judge asked me. "We're ready for a trial in this matter. We've got a jury pool here."

"He's not feeling well, your Honor. He said a deal had been worked out in this case and it was supposed to be dismissed."

Paris looked down at me from his bench like his back was hurting him more than usual that day. "Mr. Galbraith, no deal has been worked out and we are ready to proceed to trial."

"But your Honor," I pleaded, "I've never even met the Defendant and don't know anything about the case. I'm not ready to try a case."

Judge Paris was unmoved. "Mr. Galbraith, if you don't try this case, I'm holding both you and Mr. Early in contempt of this Court. What do you have to say to that?"

"I say that I'll need an hour to get ready Sir."

"You have five minutes. Now go talk to your client in the hallway and let's get this show on the road."

I guess I could say I didn't know what to do but the fact was, I had just found out. I met with the lady Defendant for a few minutes outside the Courtroom and got her story. She was charged with Fourth Degree Assault with a motor vehicle, having allegedly run up on the sidewalk trying to strike several people and actually having bruised two of them.

Why had she done that, I asked her? She explained that these same people had assaulted her two days earlier and had broken three of her teeth. She was living out of her car and they had tried to steal some of her things. When she resisted them, they turned violent and roughed her up pretty good. She had wanted to file a complaint against them but really didn't know how. But when she had seen them on the street several days later, she just couldn't help herself. She went after them with her car. Luckily, two of them had only minor injuries.

She and I went down the hallway to the Courtroom door. I stopped for a moment. My first trial, I thought to myself. I had only seen one trial before and that was when I was the Defendant in a minor matter years before. I never went to any practice trials in Law School and had never sat through one at the Courthouse. My new client and I were in deep doo doo.

I took a deep breath and tried to remember all the rules. Not one of them came to mind. My entire life flashed before my eyes. I started to freak out. "Now wait a second", I thought. "That's more like it. Hell, I can freak out with the best of them. I've been freaking out every three seconds for as long as I can remember anyway so don't worry about this anymore than you worry about anything else. Forget the rules; you already have anyway. What you need to do is go into this Courtroom and do anything you want to do, unless and until the Judge orders you to stop it. Then you might even want to see how many times he will tell you to stop it before he threatens to put you in jail. Finally, you might even need to see the inside of that jail if he tells you not to do something and you just have to do it for your client's sake. Going to jail. Hell I was even pretty good at that. The ability to handle freaking out and the ability to go to jail. Damn if those aren't the characteristics of a great trial attorney, I don't know what is."

"Okay," I said to my client. "I'm ready for trial. God Bless us both."

And He did.

Not Guilty.

A young man once asked me, "Gatewood, should I practice criminal law for a living" and I replied, "Son, any industry that's based on greed, ignorance, tragedy and human pathos is a growth industry. You'll never lack for work."

But because it deals so often with unfortunate people and circumstances, I can't think of a profession that offers more opportunities for acts of graciousness, good faith, kindness and mercy than the practice of criminal law. It's a damn shame that so much of it goes untapped.

Over the past twenty-three years I've had the opportunity to preserve people's physical and psychological freedom , their property and their dignity as human beings. I've had chances to speak to the noblest principals of human interaction and persuade individuals and groups to look for the best side of humankind. Sometimes it worked and other times it didn't but there can't be many more poignant nanoseconds in a human being's life than that time period when the Judge finishes reading the jury's verdict.

"We, the Jury, find the Defendant …."

Come on, I'm thinking. One word or two? Guilty or Not Guilty?

Maybe it's just me but next to the love of my daughters, a forty-foot putt and sex, it doesn't get much better than a Not Guilty verdict.

There is no blanket characterization of the kinds of people who get charged with crimes in this society. They can be the guy down the street or Uncle Ed or your brother or sister or your Mom or Dad or your child. There are so many laws that criminalize so much basic behavior that everyone violates a law at some time or another. Some deserve retribution and some don't, but my clients don't get any unless the Commonwealth or Federal Government proves to a jury, beyond a reasonable doubt, that they are guilty as charged. If the state can't prove it, my clients walk out of the Courtroom with me. If the state can prove the charge, I often walk out alone.

Given the human condition, only human beings should pass judgement on others. That judgement can't belong to machines or to precise mathematical formulas applied dispassionately to certain categories of crimes. Justice is all-relative, you see, just like everything else.

By example, the story is that a woman went searching for the meaning of justice in a small Eastern Kentucky town. While she sat in the Courtroom, the Judge sentenced the first fellow to three years for shooting a man and the second fellow ten years for stealing a hog. Incredulous, she approached the Judge after Court.

"Where's the justice in giving one man three years for shooting someone and a second man ten years for stealing a hog," she asked?

"Lady," replied the Judge, "here in Eastern Kentucky there's plenty of people who deserve shooting but there ain't no hog that deserves stealing."

I must confess that I am in love with the jury system in our country. It is the last bastion of freedom for the individual citizen who is beset by over-broad and misapplied statutes and over-zealous officers who apply them.

My faith in the jury is based in the fact that I would rather have twelve people from the community judge my own fate than have it done by any elected or appointed political figure. My "peers" have a better chance to empathize with me as a fellow human being, subject to the frailty of the human condition, than would any other kind of group selected in another manner.

As I found out by trial and error over the past twenty three years, the most important part of the entire trial process is the selection of the jury itself. (Called the voire dire, it means the examination of a person to discover their fitness to hear testimony.) Since discovering this, I have won about seventy-five percent of my jury trials.

In my opinion, the key to winning jury trials is the education of the juror about their role in the process. This happens in the first two or three minutes that I have an opportunity to ask them my questions to discover their qualifications.

I have never heard any other attorney use this line of approach but it is based in the law and yields great results for me and my clients. Here's how it goes.

"Hi Folks. I'm Gatewood Galbraith and I guess my first question is, how many of you Folks distrust defense attorneys in general? (laughter) After seeing us being mis-portrayed so badly on TV and in the media, how many of you feel it is my job to obfuscate the issues, pull the wool over your eyes or otherwise mislead you as to the facts of the matter to be tried here today. (No one raises their hand here but they get the point) Fine then. You all understand that my role is to protect and defend my client, the Defendant?" (They all nod their agreement)

"Now I want you'all to be a little proactive here and raise your hand if your answer to this next question is yes. How many of you, when you got up this morning and began preparing to come here today as juror, thought to yourself, 'I'm going to be a really fair juror so I'm going to be totally neutral today when I go to Court. I'm not going to be biased or prejudiced because that wouldn't be fair to either party.' Now how many of you feel that way?" (They all raise their hands.) "Next, how many of you know that my client, and every other person charged with a crime in our society is entitled to the presumption of innocence?" (Again, everyone raises their hands.)

"Fine Folks. Now tell me this. How can a presumption be neutral?" (A general unsettling comes over the jury pool.)

"You weren't brought here as jurors to be neutral. You know, before the jury system came about, whenever a charge was brought against a citizen by the King or Queen or warlord, the citizen was hauled off to the dungeon or beheaded in front of a crowd. They had no champions to defend them. Then, with a sword pointed at the throat of the King, We, the People won the right to bring twelve members of our community, our peers, into the Courtroom to help defend us against these charges, unless and until the State could prove their truthfulness beyond a reasonable doubt. In fact, it is the role of the juror to take the Defendant's side during the trial Now how many of you'all disagree with that?

How many of you feel that you cannot fulfill the juror's role of helping protect the Defendant and being just as critical of the evidence here today as I'm going to be?" (This is when I see the light bulbs go on over their heads. Some of them clued in early on, but now most all of them get it. I particularly like the ones who smile and nod their heads. They really get it.)

"So you can't be on my jury if you aren't there to help me protect the Defendant against the charges. The system won't really work otherwise and every time the system doesn't work for one of us, we all lose a little bit of our freedoms, because we could be next. Now, is there any one of you that thinks you would not be able to fulfill that role as juror? I see no hands. Thank You."

Now days, we attorneys take a lot of heat for our roles in the process and I agree that there are bad apples in the profession. But they are the ones who get the headlines when they get caught and they don't represent the hundreds of other attorneys who tend the fires of civilization that we all take for granted in our everyday lives.

I'd like to think that the good attorneys forestall more trouble than they create. I know I probably have prevented several shootings by suggesting they sue the bastard first and reserve shooting as a last resort.

Most new attorneys are not trial-ready at the time they graduate from Law School. Like any other newcomer to a profession, they need exposure and experience around the edges of a trial before they begin picking up on the nuances of a successful trial practice. In many ways the Courtroom is like the theatre, real life drama played out on a stage and it takes a while to get comfortable in your own role and to understand the role of the other players.

Especially the Clerks who keep it all going for minimal pay. Acknowledging them and treating them with respect is a necessity to a good practice. God Bless 'Em.

Ultimately, the only way to really understand it is to dive into the middle of it and take your lumps. While I knew that the law degree itself offered me some protection, I also knew that I would have to earn my spurs in the arena of the trial courtroom before I could count on being fully armed against the fascism I saw being visited on many of my fellow citizens.

I had made up my mind years earlier to become an attorney, as much for self- defense as a method of earning a living. Just getting the degree wasn't enough. I had to learn to use it.

While it's very true that a lot of legal work needs to be done, it is also true that it just doesn't come running to your door when you hang out your shingle. Unless a new attorney comes from a family of lawyers, it takes a while to build a practice on one's own. Successful results and word of mouth are the best advertisements for anyone and so it has been for me.

I guess now that I was lucky in my first trial because it was upon me before I even knew about it and I didn't have time to over-prepare or worry myself sick about it. It came and it went and I was thrilled about the entire experience. I could truthfully call myself a defense attorney now.

Still, business didn't come easily. In 1981, I had a wife and two children and money was nonexistent, so I sat beside my office phone, for days at a time, hoping it would ring, and I could make grocery money for the week. Sometimes, I didn't.

Of course, nobody had ever told me life would be easy and my experiences as an asthmatic child, adult hitch hiker, migrant worker and uneducated activist had inured me to being in difficult situations. But that was before I had taken on the responsibilities of marriage and fatherhood. The pressure was on more than ever now and I had to see if the answer actually lay within the pursuit of my long- held dreams.

❖ *Me & Politics*

That's when an old adage came to me. "An attorney who runs for public office can't lose." Simply put, someone whose business picks up because they get public exposure can't do much better than to run for office and get their name out in public.

Years earlier, I had pledged myself to become an attorney and then to become Governor of Kentucky so I could take the government off the backs of the People. I began thinking about running for the Democrat's nomination for Governor in May of 1983.

While I was pondering this, I ran into my old friend Gene Mooney, my professor from Law School. When I told him of my plan, he opined that I should probably try for a lesser office first. While that had never really occurred to me, I realized it was good advice so I began exploring which of the other statewide Constitutional offices might be pertinent to my plans. I settled on the office of Kentucky's Commissioner of Agriculture.

The Commonwealth of Kentucky, like all other states, has a Constitution, which acts as the blueprint for the organization of state government. Originally it defined 8 different constitutional offices, the holders of whom were the winners of statewide elections every four years. They included Governor, Lt. Governor, Attorney General, State Treasurer, Auditor, Secretary of State, Superintendent of Education (removed by referendum in 1983) and Commissioner of Agriculture.

Every 4 years, in May, the Democrats and Republicans hold a Primary to select their nominees for the November elections. Given my experience in farm equipment and my pledge to find other crops for our farmers, the Commissioner of Agriculture seemed like the appropriate office for my first race, so I registered to run in the Democrat's Primary in May of 1983.

In retrospect, now I can see that this decision to run was more unilateral than it ought to have been. Susie had a hard time with it and I can see why from her point of view. We barely had enough money to eat on and here I wanted to pursue a statewide political office on a platform that seemed outlandish to some and at least far-fetched to others. I saw it as an opportunity to finally speak my piece on these issues and to get my name, as an attorney, in front of the people.

Susie saw it as unnecessary expenses and a selfish pursuit of my dreams. We were both right but my decision to go forward with it was probably one of the major reasons for our ultimate breakup. The results of that first race were major losses for me on both fronts, personal and political.

I made up my mind from the start that my candidacy for Commissioner of Agriculture would be more than a token one. I traveled throughout Kentucky, attending all of the forums open to the candidates and speaking my mind on the issues of farm economies. To say that my platform shocked the hell out of many people would be the classic understatement.

I wanted a campaign slogan that was descriptive of my way of thinking yet which captured a sense of common history shared by the Kentucky voter and me. I settled on "A True Pioneer in the Kentucky Spirit." I still like it after all these years.

I traveled from Paducah (where some union members tried to drown me out and made some threats, but when I invited the ringleader outside, they quieted down a bit) to Pikeville. (where a reporter asked me why I thought I had a chance to win and I told him "There are more marijuana smokers than there are Republicans.")

My Democrat opponents included David Boswell, Ward "Butch" Burnett and Tom Harris. They all treated me with respect on the campaign trail and I returned the favor. It was not them I was really running against so much as the system itself, a system which had come to punish its own citizens because they had the audacity to consume a green natural plant that arose from the ground out of a seed. Certainly the Office of Commissioner of Agriculture was the appropriate place to seek a change in the policy.

The media, especially the two major newspapers, the Lexington Herald Leader and the Louisville Courier Journal, treated me in a more civil manner than they do now. That was because, in 1983, they were both still locally owned; the Herald by the Stoll family, from here in Lexington, and the Courier by the Bingham family in Louisville. They both still had human ties to Kentucky, its heritage and its values. The Courier was routinely named as one of the top 4 or 5 newspapers in the country and the Herald at least covered some local news.

But in 1986 the Courier was sold to the Gannett Corporation begun by Frank Gannett, a transnational corporate profiteer, and the Herald was sold to the Knight Ridder corporation, an out of state conglomerate. The Courier has since dissipated into a mouthpiece for the New World Order and the Democrats who joined in bringing us Free Trade and the decline of our middle class and its traditional values.

So, in general, I received pretty fair treatment from most of the media. Sure, I got laughed at, but never to my face. And no one proved me wrong. That was extremely important to me.

Here I was, taking it to "Them". Challenging the Status Quo with my own research and not being shot out of the water with any credible, contradictory science.

It turned out that I was right. This plant was what I claimed it was.

But I just couldn't reach out to all the corners of the Commonwealth. So when the smoke cleared and the votes were finally counted, I had received 43, 137 votes or 11.5% of the total in a four way race. I had spent $8,500 total. The winner had spent hundreds of thousands of dollars and got 132,593 votes. I was disappointed, but satisfied that I had given it my best. The powers-that-be were shocked.

The results of that race were analyzed in many different parts of the country.

How in the world could someone from nowhere score so well on such a radical platform? Several interest groups, including the Democrats and the major newspapers, pledged to make certain that it didn't happen again.

Me? I went back to work; to make up for lost time and income. My first full year of practice, 1982, I grossed $17,252. During the year 1983, when I spent the first 4 months campaigning, I grossed $24,531. In 1984 it jumped to $54,541. I may not have won my first race, but business had definitely picked up.

Still, times were very tight. Our third daughter Molly had been born in 1984 and Susie had to take to bed the last four months of her pregnancy. Things were touch and go for a while but we were blessed again and mother and child were both healthy after the delivery.

❖ *Practicing Law 1983 - 1991*

The next six years were a mad rush to make enough money to support the family. When the elections of 1987 rolled around, I decided to stay out of the races and concentrate on making a living. I still had debts from the Quadractor venture and our finances were never better than difficult. That will undermine a relationship about as quickly as anything will.

My law business kept on growing but I suffered from a condition that kept it from being lucrative. I couldn't say no to anyone in trouble, whether they had any money to pay me or not. I gave away hundreds of thousands of dollars in legal work and for three years averaged more than 30 appearances a week in the local courts at a cost of almost nothing to my clients. However, my reputation as a trial attorney was growing and people began seeking me out after they decided to go to trial rather than accept the plea offer of the prosecutors.

There are several cases and trials that stand out in my mind during these years of practice. There are none more pleasing to remember than my first big trial in Federal Court, which took place in 1989.

My client came to me with this story. From 1981 through 1987, a group of very talented smugglers had maneuvered one large load of marijuana per year into six different major ports here in the United States for a total of 650,000 pounds. Even I was impressed.

Everything had been distributed and all went well for two years after the last load had been sold. Then, a ringleader was pulled over in Florida for a traffic violation and certain records of various transactions in the car caught the eyes of the authorities. They unraveled the paperwork and discovered the smuggling ring.

The top five leaders of the group were tried in two separate trials in Federal Court in a little Auschwitz-on-the-Plains built in Benton, Illinois. They were all given Life without Parole.

The next several people in the organization began ratting-out people on down the lines of distribution, 42 in all. Every one of them pled guilty to various charges and they were given sentences ranging from 5 to 20 years. One of those lines led to Lexington and my new client had come home one day to find the business card of a DEA agent stuck in his door with instructions to give him a call.

The DEA agent informed my client that his "best friend" had confessed to being an outlet for several thousands of the aforementioned pounds and that he had named my client as one of his two outlets. My client was therefore facing a minimum of ten years and maybe life. Now if my client would just tell on everyone he knew, the agent would try to get him a break. I asked my client his response to the allegation and the offer.

"Gatewood, I don't know what he's talking about. And even if I did, I wouldn't shit on my friends like I'm being shit on. I'll go to trial and do ten years first."

Now there's a man for you. My kind of guy.

My client turned himself in to the Marshall's Office in Benton and the United States District Attorney's Office moved to hold him without bond. After a cantankerous bond hearing, his in-laws posted a piece of land worth $75,000 and he was free on bond. The U.S.D.A.'s Office was not happy.

We held a pre-trial in the matter in late 1989 and persisted in our stance of not guilty. The Judge was clearly agitated. He had presided over the convictions of the five ringleaders and the guilty pleas of the 42 other cohorts.

"This trial is going to take at least a week," he griped to me and the prosecutor standing in front of the bench. "Can't you attorneys come to some sort of agreement."

"We'll take 30 days probated for possession," I offered.

"Mr. Galbraith," he replied, " I repeat myself. This trial will take at least a week and I find it hard to take up that much time on my calendar."

I couldn't resist. "It's amazing how innocence impedes the process, isn't it your Honor."

He really didn't like me after that.

The trial took place in January of 1990. I had not yet developed my voire dire to include the concept that the role of the juror is to protect the Defendant but I knew that I wanted young people to sit on the panel. Maybe the word marijuana wouldn't scare them so much.

The trial started on a Wednesday and ended on the following Wednesday. Over a seven-day period of time the prosecution introduced a total of eleven witnesses, seven of them alleged eyewitnesses, who testified that they had dealings with my client regarding shipments of marijuana. The main witness was his "best friend" who stated that he, himself, had received more than 60 loads of marijuana over the six-year period of time and that my client had been the recipient of half of that product.

Each of these witnesses was also forced to admit that they had pled guilty to felony drug charges and were testifying because they had agreed to testify against other people in exchange for lighter sentences. Each of them also admitted that they had not paid any taxes on the proceeds of their transactions.

Still, things did not look good on the eighth day when my client took the stand for three hours and denied anything to do with the conspiracy. They had never found him in possession of even one marijuana seed and, when they investigated his net worth, he accounted for every dime of his modest income and lifestyle. He didn't know what in the hell they were talking about.

My client left the stand and the jury was recessed while the Court and the attorneys prepared the instructions. When they were reseated, it was my role to present our final argument. I had no idea what I was going to say when I stood up and approached the jury from across the room. I still don't know what got into me when I arrived in front of them and began.

"Ladies and Gentlemen, in the thirteen hundreds (sic), a jury of her peers sentenced Joan of Arc to burn at the stake based on the testimony of two young shepherds, who said they hid in the bushes along side the trail, watched Joan of Arc transform from the body of a young woman into the body of a goat, perform satanic rituals, then change back into the body of a young woman. So much for eyewitness testimony.

Why do you folks think that jury convicted that woman? Do you think it was because they were afraid of the Judge in that matter? (I gestured toward the Judge.) You don't have to be afraid of the Judge here. Was it because they were afraid of the Prosecutor? (I gestured toward the prosecutor.) You don't have to be afraid of the prosecutor here.

Do you reckon it was because of the oral testimony given by frightened people with some sort of stake in the matter? You don't have to accept their testimony as accurate evidence. You can view it as I do, torrents of sounds that arose from the throats of self-serving, impeached

sources and which crashed against the wall and fell to the floor, like so much dust, and which was swept out last night by the janitor. That's not evidence, ladies and gentlemen. That's trash.

As a matter of fact, let's look at the real, three -dimensional evidence, which has been presented against my client over the past 7 days. (I walked to the Clerk's desk where the "evidence" was located). Two files, both of which contain the guilty pleas of two of the witnesses who appeared against the Defendant. That is evidence against his accusers, not against him. That impeaches them, not him. These witnesses would have said anything to help themselves.

For instance, I accuse the prosecutor, Mr. Carr, of smuggling hot parrots across the Mexican border during the intermission of this trial and when he goes home at night. And as a matter of fact, if you give me eleven get-out-of-jail-free cards to pass out among the prison, I will get you eleven eyewitnesses who will come here and swear under oath that they helped him do it. (By this time, Mr. Carr was apoplectic. I really thought he was going to explode. He was like one of those cartoon characters, Yosemite Sam maybe, with smoke coming out of his ears. His face was beet red and his eyes wide with disbelief. I really couldn't believe it myself. I had no idea I was going to say something like that before I said it. Sometimes you just got to go with the flow.)

Now what is he going to say to the jury at his trial? Hey, he's going to say, you can get lots of folks to say most anything about somebody, but do you have any pictures with me with parrots or any of my shoes with parrot poop on them. You don't? Then you should let me go. And you would have to let Mr. Carr go ladies and gentlemen. He is right. That would not be enough to convict. It's the same thing here. You shouldn't convict Mr. Carr and you shouldn't convict my client.

Let's examine what is going on here in these terms. Let's say that you are a village sworn to protecting the innocent and a woman comes to you with a child.

There will be a crowd coming after the child, she says, to do him harm. They say he has the mark of the beast. And you, the village, examine the child and find no such mark. Will you turn the child over to the mob, when they come for him, just because they insist verbally insist that he has the mark? Of course not. You look for proof other than their allegation.

Here, we have examined the child for proof of the mark and we find none. No big bank accounts. No big cash stuffed in a mattress. An

eight-year-old truck. Helping to take care of his mom who has terminal cancer. No gold chains. This child has no marks of the beast and should not be turned over to the mob based on the allegations of criminals and tax dodgers.

Or finally, let's think of this in these terms.

Let's say that you convict my friend here and this is all over. And a year from now, you're at home and the doorbell rings. You open the door and there stands the eleven guys who testified against us here and they are all dressed in three-piece suits.

Hey. Remember us, they ask? Sure you do. You took our word on a life and death matter last year. Well, we've all turned over a new leaf and now we are investment bankers and do we have a deal for you.

It's the perfect plan for you and all you have to do is give us every one of your paychecks for the next twenty years and at the end of that time you will be well off and happy. Best of all, we'll swear to it.

Let me ask you something ladies and gentlemen. Knowing what you know about the background of these people, would you invest the next twenty years of every one of your paychecks with them based on their sworn oath? Would You?

Of course not. You wouldn't invest two red cents of your own money based on these people's word, would you?

Well, let me ask you this ladies and gentlemen. If you wouldn't invest two red cents of your own hard earned money based on these people's word, how can you invest the rest of my man's life?"

And there I left it hanging as I walked away.

Mr. Carr couldn't get to his feet quick enough. You could have fried an egg on the top of his head.

"This trial is not about Joan of Arc. And it doesn't have anything to do with my smuggling er… or Mr. Galbraith's allegations that I smuggle parrots." And from there on he attacked me in every way he could. For thirty minutes. By the end of it, I thought for sure the jury would find me guilty of something too.

Finally he flung out his last words and our part was over. The jury left the Courtroom to deliberate. My client and his family, including his wife and four-year-old son, waited in the hallway and I paced in and out of the building. I had waited on verdicts before but this was a heavyweight. My man faced a minimum of ten years on the conspiracy count if the jury believed he had anything to do with it. We kept on waiting.

I have often said that the definition of eternity is sitting in the Courtroom having to listen to that other guy talk. Waiting for verdicts also qualifies as eternities spent.

The jury was gone for three hours before they sent a note saying they had a verdict. My client and I assembled in the Courtroom before the jury was let back in. Sitting there, I heard some of the jurors laughing in the hallway and I hoped against hope that it was a good sign. When the Judge actually said the words, Not Guilty, two of the jurors waved and they all smiled.

My client and his family and I began crying together. He and I hugged for a full thirty seconds before I noticed that the prosecutors had literally fled the room in disgust and disappointment and the Judge's jaw was still on the floor. It was the first Not Guilty verdict in 4 1/2 years in that Courtroom. God Bless them parrots.

I also learned another valuable lesson on that last day. A laughing jury is much less likely to hang the Defendant.

The practice of law is full of lessons to be learned. Every story has a moral, even if it's something simple, like don't touch a live wire. Or don't play Russian roulette with a buddy's head. Others are more humorous.

"There's no doubt about it, Mr. Galbraith. Whiskey affects you differently at 82 than it does at 77," explained my elderly client, charged with his second DUI. What would he do now that he had lost his license, I inquired?

"No question Sir. Most of my pension is now going for taxi fare."

And one of my all-time favorite lines from a harried looking fellow who caught up with me on the street. "Mr. Galbraith, Mr. Galbraith," he gasped. "Can you get me a Disillusionment of Marriage?"

When I got through internally appreciating the beauty of the line, I could only respond, "Son. I can probably get you a Dissolution of Marriage but I've got to think that She has already presented you with the Disillusioned part."

Also, during this time, I was reminded of that professional attribute that the really good attorneys make available to their clients. They make the time to listen to them.

I was sitting in my cubbyhole office one summer afternoon in 1987. Business was slow and I was literally waiting and hoping for the phone to ring with someone needing my services. It was a beautiful day and I would rather have been a dozen other places, but I needed new business and this was the only way an individual practitioner like me was going to get it.

The phone rang. I answered and on the other end of the line I heard a timid and soft female voice inquire, "Is this an attorney?"

"Yes it is," I assured her.

"Sir," she almost whispered in shyness. "My husband was injured in an automobile wreck and I have an attorney but he never has time to talk with me. I've called several other attorneys but none of them have the time to talk with me.

Do you have the time to talk with me?"

I thought to myself, Dear, I have nothing but time. However, this sounds like an attorney-shopping call by a wife with a husband that has been mildly injured in some minor accident. He's probably at work while she's seeking an attorney who will take a minor injury case. Further, if they already had an attorney and he wasn't staying in touch with them, he probably didn't believe the case was worth much. All this ran through my head, but at the same time I realized that she really needed to talk with a straight shooter and I like that about my reputation.

First though, I needed to go by the ethics of the profession. "Ma'am," I informed her, " first you have to let your present attorney go before I can talk with you. Why don't you go by and pick up your file from him so you can bring it by to me and we'll talk about it. Okay?"

She agreed to do so and we set an appointment for later in the week. Several days later, when she placed the file on my desk, she told me her story.

She and her husband had been married only a short time, they had a newborn and he was in the service. He was driving down a four-lane road in Louisville and came up behind a semi tractor-trailer stopped in the right hand lane. He moved over to the left-hand lane to pass it and discovered that another car had entered the highway, in front of the truck and right in front of him. The husband took immediate evasive action but veered in front of oncoming traffic and struck another automobile head on, killing the other driver. The husband suffered terrible injuries including bruises to his brain and was now paraplegic, unable to speak or care for himself in any way.

I was flabbergasted. This looked like a major case to me, but at least one attorney didn't have the time to devote to it and several others hadn't even wanted to talk with her about it. What was wrong with this picture?

I knew this much. Every civil case needs three provable elements to have a chance to be successful. First, someone needs to have injured someone else.

Second, An actual injury needs to have occurred. Third, the injuring party has to have the capability of paying for the injury they caused.

It doesn't do much good to prove someone injured someone else and caused damages if the injuring party can't pay the judgement. Somewhere, somehow, one of these elements must be missing in this case. I needed to find out right away.

I took her case and we signed a contract espousing the usual terms of one-third if we settled and forty percent if it had to be tried. She seemed much relieved. I immediately began to get nervous.

I had never tried a personal injury case before. Almost all of my practice concerned criminal matters but I had some idea of what to do. My first task was to satisfy the question, who caused this accident? I called a private investigator I knew and hired him to go to Louisville and interview all of the witnesses listed on the accident report. He got to work the next day.

My second task was to ascertain my client's injuries. I got to work examining the medical reports. This man was as close to being killed as you can get and still survive. He had only slight movement in one arm and would be wheelchair bound for the rest of his life, unable to feed or care for himself in any way. What a tragedy. It would take a substantial amount of money to care for him and his family.

Three days later my investigator returned from Louisville with fantastic news. He had located and interviewed all of the witnesses listed on the police report and one of them had sworn in an affidavit that he had seen the semi truck driver wave to the car waiting to come onto the highway that it was okay to do so. The truck driver had never seen my client coming up behind him and he thought the road was clear. He was wrong. Almost dead wrong.

That took care of the first two elements. Someone had acted in a manner that had caused an injury to another and the damages were provable and substantial. The third element was satisfied by a call to the insurance company who covered the truck driver. Yes, he was insured and the policy was for a large amount of money. Here was a case worth waiting for.

I dove headfirst into the case and damn near paralyzed myself by hitting a solid wall of my own professional incompetence. I had never handled a case of this magnitude and I had no earthly idea of how to actually get it to the courthouse door. That's where it had to go because the insurance companies will not part with a check of any size unless they have to and they will put you off forever, unless and until you force their hand. An impending trial will sometimes do that but getting them to that point is a time-consuming venture full of pitfalls like rules and stuff that I was rather weak on. I needed some help.

During the early years of my practice I had sought the advice of Fayette Circuit Judge James Keller on various matters. More than most other Judges of that day, he made himself available to younger lawyers who were learning the ropes and I trusted his perspective.

I went to his office and explained the matter to him. Since it was in Louisville, there was no possibility of a conflict arising with his advising me on the matter.

"Gatewood, you need to talk with Pat Patterson,"J149
he said. "He's one of the best and he's now practicing in Louisville. Tell him I sent you."

I went to see Pat the next day. I showed him the case and asked him to co-counsel it with me. I said I would do whatever he told me to earn my share of the fee. He looked me over and replied, "Gatewood, I'll call you if I need you." I liked the sound of that.

Pat's philosophy of practice was simple enough. When he took a case, he didn't waste his time waiting for an insurance company to call him or inquiring as whether they want to negotiate about it. He filed suit and proceeded to relentlessly advance the case to a trial docket. If the case is worth having, it is worth trying. Time spent negotiating prior to a trial date is time wasted to Pat. I sat back and watched how a true pro does it.

Pat Patterson was the best-prepared personal injury attorney I have ever seen. Hell, he must be the best-prepared attorney anyone has ever seen, period. The first time we had to argue motions in the courtroom I met him there and he had brought three long index card files, each containing about 500 cards organized by subject matter. I asked him about them.

Pat explained that he had prepared a three by five card on every Kentucky case that he had ever read that set a legal principal in personal injury law. He knew most of them by heart but he brought along the cards for ready reference.

I was fascinated by the effect those cards had in the courtroom. Over the life of the case, the opposition filed forty some-odd motions to escape or limit their liabilities by judicial fiat but they were in vain. We (Pat) prevailed in every instance.

Finally the insurance company asked for a negotiation session. We met in their office and Pat seemed right at home. We started out fairly wide apart on the money and each time they pointed to an alleged chink in our case, Pat assured them he could handle it in front of a jury. I think we all believed that he could.

After 4 hours of back and forth our client agreed, with our recommendation, to accept an offer well over the seven-figure mark and the suspense was broken. Our client and his family had a future and I had the biggest paycheck of my career. Sometimes it pays to stop and ask the right person for directions.

It also pays to slow down and listen to people who need to be listened to. Lots of times we get so busy that we don't really listen to that voice on the other end. I learned my lesson. I always have time to listen.

The check was big but hardly big enough. Sometimes I think that my only hope for money is to out-earn my capacity to mismanage it. This money lasted a few months. Susan and I paid some old debts and got some new transportation. I also moved from Cheapside to 163 West Short Street and finally got an office where I could stretch out my legal legs. I hired a secretary and I even bought something called a computer which was supposed to help me practice law. Imagine that.

❖ *Me and the Mixmaster*

Unfortunately the big check did not resolve the problems Susan and I were having. We divorced in 1989, due as much to the time and money I had spent, and wanted to spend, pursuing my obsession with changing the system, as anything else. We were most fortunate to do it on friendly terms, which we have maintained to this day and we still share the opinion that our three wonderful daughters are our greatest achievement in life.

This didn't make meeting my child support payments any easier however and there were several periods when I would get behind but Susan never complained unless times were really tough. And they did get that way.

There just wasn't enough money to go around. As a one-man office I was effectively shut down when I was in court and a receptionist can only do so much. In addition to business overhead, I also had child support, alimony and the debt load I had taken on from the marriage. That didn't leave a lot to live on, much less contribute to a statewide effort to win the Democrat's nomination for Governor in May of 1991.

I had made up my mind to run for the nomination sometime in 1988 and it was this subject which precipitated the conversations between Susan and me that led to our breakup. I felt compelled to follow through on the oaths I had made to myself 20 years earlier and we were at odds over it. I sure can't blame her. By definition, everyone's obsessions are his or her very own. No one else should be made to bear the burdens that a true believer can put on them as the believer follows their commitment through the thickest and the thinnest of times.

As veterans of these episodes of divorce can tell you, this eventual acceptance and resolution of the matter in the friendliest terms develops over years. While you're going through it, it's like a running mix master starting at the softest point between your legs and then drilling straight through the center of your being, piercing the heart and heading for the center of your brain. It hurts like hell.

❖ *The 1991 Race for Governor: Free Trade vs. Fair Trade*

I guess you could say that I wasn't at the top of my game in 1989 as regarded either my personal life or my financial situation. But I had my dreams and the added fear that George Bush would get re-elected in 1991 and who would there be to stand up to him on personal freedoms and other issues? There were issues that absolutely had to be addressed including the already oppressive War On Drugs and the creation of the office of Drug Czar, with the appointment of the reprehensible William Bennett as its first occupant.

But the main reason I felt compelled to run was to mount a loud opposition to President George Bush's 1989 act of removing Human Rights as a factor in awarding trade status to other nations. That signaled the abdication by the United States of their stance on Human Rights and replaced our policy of Fair Trade with the corporate profit-driven policy of Free Trade. In short, America went from representing the interests of human beings to representing the interests of corporations, even when they trounced Human Rights.

When America had stood for Fair Trade, that policy exported and promoted Human Rights by insisting that any nation, which wanted to trade in our markets, must treat their citizens in a humane manner and pay them a living wage. These nations enjoyed a "most favored nation" trade status with the U.S. and the minimum tariffs and duties placed on their goods when they hit our borders reflected our desire to trade with them because of their respect for Human Rights.

When President Bush stepped in, he did not take Human Rights from first place to second or third place on the list of factors to be considered. He removed Human Rights completely as a factor in awarding trade status and, immediately, China achieved the "most favored" status, even though they routinely practice infanticide (the killing of babies, mostly female) and employ semi-slave labor.

Under Free Trade, we welcome China's slave-produced goods into our country without tariffs where they undersell our manufacturers and have been responsible for the loss of our manufacturing base (and subsequently our middle class.)

Additionally, Bush engineered a change in regulations in 1989 which allowed pharmaceutical corporations to relocate their company headquarters to Puerto Rico, where they were outside the purview of U.S. laws which prohibit the "dumping" of contaminated chemicals into third world countries. As an added perk, these companies are allowed a $40,000 per year break on their U.S. income tax for every employee they have in that country. That was worth $4 billion dollars a year for them at that time, probably even more now.

It was abundantly clear to me then and now that a nation which would abdicate human rights on an international basis was only a short step away from initiating that policy on a domestic basis. I wasn't going to let it happen without a fight. I'm still not.

I was hitting the campaign trial whenever the opportunity presented itself but it came in second to fulfilling my commitment to my law practice. Sometimes I might have a case in one part of the state, then have to drive 200 miles to attend a campaign forum in another part. Even gas money was a concern as every bit of my income went to Susan and the kids. (By the way, I still owe one of my opponents in that race, Dr. Floyd Poore, $20 that I borrowed from him for gas money to get back from a Paducah forum late one evening. Hey Doc, if this book sells, I'll get it to you real soon).

❖ *Willie & Me*

So one day I found myself in possession of $700. I was two months behind on my office rent and my office phones had been cut off but I was even with Susan. I hadn't been successful at raising money for the campaign and my exposure was very limited, so I elected to splurge this money on my campaign. I also wanted to do something different, especially to get my message broadcast onto the national stage.

I went to a local TV station and rented 30 minutes of studio time during which I sat in a stuffed chair in front of one of their cameras and spoke into the lens. I talked about the need for a change in the marijuana laws, and how our farmers could benefit from such changes. I talked about my model plan for legal marijuana and what income to the individual farmer could mean to the agrarian society in general and the small towns in particular. I laid out my campaign for the Democrats' nomination and asked for the help of any one who might be watching. Then I took the rest of my money and gave it to a satellite company to broadcast the 30 minutes over its signal. If Princess Leah could send herself out as a hologram in search of Obie Wan Kanobi, certainly I might come close to doing the same with my plea.

I literally forgot about this effort almost as soon as I delivered the film to the broadcaster. I realized it was a classic "shot in the dark" but I felt compelled to try something different, to cast my hopes to the universe and see what its response would be.

Several days later I was on my way back to Lexington from a full day trial in far Eastern Kentucky. My client had been found guilty and I made him buy lunch at noon because I didn't have a dollar to my name. It was about 6 in the evening and I was hungry, broke, tired and depressed. And I certainly did not look forward to going back to my office where the landlord was probably looking for me, and nobody could call me anyway because my phones were disconnected.

I recall that moment well because I distinctly remember what brought me out of my funk. I looked up to see a spectacular sunset right in front of me. The sun sets early in the mountains and this one was constructed specifically to lift my spirits and put me into the state of mind that life was good and that I might as well go to my office and perform due diligence on the work that had already been entrusted to me by my clients.

Still, it was with some trepidation that I approached my office door on the top floor at 163 West Short Street in downtown Lexington. The landlord was nowhere to be found but my heart sank when I saw a sheet of paper taped to the outside of my door. "Oh no," I thought. He's served me with a notice to vacate the office.

With an almost noticeable tremor, I peeled the paper from the door and found that it was a handwritten note, not a legal notice. It was signed by an attorney from an office on the 6th floor, and it said:

"Gatewood, Willie Nelson is trying to get hold of you. Call your ex-wife for details."

Minutes later I was at a pay-phone talking to Susan. She relayed what Willie had told her when he called her at home. It seems that Willie was driving down the road on his bus one afternoon, surfing the TV just like the rest of us when he came across my face and voice at the very beginning of my effort. He watched the whole thing then turned to his "family" crew.

"I want to help this guy," he said, as he picked up the phone to get my number so he could call me.

He got an operator at the GTE office in Lexington who recognized his voice.

"Willie'" she told him, "Gatewood's phone has been cut off but you can still get your message to him. I'll give you his ex-wife's number and you can call her. Also, Gatewood had handled the divorce for 6 of us operators here, including me, so I can give you the number of the law office on the floor beneath him so you can call them and ask them to leave a note on his door."

And that's exactly what Willie did. He called Susan and left his number with her, then called the office below me and they left the note. My "shot in the dark" had paid off in spades and it was one of the luckiest breaks of my life.

Let me take a moment here to tell you about my friend Willie Nelson. He is one of the most generous people I have ever met, not only with his money but also with his smile and goodwill. Willie genuinely loves everybody, especially the underdog and dispossessed. His friend, the writer and musician Kinky Friedman, calls him the "hillbilly Dali Lama" and that's pretty accurate. His entire aura is one of gentle spirituality and his eyes glitter with intelligence and mischief.

When Willie captures you with his smile, you feel bathed in light. I've seen him play for two and a half hours, then go to the front of the stage and meet thousands of people and sign whatever they hand him.

Willie has a unique talent that endears him to all that meet him. Even when there is a crowd of another several thousand people trying to get his attention, when Willie is talking to you, he's talking to YOU. He is not looking elsewhere; he's looking at you. You are the center of his focus and you can feel it. That smile he's got is for you and no one else. He makes everyone feel special.

In those few seconds that you have with Willie, you feel connected with him and when he brings closure to it by wishing you well and turns his attention to the next person, you know you have just been in the presence of an enlightened being. Nobody is ever disappointed after having met Willie. He is the "genuine article."

I got in touch with Willie on his bus and arranged to meet him in Texas several days later. I had a friend willing to underwrite the trip. When I arrived at the Dallas/Ft. Worth Airport, I was met by his wife at the gate and we went to the parking lot where Willie was driving his Mercedes.

From the time of my arrival until the time I left three days later, I was treated in the most down-home, generous manner possible. Willie's wife Annie was as hospitable as could be.

Willie and I talked life and politics as he showed me around his hometown of Abbott. ("Where the population always stays the same because every time a baby is born, a guy leaves town.")

Willie's home is within a hundred yards of where he was born. Despite all of his worldly travels, his heart obviously still resides in a little crossroads town on the plains of Texas.

We played poker with his buddies at the West Abbott Social Club, a trailer sitting on the outskirts of town. Three steps from the center of town will qualify as the "outskirts" there. Sitting around a well-worn poker table were five genuine Texas ranchers, their faces browned by the sun and etched by wind and time. They were swell guys and Willie's friends and they played me for the anxious young pup I was. It didn't take them long to empty my pockets.

My stay with Willie and his family was as good as it gets. They were generous in every respect.

One day Willie and I were riding down a golf course fairway and I had to say, "Willie, I've got to tell you how much I appreciate you spending all of this time with me. Here you are, a superstar and you could be spending all your time with kings or queens or other superstars and, instead, here you are spending it all with me."

"Well hell Gatewood," Willie eyed me intently and smiled. "You like to play golf, smoke pot and look at women. Who else would I want to spend my time with?"

Before I left, we set a date when he would do a benefit for my campaign for the Democrats' nomination for Governor.

❖ *The 1991 Campaign*

By late 1990 I had secured a living area and campaign headquarters in a large brick house on Nicholasville Road. Since I had moved out 9 months earlier and given Susan the house, I had been staying with friends or sleeping in the back of my car. I had never actually had a place where the kids could visit me overnight. This house let me give them a bedroom of their own and I still had rooms for the myriad friends and volunteers who moved in to help with the campaign. At one time, there were about 10 of us living there.

My financial condition was a wreck. I could no longer afford a separate law office so I ran my practice from the same building as my campaign. Business, however, was slow and many days each of the crew ate one meal only. God, that was a dedicated bunch of people. Danny Pigman, who has had more than 150 letters to Editors published about medical marijuana and Dan Wooton, Jackie and Kurt, Chris and Sue. Thank You so Much and God Bless You All!

Meanwhile, my campaign was not setting well with the Democratic Party. They ignored me completely and considered it an invasion when I did show up at any of their functions, uninvited and unwelcome. The Party leaders were arrogant and corrupt and had an agenda, which had paid them well for years. Take big money from special interest contributors and reward them with state contracts and taxpayer's dollars. Quid pro quo. You scratch my back and I'll scratch yours. No matter how much public money it takes.

When I did get a chance to speak, I told of the poverty and despair within the Commonwealth. I pointed out Kentucky's extremely low ratings in all of the major standard of living indexes and insisted we could do better. I spoke of cannabis, as both an industrial/textile and medicinal cash crop, which would alleviate poverty and lower the cost of medicine for everyone. I also encouraged an international sweepstakes on the Kentucky Derby, akin to the Irish Sweepstakes. It promised new money coming into Kentucky from around the world and it didn't make noise or pollute the atmosphere.

The most important speech I made was at the Fancy Farm Picnic, an annual barbecue and political speaking event, 125 years old, which is held on the first Saturday in August. Thousands of people, political and non-political, gather on the lawn of the Fancy Farm Catholic Church, eat pork, beef and mutton by the ton, play bingo (ah, Catholics and Bingo) and listen to the candidates for statewide office give their best five minutes.

I spoke about cannabis as a cash crop and the International Sweepstakes as a moneymaker. Then I devoted the last two minutes talking about the United States Congress and the New World Order and their plans to ratify a treaty called G.A.T.T. (General Agreement on Trade and Tariffs) that would codify Free Trade as our official policy. I explained that it would decimate our manufacturing base in Kentucky, move tens of thousands of jobs overseas, allow slave-produced goods to flood our markets and subvert worker's rights.

My words had little effect on most of the audience but there were a few people who were real interested in what I had to say. They were primarily 2nd Amendment proponents and veterans. They approached me after I finished and invited me to their booth. Once there, they furnished me with additional information they had compiled on the dangers of the New World Order. They distrusted it as much as I did.

Finally, I had found an existing group which shared many of my views on self-determination and the preservation of our individual and national sovereignty. We didn't see eye-to-eye on everything but we could unanimously agree that our Constitutional guarantees were being threatened by our very own government. It was the start of a long and welcome relationship.

My relationship with the media and the Democrats, however, did not improve. I just couldn't then, and can't now, let them get away with being voluntarily ignorant. I am committed to telling them the truth every chance I get.

I was especially happy to get the opportunity to speak my mind in January '91 to the Kentucky Press Association in Lexington. None of them reported it.

SPEECH TO THE KENTUCKY PRESS ASSOCIATION

"I read an editorial in a Kentucky paper several months ago decrying the lack of Statesmen within Kentucky and wondering aloud why men and women of high principal are not drawn to politics and the electoral process, why it seems that only those who are wealthy are able to offer themselves for

public office. Ladies and gentlemen of the media, the 'Statespersons' of Kentucky, just like the solutions to the problems of Kentucky, may very well be right before your eyes, but my question is, 'Would you recognize them if they did present themselves to you?'

Is it possible that the problems of Kentucky are not being addressed or that all possible solutions are not considered because of constraints imposed by the emotional and intellectual parameters of the political reporters and analysts of the media? Do the prejudices carried by you at the reporter level, the editorial level and the ownership level act as barriers to your giving fair treatment to ideas that, though adverse to your own line of thought, may present common-sense solutions to chronic social problems heretofore unsolved?

Is it possible that you, the media, compound the problems by dismissing, out of hand, candidates and possible candidates whose checkbooks are not swollen with special interest donations or whose platforms fall outside some vested government interests such as protecting the monopolies of the petrochemical and pharmaceutical industries?

Is it possible that my own specific proposals for lifting Kentucky out of poverty are dismissed by you because you are too smug to accomplish the one honorable basis for dismissing my candidacy - that is to PROVE ME WRONG?

That's right, PROVE ME WRONG! Instead of dwelling on my physical attributes or the fact that I am broke, how about using your vast investigative resources to discover whether my platform is based in scientific fact? This should be easy enough to discover because my platform is not tied to futuristic visions but is rooted in our own history and heritage.

PROVE ME WRONG when I say that an International Sweepstakes on the Kentucky Derby would raise millions of dollars for our Commonwealth and that by cleaning up our air and water and seeking non-polluting intellectual industries to locate here, we could become a center of tourism and new industries such as telecommunications.

PROVE ME WRONG when I say that Cannabis is the most beneficial medicine known to mankind in the treatment of stress, glaucoma, anorexia, nausea, migraine headaches, asthma and epilepsy.

PROVE ME WRONG when I say that if we license and regulate the marijuana plant and remove people who smoke it from the criminal category, then we can turn loose our law-enforcement and medical treatment personnel and rid Kentucky of crack, cocaine and heroin, those synthetic man-made addictive drugs.

PROVE ME WRONG when I say that one acre of hemp produces the same amount of paper pulp as 4.1 acres of trees and that we can stop global deforestation on a vast scale by using hemp pulp instead of wood pulp for our paper, while restoring a much needed ecological balance.

PROVE ME WRONG when I say that hemp is the very best source for agricultural fuel - methanol - and that methanol is the future fuel of choice. This year, Volkswagen has introduced for sale a multi-fuel, top-of-the-line vehicle that runs on methanol as well as gasoline. This is reunified Germany placing some big bets on the nature and source of the world's future fuel needs. We can no longer rely totally on oil, especially foreign oil as our major energy source because it is wrecking our environment and holds an inordinate sway over our foreign and military policies.

PROVE ME WRONG when I tell you that over the next twenty years, trillions of dollars will be redirected from accounts of the fossil-fuel petroleum cartels into the hands of those agricultural fuel producers who poise themselves to take advantage of this transition. I believe this economic transition represents Kentucky's one spectacular opportunity, the chance of a century, to raise itself from poverty to wealth, and from an ignored status to an esteemed position.

PROVE ME WRONG when I assert that no valid reason exists, except perhaps our own limited vision, that should prohibit Kentucky from asserting its heritage as the world's largest producer of hemp for over a hundred years, and stepping up and insisting on a lion's share of that agricultural fuel market, to the immense benefit of our farmers, our business community and our tax revenues.

I challenge you to PROVE ME WRONG on these and the multitude of other issues which you have heretofore ignored and which have comprised my campaign platform from the beginning. And when you cannot, then I offer you a second and even bigger challenge. Write an editorial in answer to the question,

"What could it mean to Kentucky if Galbraith is right?"

My campaign slogan for this race was simple. "Choice." We laid it all out in an eight-page newspaper entitled "Choice." It is a work of which I am still quite proud. We distributed 300,000 of them, which was necessary because my campaign was not being covered by the media. The Courier Journal refused to mention my name as a candidate in any of its coverage of the campaign, a policy it continues to this day. Various associations and political groups and clubs holding forums "forgot" to invite me and it was only by insistence that I was included in the candidate's forum televised statewide by Kentucky Educational Television KET.

In preparation for this event, KET asked the candidates to write a paragraph or two describing what they considered to be their greatest accomplishments. I wrote and rewrote several paragraphs listing this and that but none of it rang true. Achievements aren't the same thing as accomplishments. I had achieved a law degree but I hadn't accomplished much with it. I dug a little deeper into what I was really proud of and came up with this.

"My greatest accomplishment was learning to believe in myself and trust in the natural cycle of things."

I still believe that today.

Finally the day came (Oct. 13, 1990) when Willie arrived in Kentucky to play a benefit for me and to endorse my candidacy. We held a news conference in front of the Fayette County Courthouse on Main Street and Willie and I poured a gallon of pure hemp seed oil into the gas tank of my Mercedes diesel and led a two-hundred car caravan of supporters from Lexington to the concert in Louisville, stopping in Frankfort to attend a rally of the Democrats' Party.

As far as we know, that was the first time in at least 50 years that an automobile had been driven on an American highway powered by hemp oil. Willie and I both thought it made a hell of a campaign event. That story and Willie's benefit for me that evening made both the front and back cover of the January 1991 issue of High Times magazine. Damn, I looked good.

Willie's appearance made the news in some places but not the Courier Journal. They would not include my name in any story on the Governor's race and they wouldn't include my name as candidate in any of the polls they took.

With three weeks to go they did use my name in the Bluegrass Poll and reported that I would receive less than 1 percent of the vote. I was offended and believed then and now that the figures were rigged and the Courier was patently trying to manipulate an election.

I had met with their editorial board several months prior to the race and their entire demeanor was condescending and smug. There were nine or ten of them and as the meeting began, several of them looked at their watches and said they only had a few minutes and they were sorry to have to leave early.

We took a seat around a large conference table and one of them asked me a question. I responded that if they would give me five minutes, I would explain my basic platform and they could ask me questions based on that. They agreed.

One hour and fifteen minutes later I quit talking. No one else had uttered one syllable and no one had left the room. "Any questions," I asked.

They were shell-shocked. They had never heard my version of history before. They were as far removed from the reality of the natural cycle as people could be and still dress themselves. They struggled to respond.

"I wrote an editorial once about medical marijuana," stammered a younger man. I wasn't impressed.

"What have you done lately to get that medicine to sick and dying Kentuckians," I asked? No one said anything.

I pressed my point. "Does anyone in this room not believe what I've said today about this plant?" Again, no response.

I laid a stack of material on the table and said, "It's all government studies."

No one moved to pick up the studies as the meeting broke up and they left the room. I took them with me when I left.

I called a news conference to be held in front of the Courier Journal's office building in downtown Louisville. I challenged the Poll and its integrity. I challenged the editors and their integrity. I said that it was basically unfair to exclude a legitimate candidate and their issues from a statewide race. It arbitrarily excludes what may be viable issues from being examined in the marketplace of ideas and is a disservice to the people and the political process.

I issued them this challenge. If my vote total did not exceed their reported 1 percent plus their Poll's margin of error of 3.5 percent, I would retire from politics. With that much on the line, I redoubled my efforts. Where I had been campaigning 70 hours a week, I now went 80 to 90, sometimes shaking 3 to 4 thousand hands a day. Finally, with two weeks to go, my body simply wore out.

I was hosting a campaign rally called Gatewoodstock on a hilltop in Montgomery County when I began having severe chest pains. My friends rushed me to Central Baptist where I was diagnosed with exhaustion and bronchitis. I had lost 32 pounds during the campaign and total rest was the cure. They didn't have a cure for my anxiety.

You could say that I was mighty relieved when I got 25,834 votes on Election Day, for 5.3 percent of the vote. I was too young to retire from political life. And I had already decided that, if I beat the Courier's effort to ignore me in the polls, I would go again for Governor in 1995.

❖ *Trying to Get My Act Together*

But for now, May 1991, I was not only was physically exhausted, I was also deeply in debt, homeless, responsible for several thousand dollars a month for child support and maintenance and lacking an office from which to conduct a law practice.

It was one of my lowest points and that seems to be when you find out who your friends are. I approached the owner of a local hotel and explained my situation. He arranged for me to take a small room and let me pay him when I could. I lapsed into a mild but chronic depression and there were times when I struggled to maintain a positive outlook; but then I would get a phone call that said, "God bless you Gatewood for all that you do. Uncle Willie had cancer and hadn't slept through the night for three years until he came to live with us and we told him what you said about marijuana as a medicine. He tried it and slept like a baby for the last year of his life. Don't give up Gatewood. Please don't give up."

There were other days when I had lots of energy and tried to use it to advance the cause. I held several public exhibits of hemp products such as shirts, jeans, shoes, oil and paper products which the media scrupulously avoided covering.

I also maintained my national presence, which had begun in the late '70s, with the publication of my plan to revitalize the rural economy by reintroducing cannabis. Nationally, readers of High Times recognized me as did those who saw my picture on the front page of USA Today, dressed in a pin striped suit and peering from among a patch of wild cannabis in Central Kentucky. My biggest political boost, obviously, came from my endorsement by Willie.

I traveled when I could to network the issues and tried to write about it so that I could reach others.

In '92, I was invited to an anti-nuclear rally in Nevada called the 100th Monkey Project. They were protesting the nuclear tests at the range within wind-borne distance of Las Vegas (and other life one would suppose).

I saw this as an excellent opportunity to match up the cannabis movement with another activist group with an already-existent infrastructure. Networks and coalitions are basic politics and God knows that is what I am about.

While there, I met with various organizers, alerting them to marijuana's medicinal benefits for radiation sickness and a myriad of cancer cases. In turn, they arranged for me to enter an Indian village of tepees and address a council of elders. We sat in the traditional circle but they graciously declined my offer to add to any peace pipe which might circulate.

I explained cannabis in some detail, its industrial/textile and medical properties. Then I suggested that the tribes situated on Reservations exert their National Sovereignty, plant the hell out of cannabis and market the products.

I foresaw a situation where the tribes could construct "healing centers" on their land, where patients who needed cannabis could come for treatment or recuperation. I thought they made a great alternative to casinos.

The elders sat and listened graciously then agreed to take it under advisement. I never heard back from them but it warms my soul that, at the time of this writing, the Lakota Sioux tribe, of Pine Ridge Reservation in South Dakota, are exerting their sovereignty as a nation and cultivating cannabis hemp as an industrial textile crop. Say, you guys named Sioux, has anyone ever talked to you'all about healing centers?

But I have never been willing to give up the fight just because I had lost an election, the media was ignoring me or potential friends hadn't seen the utility of forming coalitions. I did what I had to do: get back to the practice of law and continue to educate Kentucky's citizens without the necessity of co-operation by the media or anyone else.

The best way to get around a co-opted and corrupt media is to write the truth and distribute it yourself. I decided to do that and started on a book about the campaign. I began the first draft in late '91 and finished several chapters but it just didn't come together for me like this one has. Still, there is one chapter which gives full flavor to my first campaign for Governor and it deserves to be included here because it is the voices of the people who watched and took part in the effort.

❖ *"Letter to a Politician from the Grassroots"*

Letters...
We got letters...
We got piles and piles of letters...
Dear Gatewood...

They came from France and they came from Amsterdam, they came from New York and California, Arizona and Vermont and all places between.

They came in long envelopes, short envelopes and no envelopes, thin with money and thick with bad news and good tidings. Big envelopes and little envelopes, some with brash statements as to their politics on the outside, painted to catch the eye of everyone they could and others came bare of signature both inside and out as if by signing their name or their return address they might become immediate suspects. They might have.

The letters on the inside ranged from one word to tens of thousands, from hand-written scrawls to professionally printed information sheets.

They came with lots of money in them and a little money in them, no money in them and some of them asked for money.

The ones I remember the most were those with one dollar or two or three dollars in them, dozens of them with no note or letter, just a dollar bill between two sheets of white paper, no track to trace from, no tale to tell. I tried to imagine the human circumstance of the people who mailed these to me and how they would want me to use their dollars and their representation. I felt very humbled and very empowered by their actions. Their tokens of hope and support never failed to lift my spirits and resolve that yes, Damn It!, our voices will be heard.

Most letters were filled with their own voice, seeking further information and literature, offering advice and encouragement, seeking answers and often solace. There were endless renditions of tragedy visited upon everyday people by the police state depicted elsewhere in this book and present everywhere in this country. They told of warrantless midnight searches by dozens of mean, heavily-armed "peace officers" with an attitude, guns drawn and pointed at parents while the awakened children watched their moms and dads get violated and harassed, physically and verbally. Sometimes the parents would get arrested and the children put in a foster home if contraband was found (even if it was not what was expected to be found in the affidavit for the warrant) and sometimes there was nothing found. Routinely, where nothing was found, and many times with the house virtually destroyed in the search, the parents were threatened with further investigation and the "officers" left without so much as an apology much less an offer to help clean up.

These kinds of letters came from everywhere and they convince me that there is a nation-wide and uniform effort by the Federal Government to encourage this kind of treatment of individual citizens at the hands of Federal and State agents...

Dear Gatewood...

"We are a small group of veteran police officers who feel that it is our civic duty to expose certain unwritten policies, and attitudes of our officials and fellow officers, regarding (sic) the 'war on drugs', an attitude that the civilian population is the enemy and the policy is to advance and attack. Another attitude is that we must assist our department in obtaining more funding and to expand our powers to the point that we have totally disregarded the rights of others. We have all participated in a large number of drug raids and over the last few months, the nature of these raids has changed. Slowly, but steadily, it has become an unwritten policy and practice with some of our fellow officers to carry what is known as 'throw away' drugs, just as it has always been the practice for some officers to carry 'throw away' pistols. Until a few months ago, it was rare to use these throw-aways unless we had strong circumstantial evidence that the suspect was a dealer or user of drugs.

We know that because of the stepped-up efforts in enforcement, that a good share of the raids that we go on are instituted by a vindictive neighbor, an overzealous neighborhood watch participant or maybe an angry relative or something of that nature. We know that some of the officers are dumping drugs on these people during raids but we don't know how many innocents are affected by this practice.

To our amazement, we are able to obtain a search warrent (sic) from almost any judge by giving nothing more than the person's name and address.

During our weekly card games, our group has discussed this matter at length and we feel that if left unchecked, the system will reduce us as officers to nothing more than feared S.S. officers.

We know that we are systematically displacing large numbers of black males and poor white males through arrest and imprisonment and we are getting

increased pressure to get into the middle-class areas, to confiscate more property of higher value.
We are not offering any political solutions to the situation and we are not suggesting that we stop the war on crime, but we feel that the public and the courts should be more concerned with individual civil rights if we are not to become a brutal police state.

Unfortunately, already we as police officers must protect our identity and our location from our union, department heads and fellow officers in fear of serious reprisals from within for voicing our criticisms; therefore we are mailing this letter at our own expense to various people whom we feel may effectively inform the public in one way or another...

Before it is too late please help us: Recopy and Redistribute!
Lawman X

Thanks Officers. I really admire your appreciation of the balances in a free society. Thanks also to another Lawman X for his note from the northeast, telling me that he has been in the room with various DEA agents who spoke with relish of my ultimate "demise"; and also to the several other law-enforcement agents and elected officials who wrote anonymously to wish us luck.

Hundreds of letters came to us from the victims of this run-away War on Drugs, those men and women locked away behind bricks and steel for major parts of their lives because of their association with a green, natural plant. What kind of free society outlaws its own farmers?

These letters came from everywhere but mostly they came from the heart, from hearts filled with pain and grief to hearts filled with hope and expectation. Mostly those hearts are better writers than I am so I will let them tell you their story...

Dear Gatewood...

I am incarcerated at Wyoming Correctional Facility and would like to congratulate you on your stand on hemp. I know what it means to have your Constitutional rights violated with no hope. Let's put it this way, I will be receiving a "random" urine test for just writing this. Myself, I can never touch it for a long time but I will be getting out soon and I am glad after all that is happening in this world that there are still people like you out there. This system we are in is more corrupt than the people in here.
Dear Gatewood...

I pray for you each and every day. If I had money I would be more than happy to send a contribution. Unfortunately what you are fighting for (is what)

I am in prison for and can't send you anything except for my most humble gratitude and prayers... I just want to tell you on behalf of all those incarcerated because their freedom has been taken away because of the prohibition of pot.

Dear Gatewood...

I am an inmate serving a seven year sentence at FCI (Federal Correctional Institute), Lexington, for importation of marijuana. My hope is that one day marijuana will become legal.

I admire your courage. These are very difficult times for the American public. Many of us are victims of this witch-hunt called the "Drug War." My offense is categorized and treated equal to cocaine and heroin crimes-the government classifies marijuana as a narcotic. Because of this I am housed in a medium security facility, with no chance of camp (minimum security) placement and eventual half-way house.

Dear Gatewood...

we had seven small plants growing on our front porch in North Dakota. We are both facing Class B felonies for this. All kinds of scare tactics are being used by our fine police detective; he has spread more untrue stories against us (among) my ob/gyn doctor and

people we don't even know personally. The informant was supposed to be a friend of ours. We were sharing our food and money with him that we didn't really have to give. He was in trouble for something in Minnesota non-drug related. He ratted on us to save his own ass.

Dear Gatewood...

I am a Vietnam veteran presently incarcerated for my indulgence in the pleasures of cannabis. Branded a criminal, due to a law that I consider unjust, I am otherwise an honest, peace-loving citizen who bothers no one and expects the same in return.

As our basic rights and freedoms are being eroded in the "War on Drugs", I am becoming increasingly concerned, not just over my present suffering, but that of future victims. Our current laws are not only draconian but also de facto. I correlate the present situation, which I consider a holocaust on our own people, to the history of alcohol prohibition.

For America to be truly free, adults should justly have the right of personal choice. I oppose appropriation of additional funds to expand the repressive police state that has been forming, and suggest using now wasted funds for education and social programs, rather than persecuting casual users.

Alternatives such as decriminalization and licensing would devalue what is now contraband and effectively eliminate some facets of organized crime, reduce street crime and violence, and improve our sagging economy by keeping the money circulating within our borders. As evidenced by the Dutch, who legalized marijuana in 1972, consumption would decrease, contrary to myths being propagated by the Bush and Bennett regime.

I further urge reclassification of marijuana, which is now classed with hard drugs. Its mild euphoric properties, along with many recognized medical uses, can hardly be compared to other drugs (legal and illegal) especially what many consider the most dangerous, alcohol.

I have used marijuana for almost 25 years since my introduction in Vietnam. I find it is mildly relaxing, stimulates my appetite and enjoyment of food, and enhances my sex life. I defend my personal and private usage and resent Government intervention.

I am confident my views are shared not only by the estimated thirty million plus Americans who indulge in marijuana but also free thinking individuals who are sympathetic to our plight and believe in freedom and liberty. I pray logic will prevail.
Signed, P.O.W.

Millions and millions and millions of Americans, millions of people exactly like you and me, have been arrested for associating with or being in the proximity of a green natural plant, a plant, in fact, which was the largest cash-crop in Kentucky just 80 years ago. And where the taxes from hemp were used to build new "temples of justice" in Kentucky around the 1900s, thousands of men and women are now led, shackled and chained, through the newly renovated "courthouses" and branded as criminals because they farmed a crop that their granddaddies did. And the insanity of the situation is not only visited upon the adults...

Dear Gatewood...

I am a hard-working, respected, and law-abiding citizen. I pay my taxes, go to church, wear my seatbelt and try to teach my children to act within the law. I also smoke pot. I resent the fact that because of this minor and harmless vice, I am a criminal!

I live in rural Kentucky and there are a lot of growers in this area. I have to watch that my children don't wander into neighbor's fields during the growing season. Pot stealing is as common as pot growing. Taking a walk is dangerous. Legalization would take care of this problem.

At a time when dollars are being cut from school lunch programs, with more children falling below the poverty level and with education in shambles across most of the nation, why are our precious tax dollars being spent testing the urine of our brothers and sisters?

Good question. The answer is that this is the growth of the "People Processing Industry", (PPI) where people with degrees in law enforcement, criminal justice and prison management and those with careers as prison guards and jail guards, bailiffs and deputies, police officers and probation officers, social workers and domestic supervisors, judges and lawyers all need human beings to pass before them as grist for the mill, fodder and fuel for the life of a machine that depends upon coercing human beings into it on an increasing scale in order to justify the existence of a career and employment in the growth industry of law enforcement. Have we accomplished full-employment when half of our sons and daughters are prison guards and the other half prisoners?

This new prohibitionist mentality is the cornerstone of a new, yet old, form of slavery where the "status" criminal is the fodder for dealing anew in human beings. Fathers and mothers are condemned to extraordinary prison terms, torn from the arms of their distraught wives and grieving children, replaying those tragic scenes of forced family separation on the auction block 150 years ago. The privatization of prisons has further institutionalized this dealing in human beings as a form of commerce and it is just as immoral and unchristian in this century as it was in the past. The madness of slavery revisited!

Couldn't we at least use these tax dollars currently being spent against marijuana to search for the Jeffrey Dahmers of the world before they claim 17 victims?

Even more inhumane than the treatment of prisoners trapped within bricks and bars is the treatment of millions of Americans who are imprisoned within diseases and debilitations and for whom marijuana is the safest, most therapeutically active agent for their treatment. What must it be like to know from medical literature and common experience that marijuana could save your sight, or help your son or daughter eat and keep their weight on during cancer treatment or a myriad of other beneficial medical results and then to know that your government forbids its prescription and use?

All because it interferes with the corporate profits being enjoyed by shareholders (including Bush and Quayle) of pharmaceutical companies who have a monopoly on medicine in the United States?

How truly free is an individual who can not medicate himself or herself with a green natural plant that is the best medicine on the planet?

At a time when the government seems powerless to stop Dr. Kovorkian, the "suicide machine", or the right of a person to pull the plug on themselves through "living wills" or the right of a person to voluntarily risk their lives by joining the armed services and engaging in unnecessary political wars, being fought for corporate profits, then it seems contradictory, wasteful and illogical to spend scarce tax dollars to criminalize and enforce laws against patients and adults consuming this most beneficial and least harmful of all the green, natural plants given to us by our Maker.

Marijuana is the least expensive medicine on earth but its competitors, Bush, Lily and the gang, want to raise the cost of its acquisition and use by making it illegal and burdened with black-market profiteering. They can't stand better and cheaper competition and they can't stand losing a dollar's profit. I wonder how they can stand their own consciences.

Dear Gatewood...

A short letter to the point. I am being sentenced to 7 years for a crime described as Intent to Deliver 5 pounds of marijuana.

I had 3 or 4 pounds of hemp seed and some hemp leaves, not cleaned, and weight may have included dirt or soil. I personally have not purchased any marijuana for over 2 years and this was road-side, fence-line-growing wild stuff. Whereas the highway ditch and the farmland was maintained, hemp only grew on the fence line, like wild asparagus. I know there isn't any THC in it and it didn't even look right, for it was dark gray to black in color and smelled bad. Believe it or not, I was going to use it for bird food... The only plea bargain I got was 5 to 10 years and the judge gave me 7 years.

...Also, the only people I've been in contact personally (with) is a parole man a week ago & I gave him past history, which my lawyer never asked for, the only time I talked to lawyer was 5 min each time before I approached the Judge...

I have been a pot smoker. But after this, I know that to be just, you have to obey the law of the land along with God's. I am a Christian, and my family is against my using pot. I've held out because of an excuse that I thought important. My right eye which has glaucoma. I take steroids, a legal drug, to combat it, however, I know that pot does help and when I have it I don't need the drops; but now, I will receive laser surgery when it occurs again. My ailment is rare. It is called recurring glaucoma crisis. But I'd rather have one good eye and be free than both eyes and in jail.

I know I was wrong. Hemp and marijuana are the same under the law, but the balance is kind of crooked. Education is the answer. My doctor doesn't agree with me either but I know from experience from the past 9 years of this eye trouble. The doctor says the steroids will cause cataracts but no problem with the laser and he wants to do laser surgery.

Now to come clean, I have no health insurance. I have no money! I give all to forward Christ. And even that hemp, if someone wanted it, I'd give it to em.

Dear Mr. Galbraith...

...legalizing pot is a good idea. The people who need it cannot get it. I have a friend who died of cancer, suffered every day and would have had an easier time if we could have pot. She didn't even know where to get it.

I have glaucoma and with high pressure most of the time and medicine does not help all of the time. If you mention this to the doctor, he looks like he thinks I'm crazy.

Do you know of anyone who can help me get pot for my eyes? Also my daughter, at a young age has it, with some lost sight already. Please let me know if you have any idea how I can get it for my health. I have had glaucoma for 20 years.

Dear Ma'am. Bless your heart and those of the other millions of ailing Americans who could benefit in the next FIVE MINUTES from marijuana as a medicine. You are being deprived of this medicine because of the politics and greed of the pharmaceutical industries as represented by George Bush and Dan Quayle. The only way we can overcome these tragic barriers is to assume control of the political system that has spawned them, casting them from positions of power with our votes and creating a new relationship between government and the individual. We must begin immediately because there are countless people whose day-to-day quality of life and health depends on us.

Dear Mr. Galbraith...

Remember that Oliver Twist wanted "some more?" What he wanted more of was gruel, which is hemp seed cereal. This may seem a simple idea but believe me it is powerful, effective and inexpensive. Hemp seed, high in linoleic acid, will be an effective nutrient in allergic and immunity disorders, will lower cholesterol and will aid in multiple sclerosis, arthritis and heart disease.

Thanks for the tip Doctor! In addition to being effective, accessibility to cannabis as a medicine will significantly lower the cost of health care for millions of Americans. It can be produced at a fraction of the cost of less-effective synthetic medicines and by letting our farmers grow it in competition with the industrial medicine, we are breaking up the Monopolies of the pharmaceutical giants whose control of the market has lead to price-fixing, gouging and contempt for the needs of our people.

Dear Mr. Galbraith...

I know you are a fair man and you care about people. I am writing you seeking help. My husband is suffering from a disease called AIDS. The Doctor has given him six months to live. Ha was diagnosed in September 1989. He has *cryptococcal meningitis, shingles in his eyes and is now fighting a lung infection called ronducoccus equi pneumonia. The medicine he needs to keep him alive is very expensive. He had a medical card when he was getting SSI, but when his social security disability came through he made too much ($820) to get SSI also so he lost his medical card. I had to go apply for a spenddown medical card which is based on your income. I have not got the decision back on it yet, but they expect us to come up with $1,599 to be eligible and then that amount thereafter every three months. We do not have that kind of money. I would pay for Barry's bills but I do not have that kind of money; just his prescriptions cost about $5,000 a month.*

I feel that the system is keeping my husband from getting the medical card he so desperately needs. Therefore it is keeping him from getting the medical attention and medicines he so desperately needs to stay alive.

We both have been hardworking people that pay their taxes. I am hoping maybe you can help us. The government needs this situation to be brought to its attention and something needs to change. As an American and as a human being I feel every one of us deserves the medical care we need no matter what our financial situation is. It is bad enough to deal with a loved one who is dying much less have to worry about how in the world you are going to get it for them, thus keep them alive and comfortable for as long as they can.

I have read that kidney disease persons get automatic Medicare cards, why than can't people with other terminal illnesses (AIDS, cancer) get the same treatment and get a Medicare card also? These diseases are just as serious and need as much attention.

Please, Please help us. I know this is a good country and there are people that are willing to help. I hope you are one of them.

This letter was one of many sent to us by desperate people everywhere whose lives, families and futures have been decimated by medical necessities. Medical care and affordable medicine can be had when we bust up the pharmaceutical monopolies AND redirect the expenditure of scarce tax dollars from detecting, arresting, prosecuting and imprisoning marijuana smokers to underwriting health care in this country. Please add your voice to the effort.

So many voices came to us during our 1991 Campaign that it is impossible to acknowledge, much less quote, those marvelous individuals who sent us their insights on politics and the Human Condition. Desperate pleas and shrewd observations, naivete and cynicism, came to us in the form of letters and songs, poems and artwork. We have come to realize that these issues seem to tap a creative streak in people, giving them direction and purpose and uplifting and satisfying in them the need to feel useful to themselves and helpful to others.

Many of the songs were delightful and the music topnotch. Take a note, you activists, that artists and musical groups everywhere are willing to lend their talent and effort to the cause. Contact these people in your area for fundraising and political activism. You can tell 'em that Gatewood sent you.

Dear Gatewood...

...The Problems our past and current government has caused are beginning to take the strength out of our nation; People are becoming dishonest with themselves and others, we are being force-fed a large amount of media generated morality, not much of which is realistic. I think it's about time concerned individuals nationwide take a stance with a new direction and new ideas before it's too late for freewill. It's good to know that people such as those who are supporters of your organization are starting to hear the message and come forward. But for a clear victory over conservative squabble, every freedom-loving individual must speak out!

Being in the entertainment business I have met a lot of really cool people and a lot of snakes. Now in ever increasing numbers government informers and spies are trying to blame everything from most of the drug trafficking to teen suicide on those who work in the music industry. It's all lies and has made for stiff creativity and bad karma throughout the music world. Now, THANK GOD, if people stand up and take up for themselves the tide can turn!

When your organization needs entertainment for your functions, don't hesitate to call on me. (My record company) has over two dozen available artists representing every type of music ready to perform when needed. We're open to benefits and parties, if there is any cost, it will be slight... We're ready to rock!!!!!

Long live rock and roll and country and western and every other music that sparks the human expression to creativity. Hands off the Arts, Government, you can't gag Music! I'll be damned, Jesse Helms, if I'll let you be the arbiter of My morality!

Our country is in great need, right this instant, of a renaissance of personal and creative expression from artists, writers, musicians and performers affirming the worth of the individual, their capacities and their rights as human beings. Dozens of local bands and performers graced our campaign with their efforts and talent for which we will be forever grateful.

But among the superstars of the music and entertainment world, only one man had the knowledge, the fortitude and the sensitivities to step forward and offer his voice to our efforts and may the name Willie Nelson be forever inscribed among the names of our true patriots.

Willie Hugh Nelson, "Willie" to tens of millions, friend to them all. One of the most familiar voices and faces on this planet, Willie is a man of, by and for the people. His albums have sold tens of millions and he walks with Kings and Queens yet no entertainer of any stature has ever performed more benefits for down-and-out folks, that you and I never heard of, than Willie.

Willie tells it like it is and I've never seen him back down from lending his weight in the fight for truth and justice. He knows that the farmer sorely needs cannabis as a cash crop for it's medicinal and industrial properties and what it would mean to the environment to use hemp as a fuel, fiber and paper crop.

Willie knows too of the value of cannabis as a medicine and it's potential for relieving the ills of vast numbers of people. Willie knows and he's big enough to do something about it. He gave a benefit concert for my campaign and toured Kentucky with me in a hemp oil fueled diesel station wagon. He sang to the Kentucky Democratic Party on my behalf and gave over forty interviews in a day, supporting my candidacy, my rural economic and environmental platforms. He was a Titan and a walking truth teller and his message, our message, came out loud and clear and was heard by many in a new light and understanding.

But where are the others with vision and understanding who occupy a similar superstar spotlight?

Paul McCartney, please step forward and let your voice be heard again as in the past when you have defended your use of hemp, as well you should. The world needs you, Paul, to take an active role in helping to create a change. We need successful people with resources and the ability to generate synergy to commit their names and support...

And you, too, Bruce and Jerry and John and Neil and Ringo... Our generation, your generation, this generation has made you rich and famous, spokespersons for what matters to us; but this issue of cannabis has festered in the dark government world of shadow and crime and now it is time for you to step forward and help us demand it's empirical examination and accommodation in an open society.

And you too, Joe Kennedy and Professor Ginsberg and Al Gore and Bill Clinton, quit this "Well, I tried it while I was in college but, you know, it was just a period of experimentation." That's bull and you know it. If you still smoke marijuana occasionally, let the people know it. And that you favor a change in the laws regarding it. You need not apologize to anyone for it. Your stance will be based on strong scientific evidence and democratic principals and you will feel better about it, and yourself, when you get honest about it.

And you, William F. Buckley; get off this position of yours, where you state that marijuana should be decriminalized but those who sell it to minors should be shot. That kind of blather adds little to the weight needed to bring a practical and beneficial change to these laws. Your stature mandates a thoughtful position where you emphasize your conservatism by helping us take the government off the backs and out of the blood streams and bedrooms of the people. "The least government is the best government," Bill.

And you wonderful, wonderful activists. Where would America be without you? Lending your voices and your time, your freedom and your physical well being to your visions of truth and justice, so far removed from the corrupt vision and policies of today's politicians. You are America's true heroes...

You, the long-distance trucker, spreading the word across the country and dropping us a postcard from Route 66;

You, the older gentleman who will never smoke marijuana but who so dearly believes in the right of choice that you sent a generous contribution in support of individual rights;

You, the ex-cocaine addict, who understands that where marijuana is available, hard drug use diminishes and who prays that marijuana is removed from the Black Market and made available under license and regulation;

You, the small farmer, losing your heritage and your dignity and wondering why you are not allowed to make your living from the land; criminalized, with armed gun ships hovering over your house and your fields. America has become an "occupied territory" complete with armed troops in your barns and an official line of propaganda which you had better espouse. I wonder if we can get some tips on how to resist this occupation by surviving members of the French Resistance who battled the Nazis.

You, Woodie, the NRA supporter, who astutely understands that the disarming of our population is of rights as well as weapons and that we must band together in a mutual battle to protect our entire spectrum of rights and privacy;

You, the Peace Park Vigilist , standing in front of the White House everyday of the year, all day and night long, in all weather until nuclear disarmament is a reality and your children are safe;

And You, the environmentalist, whose letter to National Public Radio's "All Things Considered" was so on point:

Ladies and Gentlemen:

...First, I have recently become an activist for the re-establishment of commerce in cannabis hemp. There are others who have long been advocates for the legalization of marijuana for recreational use, and have stumbled upon the environmental aspect of this issue. My motivation is based solely on environmental and economic concerns.

Second, the grass-roots effort that is presently underway to bring hemp back to the agricultural sector is on the verge of becoming a national issue...

I have been stunned by the potential uses of cannabis hemp to replace petroleum-derived products. Further, I have concluded that our country's "War on Drugs" is quickly approaching a ludicrous, but dangerous, Orwellian nightmare. Considering that we are almost at war with Iraq over our own wasteful dependency on oil, this story may well be one of the most important for "All Things Considered"

Enclosed is a copy of "The Emperor Wears No Clothes" and a video cassette of the United States Department of Agriculture's film, "HEMP FOR VICTORY" (1942, fourteen minutes). I was personally shocked by the content of these materials. Please try to read at least pages 1-22 and 43-47 of "Emperor".

These materials discuss the commercial, agricultural, and home use of cannabis hemp. Presented are documents, some of which were prepared by our own government (United States Department of Agriculture Bulletin 404 on paper-making from hemp hurds) that validate their claims. Cannabis hemp is agriculturally sustainable and environmentally friendly to grow ... especially when compared to crops such as cotton. It has grown for over one hundred years in the same location without crop rotation. It is a truly superior textile product. Then consider the other uses of the plant... a natural resource that could replace synthetic fibers, numerous petroleum-based products including automotive fuel, wood-based paper, and pharmaceuticals.

Although the tone of Emperor is inflammatory and statistical values questionable, the information may potentially be a basis for one of the largest economic and environmental changes of our lives. I refer to a transfer of capital from the petrochemical. paper, and pharmaceutical industries to the agricultural sector. Billions of dollars may be at stake, as well as our own civil liberties and the health of our biosphere.

I do not use marijuana as a drug. Crack and ice are killers. And I firmly believe that no one should be allowed to endanger the safety of others while under the influence of any drug. But the US Government's "War on Drugs" is actually making the problem worse. Please read the letter on page 147 from Milton Friedman, one of the most respected economists in the world. This opinion is shared by a growing number of people, including former Secretary of State George Schultz and conservative columnist William F. Buckley, Jr.

Quite simply, this issue is monetary. Our government's marijuana eradication efforts serve only to:

1) Keep an environmentally friendly agricultural commodity away from industries that may well benefit from the use of cannabis hemp.

2) Protect the revenues of petrochemical industries, maintain antiquated agricultural subsidies, and protect the US Government's own tax revenues from the sale of alcoholic beverages. It is hypocrisy not to include alcohol in the "War on Drugs".

3) Reduce the availability of a "harmless" drug, thus promoting the use of truly dangerous drugs such as crack.

4) Endanger the lives of law enforcement personnel unnecessarily while wasting taxpayer's money. We need criminal justice funds spent on real crimes such as Savings and Loan fraud.

5) Maintain the profitability of the illegal drug trade. Prohibition did not work with alcohol; and it will not work with marijuana.

Enough on drugs. I realize that I am editorializing. The true issue is re-establishment of the commercial hemp industry.

My profession is both Electrical and Industrial Engineering. I have worked extensively in the paper, textile, and plastic industries. I have set up machines that make fiber from recycled plastic bottles and machines that make paper from tobacco stems. I know that changes to industries and manufacturing processes are possible. Unfortunately, modern agricultural and manufacturing processes have never been applied to cannabis hemp, due to marijuana prohibition. The article from POPULAR MECHANICS (February, 1938), reprinted on pages 16-18 of the "Emperor", discusses a breakthrough in processing, decorticating, that would enable the same crop to be used for both textiles and paper manufacturing. Allegations of conspiracy between companies such as DuPont, timber interests, and the US Government are supported by the onset of decortication and the rapid expansion of hemp acreage in the early 1930's.

My motivation is solely as an environmentalist. I am seeking out people such as yourself who are in a position to bring this issue to the attention of the American people. In particular, I am seeking out collegiate educators in the fields of pulp and paper manufacturing, textile science, and economics, as well as regional and national media organizations such as National Public Radio. My job responsibilities have allowed me to make contact with people in industries that would benefit by utilizing cannabis hemp in manufacturing. I am not seeking publicity, nor am I publicly mentioning the names of people who I have discussed this issue with. Consider this package a message in a bottle, one that I am proud to have sent.

I request that you at NPR review these materials, contact Mr. Galbraith's campaign office, and consider re-establishment of commerce in cannabis hemp for a story on "All Things Considered."

P.S. See the new Johns Hopkins/World Health Organization study! I am outraged to learn of our government's use of military resources in the enforcement of domestic laws. This is prohibited by our Constitution and is in contradiction to every democratic principle that our country stands for.

There are numerous people who at this very moment are advocating the re-establishment of commerce in cannabis hemp (the buds of which are referred to as marijuana) as an environmentally friendly alternative to numerous petroleum products, including automotive fuel. Our own U.S. Department of Agriculture has published reports that one acre of cannabis can produce as much as four acres of trees in a twenty-year cycle.

As a taxpayer, I abhor the expenditure of $700,000 for Operation Greensweep. To dress and equip employees of the Bureau of Land Management as commandos and terrorize the local populace is a crime.

It is questionable that we should even be eradicating a useful agricultural commodity such as cannabis hemp. To use the military forces of our country in this effort is a prime example that "Reefer Madness" is alive and well after fifty-three years. I commend the individual citizens that have challenged this use of military force with their lawsuits against the U.S. Government.

What can I say, Mr. Engineer, that you haven't already said so well. Exactly what we are talking about is the re-direction of Hundreds of Billions of Dollars from the hands of the synthetic manufacturers into the hands of the farmers and the rural economy, the People. But don't depend on the national media to bring all of this information to the public's attention, although NPR has contacted and interviewed me on several occasions. As discussed elsewhere in this book, the national networks are now owned by these synthetic manufacturers, and they will sit on this story until hell freezes over. What do you expect from a government which is boycotting the most important environmental conference ever held, where over 120 other countries will be present to discuss acid rain, global warming and the destruction of the ozone?

Dear Gatewood...

I wish to call your attention to the fact that the United Nations is sponsoring a world conference on the climate and sustainable development, dubbed an "Earth Summit"...for purposes of developing a "global response strategy" to the current dilemma of climate change, exhaustion of non-renewable resources, et cetera. The UN General Assembly has authorized the participation – to an unprecedented extent- of "non governmental organizations" (NGO's) which can demonstrate both competency and relevancy on this matter. I feel it is incumbent on the American Hemp Council to participate in these proceedings, which are already underway...

I hope we can use the ACH as a sounding board on this matter to pull together a coordinated effort in presenting this case to the relevant United Nations organizations in the most dignified and professional manner possible in the time yet available.

This "Earth Summit" is a perfect forum for our information, but it is damned hard to overcome the significant lack of resources of the various activist groups, which could so ably represent us. We need someone who can jump-start us in this effort, someone who has told the government and the other major networks to "take a leap."

Say, how about Ted Turner, who seems to have a mind of his own and a network to match? Come on Jane and Ted - you know what we're talking about here. Lend your voices to what's right. Other folks in positions of responsibility are...

Dear Gatewood...

The DSM Reform Initiative has just asked the American Psychiatric Association to remove the cannabis (marijuana)... category from the Diagnostic and Statistical Manual of Mental Disorders (DSM) to present a more balanced view of cannabis...

The DSM Reform Initiative is a network of activists, scholars, mental health professionals (including psychiatrists), survivors of drug "rehab" and other concerned citizens. 44 are exposing psychiatric labels as a key political issue within drug policy to increase the effectiveness of re-legalization activists. This is to provide society with the necessary stimulus to improve the legal standing of people who use cannabis... to speed up the repeal of their prohibition.

There is an urgent need for radical changes in drug policy. Leading drug warriors such as George Bush, the heads of the DEA, National Institute on Drug Abuse, the FBI and the General Accounting Office among others, are unable to cite a single study that demonstrates benefits of drug prohibition when weighed against the costs. Most of the harm attributed to illegal drugs is actually due to black market factors caused by prohibition. The rights of all citizens are being increasingly sacrificed for this costly mistake.

Psychiatry (through the DSM) provides the main ideological prop for prohibition by calling the users of cannabis...mentally ill. This opinion has a powerful impact on drug policy and drug abuse education – (US PL 91-513). It also legitimizes social prejudice and discrimination against users. In the form of drug "rehab" treatment and misguided laws psychiatry adds to the cost of prohibition.

According to Stanton Peele, treatment actually sets people up for relapse by convincing them that they are sick, and is worse than no treatment at all. The pursuit of intoxication cannot be an illness as drug-taking behavior is so widespread in the animal kingdom that Dr. Ronald Siegel calls it the fourth biological drive after hunger, sex and thirst.... Norman E. Zinberg found that most drug users learn informal social rules that protect against abuse. The Merck Manual (15th edition) says that the chief opposition to cannabis is based on moral and political grounds rather than toxicology. Cannabis is a safe, nontoxic and effective herbal medication for glaucoma and a variety of other physical ills including AIDS. A recent survey of oncologists (cancer doctors) showed that 48% would prescribe cannabis if it were legally available. 44% have already advised some patients to acquire pot for their cancer treatment. The moral opposition to cannabis that denies medical marijuana to people in need is a direct cause of suffering and contributes to blindness and death. Environmentalists are increasingly calling for cannabis re-legalization to improve the quality of human life because the cannabis plant can meet basic needs for food, fuel, fiber and industry with benign ecological consequences. The APA's DSM categories for cannabis...are inappropriate, misleading and are not humane or helpful.

The DSM Reform Initiative urges people who favor the re-legalization of cannabis to write letters in support of the APA removing the unfortunate cannabis category from the DSM. Activists should also write directly to the Nomenclature Committee of the American Psychiatric Association 1400 K Street NW, Washington D.C. 20005

And You All, the Christian, the gay, the farmer, the union member, the feminist, the black, the poor, the handicapped, the imprisoned and the elderly who wrote and called us with your stories and your support. All of you were so kind to me. Don't lose faith just because we didn't win this time out.

Ours is the eternal struggle between right and wrong, good and evil, freedom and slavery, light and darkness, understanding and ignorance. Our issues will not fade, they are not transitory and they are achievable at the election booth despite the fraud of those who oppose us.

Dear Gatewood...

I voted for you along with my entire family but you came out with 0 votes in our precinct. I registered a complaint with the Attorney General's Office but they said we all must have pushed the wrong button...

We are not the first generation of freedom seekers nor will we be the last. As my Journalism professor once wrote, "Every generation must win it's own freedoms." It's time that my generation and yours marshaled our forces as our forefathers did and stand for self-determination and personal sovereignty with all our might. We must do all of this or risk kneeling before our "Masters" in a New World Order, as the first American generation to abdicate our freedoms through lack of courage and will.

Many of us will not kneel, no matter what the odds, and we are already at work in the battle of a lifetime.

Dear Gatewood...

It is the night before the Kentucky election and I know you are anxious for the big day to come and go. I will vote six o'clock in the morning and the people I have registered to vote on your behalf will vote sometime throughout the day. We intend to get together and watch the primary's return on television. No matter what the outcome, you will be the only winner.

As I reflect on the way I and my friends behaved during the campaign period, I look back ashamed. We had got the idea to put 10,000 Choices in our local paper yet it always seemed like too much money and we were afraid to do it because you had to give your name to the paper to get it inserted. Yet you were not afraid. We made hand-made posters using the slogan "Gatewood for Me" and "Gatewood for Freedom", but as soon as we would put them up someone would tear them down. We put up a huge sign that said "Stop the War, Legalize Marijuana", but the local police decided to take that down. Why are we afraid? Don't they realize that when my freedom goes, so will theirs? I have heard you speak and I have you on tape and I honestly believe if not tomorrow then one day you will lead Kentucky and maybe even the United States away from its path of self destructive fascism that has swept across the country.

You have sacrificed so much for those who have sacrificed so little. But you have shown that to live in fear of the modern day Nazis is just as bad as being held prisoner by them. The fight will go on. Many of us have found new courage. We must win, they must not. We must not let them win, because if they do, our grandchildren will lose. I will not, we must not ever stop the fight for freedom. You have paved the way and we will never turn back, NEVER.

❖ *Letter to the Soviets*

It was during this time that the Soviet Republic (USSR) was breaking apart and that first draft of my book also included a letter to the Russians explaining my view of history. I think it stands on its own today.

Greetings,

The great events of change sweeping your political lives and geographical boundaries offer an exceptional opportunity for you to replace the centralized, totalitarian government you have overthrown with a system that enacts safeguards for your individual and personal sovereignty far beyond that which exists in the United States today.

The breakup of the centralized Federal power base opens up the possibility that local jurisdictions will fill the role of government in such ways that humaneness, individuality and liberty are the result of a new accessibility, accountability and proximity.

However, the seeming defeat of the old lines of power-of the totalitarian regime which put itself first, the state second and the people wherever they fell - is no guarantee of the attainment of freedom.

There lurks on the horizon a presence just as stultifying to the individual, just as demeaning to the human potential and just as likely to use the power of the state to force compliance with their own personalized agenda. This force carries the flag of the "New World Order" and it resides in the minds and the corporate plans of the Western world's petrochemical-pharmaceutical-military-industrial complex. And while its dominance may result in the presence of synthetic consumer goods on your shelves, that dominance will also extend to your private lives and lifestyles, just as surely and completely as the now deposed Politburo once dominated your lives.

This New World Order also follows the maxim, "In order to have a controlled economy, it is vitally necessary to have a controlled population." Sounds familiar, doesn't it?

The United States today does not represent, in any way, a free-market economy nor is it the bastion of individual freedom and self-determination that our forefathers fought and died for.

Over the past one hundred years, our basic form of government has been bastardized by the petrochemical and pharmaceutical interests, who have seized the reins of power by buying Congress and the White House. They formally staged their coup in the 1930's by the passage of the "New Deal" legislation whereby government and business worked out a new relationship between themselves which involved usurping great power and policy prerogatives from local and state governments and the individual. They have used this power to promote and protect certain industries from competition. Unfortunately, in the formation of the authoritarian New Deal, the people were left out of the negotiation process.

By the passage of this legislation, the Commerce Clause of the United States Constitution was given pre-eminence over the worth of human beings, individually and collectively. Farmers could be told what to grow on the pretext that their crop, no matter show small, affected "Interstate Commerce." The corporate bottom line of the DuPonts and the Rockefellers was then, and is now, the supreme measure of America, with their profit motive supplanting our human dignity, privacy and potential.

Our present system of government checks and balances seems unable to correct this situation because the two major parties, supposedly competing to represent the best interests of the people, have vigorously abandoned that principal and are continuously, in common, chasing personal wealth from, and influence with, the oil, chemical and pharmaceutical barons.

The labels of Democrats or Republican are merged at the feeding trough. Neither seems able to distinguish itself from the other through policies of compassion, fulfilling true human needs and the rights of personal sovereignty. Their policies and their actions always and ultimately serve the large corporations, and are doing great harm to the vast majority of people.

The powers-that-be view the land and its produce as adversarial, to be exploited or else destroyed, eliminated as competition and removed as a means of production of wealth.

They will offer you large doses of chemicals, free or on credit, just like the heroin pusher. These pusher's drugs are synthetic fertilizers, pesticides and herbicides in the agriculture sector and synthetic drugs, fibers, fuels and foods in the marketplace. They will seek to remove the farmer from competition with their synthetic monopolies and they will stop at nothing to do so including the jailing of large segments of the population who resist by insisting on procuring their medicine, fiber and food from the natural farming cycle. The poisoning of America's water wells from chemical run-off shows the results of the USA's habitual abuse and dependence on toxic chemicals Please heed this warning.

These synthetic monopolies have already taken control of our form of government and we now have more prisoners per capita than any other country on the world. "You cannot have a controlled economy unless you have a controlled population", and there is no doubt that the United States today has the most controlled economy on the planet. You can bet that this New World Order envisions the same policies and controls being implemented in your societies as you move through change and toward economic revitalization.

You do, in fact, stand at a pivotal time in global affairs as you prepare to negotiate a "New Deal" in your own country between the government and business interests, both within and without your borders. Do not let these negotiations take place without having the people represented in the highest capacity as to their rights and privacies and do not fail to protect the earth and its produce for access by the public. Do not let the new governments outlaw the growth and consumption of hemp nor any other natural product by your people. No truly free society makes outlaws of their farmers and you folks have the opportunity to affect a revolution in the government's policy of policing private behavior. Don't blow it for a few synthetic trinkets in shiny packages...

❖ The Science & Truth Hearings

I believe Mark Twain was correct when he opined, "Everybody's ignorant. Just about different things." What bothers me is when someone has an opportunity to learn something important with which he or she may do good for others and they choose to remain voluntarily ignorant of the matter. That's the way I feel about the media now and then and their treatment of the cannabis issue.

However, I was still ready to give them the benefit of the doubt regarding medical marijuana. I thought that they hadn't been able to find out the facts because they were so hidden among the tripe generated by the architects of the War on Drugs, so I decided to make it as clear as possible to them.

On January 18, 1993, I paid for and hosted the Science and Truth Hearings at the Hyatt Regency Hotel in downtown Lexington. These were public hearings, open to everyone and members of every media outlet were invited. None of them attended.

At this hearing, a four-member panel, consisting of myself, Lexington media-stalwart Sue Wiley, Fayette County Public Health Director Dr. John Poundstone and President of the University of Kentucky Medical Center, Dr. Phillip DeSimone received and cross-examined testimony from three of the world's top doctors/medical experts on the utility of cannabis as a medicine. Then we heard the stories from four patients who were using it to alleviate the symptoms of AIDS, multiple sclerosis, glaucoma and cancer.

The testimony of the patients was graphic and poignant. They all testified that marijuana brought them more relief than any other medicine they had tried and they had all heard about it from friends. No doctor had ever told them about it.

Each of the three world-renowned doctors had impeccable credentials. Doctor Lester Grinspoon is Associate Professor of Psychiatry at Harvard Medical School and has sat on every significant national drug-policy board since the early 1970s. He has written and/or edited 13 books and 300 papers on drugs and humans and received a dozen national awards for his research. His book, *Marijuana Reconsidered*, published in 1971, and updated regularly, is a classic in the field.

Doctor John Morgan is Professor of Pharmacology at the City University of New York and at Mount Sinai Hospital. His book, *Marijuana Myths, Marijuana Facts*, sets the scientific record straight in a common sense approach to educating the public. Dr. Morgan has testified that marijuana is safer than fast-food hamburgers. Recent research shows he is absolutely correct.

Doctor Tod Mikuryia is a Berkeley psychiatrist who, in 1973, published the first modern book on marijuana's historic use as a medicine, *THE MARIJUANA MEDICAL PAPERS*. He broke a lot of ground on the matter.

All three of these experts were equally adamant about the state of research and how cannabis had brought relief to their own patients. All of the testimony presented was un-impeached by the panel, which included two "establishment" doctors, a journalist/critic and me. Surprisingly, I asked the hardest questions of any of them, because I wanted to know the truth.

The results of that hearing were encapsulated in the Science and Truth Hearings which are set out on my web site at gatewood.com. A synopsis of the hearings is as follows:

Active medicinal ingredients in marijuana, especially tetrahydrocannabinol, are among the safest and most widely applicable therapeutic substances known to man. Marijuana relieves suffering in patients afflicted with AIDS, glaucoma, multiple sclerosis, anorexia associated with chemo and radiation-therapy for cancer, the "wasting" effect of tuberculosis, AIDS and cancer, migraines and spasticity both by relieving the symptoms of their affliction and by allowing them to by-pass certain other medicines which have demonstrable debilitating side-effects. The evidence indicates that marijuana is highly therapeutic in the treatment of itching, dystonia, chronic pain, as an antitussive, antidepressant, tranquilizer, and topical anesthetic and uterus stimulator. It seems that no other single medicine has been discovered that has such a wide range of applications and is as completely safe to use as tetrahydrocannabinol.

There it was, the truth for all to see and yet the newspapers of Kentucky, then and now, have categorically avoided this issue on all levels. I have set all of the research and studies in front of them time and again and they won't discuss it. They are incapable of considering the merits of any view alternate to their corporate agenda. They have given up relying on science and truth as a compass. They have morphed from voluntary ignorance to intellectual eunuchs, unable to erect thought processes on their own. They have no shame.

❖ *Daisy & Me*

After my divorce in '89, I had gone into a three-year long state of emotional isolation. I didn't date or attend parties or look for another relationship. I tried to fill the void with my girls, my law practice and my politics but even they weren't enough to stem my aloneness.

I figured I had to face reality. I was 45, divorced, with 3 young daughters and a healthy child support commitment. Besides that I love my ex-wife. (Hey, if you can't maintain love for the mother of your children, what the Hell are you thinking about having children anyway?) I mean, not in a way that I thought we would ever get back together, but I just decided I was going to be the best ex-husband any woman could have. I hope I've done a good job.

Add all that to the fact that I am an unelected, unrepentant radical political activist and it was certain that a vast segment of the female population opted themselves out of the pool of possible new lady friends for Gatewood.

So I resigned myself to trusting in the natural cycle of things, even if it meant I had to go it alone, for God knows how long. I wasn't even certain I knew how romance and love was supposed to work anyway.

And I sure as hell didn't plan on falling in love with a beautiful young woman who understood why I have to do what it is that I do. But it happened.

And what was really amazing is that she learned to love me back. And I was reminded of a quote by Ed Howe. "No woman ever falls in love with a man unless she has a better opinion of him than he deserves." That probably explains it.

I met her at Gatewoodstock, a fundraising concert in Montgomery County in 1992. She smiled at me and every resolution I had against getting emotionally involved with women again went kaput.

I tried to be wary, maybe to an extreme, but it didn't work. Within seconds, I was lost in her eyes and her aura. Damn it, if I was going to get my heart broken again, this was the woman I wanted to do it.

Over the next few weeks we approached each other cautiously. I was thinking all along that she would come to her senses and detour around me but it didn't happen. We began spending more time with each other and you know how those things go. One thing led to another and before you know it, I was head over heels in Love with her. Another resolve bites the dust.

In Love. The big L. Which calls for the big R. Romance. What the hell do I know about Romance?

I fumbled and faltered. She observed and surmised. It was a damn fine match. Add it all to the fact she is a Gemini and it's like I'm dating two different women anyway, so it's always exciting.

That began my 12 year dance with a beautiful Flower Child I'll call Daisy, a dance that's been a vast learning experience for us both.

My girls, then 7, 9 and 11, took to her immediately and she to them. It didn't take her long to find out that they wouldn't mind her just as readily as they wouldn't mind me or their mother, so she felt right at home.

The rest of my family was flabbergasted and immediately questioned her sanity. When they found out she had a pretty good grasp on reality, they welcomed her with open arms.

Daisy and I have had our troubles no doubt. I must be maddening to those folks who look for a little economic stability in their lives. All my money comes in clumps and I never know when it's going to come through the door.

And it is a fact that I wasn't able to resist the bugle call of Kentucky Politics in '95,'99, '00, '02 and '03 and I've been on the road a lot. Ummmm? Broke and absent. Maybe Daisy had a point there when she said she couldn't put up with it.

But it took her a while to come to that conclusion. About 8 years to be exact.

During that time we had a hell of a lot of fun. Road trips were a blast. New York, Atlanta and San Francisco and a lot of other sites where demonstrations were being held for a change in the laws. After a while, the activists were happier to see Daisy arrive than me.

And of one thing there was no doubt. Daisy made me look good. I rarely got a second glance but the third, fourth and fifth glances she got more than made up for it. And the really great part of it is that she has fine mind to go along with all the rest of it. And a Spirit that speaks out against injustice, corruption and the exploitation of the weakest among us. Daisy's the total package.

Of course I asked her to marry me. Who wouldn't? Twice!

And, of course, she turned me down. Twice!

She knew I wasn't finished with political races and the campaign trail is no place for a fine romance much less a marriage and honeymoon. I couldn't blame her.

Things became even harder on her, and me, when the races came even closer together. The '99 Governor's race and the 2000 Congressional effort took their toll on us both, financially and otherwise. She told me she was looking for something else in life and so we split and so did my heart.

I had sworn that I would never let that mix master near my heart again but there it was, running full throttle and doing a bang-up job of tearing me apart. An almost overwhelming loneliness set itself up in my life. For the first time I could remember I didn't sleep through the night. Let me tell you that waking up at 4 in the morning, heartbroken and alone, is a real drag. I hope you don't know what I'm talking about.

One thing's for sure. It's easier on me to lose an election than someone I love.

So Daisy struck out to follow her own path and has made it, just like I knew she would. She's an Independent Cuss and that's one of the things I admire. Independence.

For the next two years I retired back into my confirmed bachelorhood but I made up my mind that I was not going to lose Daisy as a friend. We had gone through too much and had been there for each other too often. We made it a point to keep our communication open and I tried to develop my ability to hold her with an open hand.

Some folks just can't take being held prisoner in a relationship. When their partner tries to grab and hold on, they feel trapped and subsumed. They will resist in direct proportion to the effort expended to hold them down.

An open hand is the invitation to join the person who extends it and know that you can rest here, in confidence that your friend will not try to bind you with mind games or servitude. You are free to leave and that is what makes you want to stay. With the open hand, you have that choice.

So instead of breaking it off with Daisy, I made sure she knows that my open hand will always be there for her and I think she might be more aware of it now than ever. Our Friendship is alive and well and, as a result, my heart "soars like an Eagle" whenever I see her. Which is as often as I can.

Because I Love You Baby and I Always will.

❖ *Rules & Me*

But, hey, all of IT was not, and is not, necessarily life-or-death with me. I take life seriously but I'm also trying to find humor anywhere I can.

The chance for that came from an odd source around this time. As happened all too frequently during the campaign, I got pulled over for speeding on I-75 in Richmond. Some of the times I just got a warning but this was a no-nonsense officer and I got a ticket.

I appeared in front of Madison District Court Judge Robbins and he presented me with the same choice he gave other speeders in his Court. I could pay a fine or write a 500-word essay on speeding. I was broke, so I agreed to the essay. Two weeks later, I submitted this to the Court.

RULES

Rules are made for fools like me,
Who try the leash to feel the free,
Who love the motion down the highway,
To feel the rush, to do life "my way."

Rules are tools for fools like me,
To judge the lines within which to be,
To toe that line, rub in some dust,
To ride that line, to risk that bust

Rules are for who'll pay attention you see,
Regarding auto traffic, they're very necessary.
To best do that job, radar is needed,
To stop fools like me who sometime have speeded.

Rules aren't cruel but fools think they are,
Them's the fools to keep out from behind the wheel of a car,
The ones who go ninety, just to show "sweetie,"
How "sweet it is" when their chariot goes speedy

Rules are jewels of wisdom and actually,
Should be based on behavior that can be proven factually,
And everyone knows, including the seeker of thrills,
That everyone knows, for sure speed kills.

Rules prevent ghouls from crashes to view,
Are they hurt, are they dead, is it one body or two?
Drive by more slowly, let's have a look,
At the hurt on the people, whom luck has forsook.

Rules are our schools, our learning at work,
Not meant to be bent by every high-flying jerk,
For whom lessons of safety are rules to be broken,
Compliance with which is only a token.

Rules are pools of agreement with which,
We can all agree who's the son-of-a-bitch,
That's stepping out of bounds, making that wave,
Taking that chance, a minute to save.

Rules are for mules, which people often are,
Stubborn when they plow through traffic in their car.
People get planted all in a row,
And it's not always the mules who must reap what they sow.

Rules are renewals of our social pact,
We agree what to do, agree how to act.
They are relied on by friends, relied on by strangers,
To avoid the unexpected, to cut down the dangers.

Rules keep from duels, the modern weapon cars,
People hurting people, it gets so bizarre.
So many monkeys expected to obey
Stay out of the way if one's had a bad day.

Rules keep the fuels of impulse from flaming,
Keep people from hurting, keep them from maiming.
Treat others right, do unto others…
They too have family, sisters and brothers.

Rules keep things cool, keep tempers from flaring,
They mitigate anarchy, their need is quite glaring.
If they weren't existent to keep predators in place,
The strong would overbear, they would "pusha youse face."

Rules are not bull, they have their own function,
They tell who goes first, if two arrive at the same junction.
How else can we judge who's wrong or who's right,
You do so by laws, not money or might.

I know now what rules are, their reasons and rhymes,
I shan't break so many, as in previous times.
If I get caught again, there'll be many sobbins,
If I have to again, write poems for Judge Robbins.

❖ *Amsterdam*

Another opportunity for a good time came when I was selected by the Freedom Fighters Association as Freedom Fighter of the Year 1993. I was modestly going to suggest that the title be awarded to some other deserving activists until they told me that the winner got an all-expense paid trip to Amsterdam where they would be one of 60 judges in the annual High Times Cannabis Cup competition. I modestly changed my mind and accepted it.

Amsterdam is a city of some 700,000 situated in the Netherlands. It has been a crossroads of world culture since the Renaissance and is renowned for its art, its architecture and its policies of accommodating people's vices in a reasonable and safe manner rather than criminalizing them and forcing people to deal with the underground element of career criminals.

Amsterdam has set up a "red light" district in a central part of the city and just about anything you want can be found there. Brothels and live sex shows are the norm and paying customers abound. In the center of this district is a one square block park where hard drug users may "shoot up" their drugs without police interference. If they do it any place else in the city, they are subject to arrest. This policy has resulted in the decrease of hard drug users in Amsterdam because no one else has to be recruited by the users.

Another accommodation of the people's desires is the proliferation of coffeehouses throughout the country where marijuana and hashish can be purchased and consumed along with espresso and lattes. Each coffeehouse has its own menu and special brand of herb. Many of the houses grow their own cannabis plants right on the premises and they are gorgeous plants to behold, when you have the time to tend to them and don't have to duck the helicopters, as we do in the U.S.

Each year, High Times magazine holds its annual Cannabis Cup Competition, where marijuana smokers from around the world meet for a week to try the best strains of marijuana available and judge them for their quality. At the end of the week, the winners are announced. It's a big time event and all the coffeehouses are anxious for their product to be recognized as among the best.

When I got off the plane at the Amsterdam Airport, I was met by Steve Hager, editor of High Times. He was in the back of a limousine and he smiled as he handed me a brown bag. "Gatewood," he began, "in this bag are twelve of the best brands of marijuana in the world, donated by the four biggest seed companies in Europe. Also, here is a list of the forty coffee shops taking part in this year's contest. Finally, here's a score sheet on which to rate each brand. Most people are not going to get around to all these shops, so just do the best you can."

I readily accepted the challenge and was driven to the hotel that had been arranged for me. I was going to share a room with another judge and imagine my great surprise and happiness when I learned it was my hero, Jack Herer.

While we were getting reacquainted, another judge recognized Jack and asked to join the group while we explored the city for the first time. It was Sebastian Bach, leader of Skid Row, a heavy metal band with record sales exceeding 11 million albums. He had been to Amsterdam before and knew the really good spots. He made a hell a tour guide.

And we had a hell of a time. The city and the coffeehouses were glad to host the competition and the 60 or so judges were treated graciously everywhere we went. You might find us at any time, anywhere in the city, taking in the sights.

One of the most remarkable things I remember was the lack of emergency sirens in the city and the lack of policemen on the streets. The thing was that you never felt any danger walking around at any hour of the day or night, either on the well-lit main boulevards or the narrow and winding unlit alleyways. No one needed to rob anyone to feed their drug habits and street crime was rare.

The only negative thing I remember is that both Jack and Sebastian were international stars and they got approached all the time by fans who passionately hugged and kissed them. No one knew who I was except for those Americans who had come for the Cup.

However, they knew me well enough to elect me Judge of Judges at the end of it all. That meant that I took all the scorecards, added, divided, multiplied, bent spindled and mutilated them and figured the results. Then I announced the winners at the party on the seventh day. A "Northern Light" strain crossed with a fine "Purple Haze" took the top prize for cannabis and the Green House Coffee Shop won for best Shop.

Afterwards I was interviewed by a lady from the Amsterdam newspaper who covered the event. She was definitely intrigued.

"Now let me get this straight Mr. Galbraith. You came to Amsterdam and in six days you tried 52 of the best brands of marijuana in Europe and graded them in eight different categories including the duration of each of their 'highs'. Correct?"

"Yes ma'am," I replied. "That is correct."

She eyed me skeptically. "Mr. Galbraith," she intoned, "how were you able to do that?"

"Young lady, that's the reason I'm the only one who had all his expenses paid to come over here. I'm one of the very few people in the world who can do that."

That must have impressed someone because the next day my picture went up on the wall of the Museum of Hashish. I was honored but I didn't let them know that the very best marijuana I smoked during those seven days was a joint of California weed that had been smuggled in from the states by one of the judges. It's very hard to beat those California wizards.

❖ Cannabis and Sustainable Development

One of the events of 1994 that stands out in my mind was the "From Rio to the Capitols" convention held in Louisville by the Governor's Office. This was an offshoot of the Rio Convention of 1993 where more than 100 Countries gathered in Rio de Janeiro to pay homage to the concept of "Sustainable Development." That's the idea that the earth's development could only be sustained if we got off fossil fuels as the basis of it's energy and switched to alternatives such as bio fuel, hydroelectric and wind energy. I think it's called Environmentalism.

The plan of its authors was to get an agreement in general and then to market it to the American public. The year after Rio, 1994, Kentucky agreed to host the first U.S. convention in Louisville.

Environmentalism. Sustainable Development. Bio Fuels. Hell, they were talking Cannabis. Hemp. The number one fiber, food, medicine and fuel crop on the planet. A crop that could make the United States energy independent just like I told the Kentucky Press Association years earlier. I couldn't stay away.

The event was being sponsored by the Kentucky Governor's Office, occupied by Democrat Brereton Jones, a transplanted West Virginian who had been their Republican Speaker of the House. Brereton had beaten me in the May 1991 Primary but we had a friendly relationship and I was a little surprised when I was told by the event staff that I couldn't set up a display at the convention to show hemp as a mainstay of sustainable development.

In fact, groundwork had already been laid by one particularly fascist asshole to keep me from possessing or showing hemp anywhere in Kentucky, as I had done throughout the race in 1991.

When the 1937 Marijuana Tax Act had been passed by Congress, it had differentiated marijuana from hemp and allowed licenses to grow the latter, especially during WWII. Every other state in the Union adopted that law in total, including Kentucky. Each state law recognized the difference and it was on this basis that I had gathered and shown hemp products throughout the state.

However, after the '91 race, in an effort to quell my political uprising, a reprehensible state representative, named Bill Lear, engineered an amendment to Kentucky's law which sought to include hemp in the definition of marijuana.

Bill has always been for sale to big money so I wasn't surprised by his actions in carrying out their plan to keep me from promoting hemp as a possible solution to our economic woes. His act was deliberate and malicious, filled with intent to deprive me of hemp as an issue no matter what the long-term harm to the farmers. Besides, Bill has always sided with big money against the people.

Under this modified law, the convention organizers claimed that hemp was the same as marijuana and therefore illegal to possess. I had fiber, paper and oil to display and felt they did not meet the definition of illegal substances. It was time for a judicial showdown.

I filed a Motion for Injunctive Relief in the Franklin Circuit Court and drew Judge Roger Crittenden to hear the matter. In my Motion, I asked the Court to hold that Kentucky's modified marijuana statute did not preclude hemp as a legal crop. I further pointed out that the hemp items I possessed, oil, paper and fiber, were purchased in Interstate Commerce and therefore were regulated by Congress and outside the purview of Kentucky's legislature. The Commonwealth argued that the sheets of paper, the gallon of oil and the hemp suit I was wearing were all marijuana. The Judge was as unimpressed as I was.

Judge Crittenden ruled that the products I possessed were acquired from interstate commerce, which was protected by the Constitution from state interference and that they were so far down the line from the natural plant that they did not fit the definition of marijuana. He gave me an injunction which prohibited the state from interfering with my showing hemp at the convention. We were in.

The Rio event was held in the Convention Center in downtown Louisville and consisted of more than 100 displays of items and themes ranging from catfish farms to NASA rockets. Every major environmental group in the U.S had representatives and displays there as did several dozen other countries.

It was designed to be a sophisticated affair and it was well presented. Because we were late getting in, we were assigned one eight-foot table in the middle of a room dedicated to rockets and machinery. I guess they thought we would get lost.

We probably were lost for a while but within a half a day we were the hottest exhibit in the whole damn show. When word got out, people began streaming in from the other rooms, including those who were there to exhibit their own wares.

What seemed to generate the most interest in these people was the opportunity to actually touch our materials. They would stand and look with open skepticism while we explained what we had. I let them feel the paper and the fiber which was soft as silk Then I would take a thimble full of oil and invite them to dip their fingertip into it, then rub it between their fingers until it evaporated on their hands.

Warily they would get some on a fingertip then begin to spread it over their hands. Their eyes would widen in amazement as the oil kept spreading wider and wider until both of their hands were covered in a lotion that the skin soon readily absorbed. It spread like the finest of lotions, which it is.

Representatives from the United Nations and dozens of countries came to the table over the next three days and we were the most popular exhibit, by far. What struck me most was the lack of knowledge of this plant on the part of all these supposed scientists who were looking for an answer to the worldwide degradation of our environment. They too had been "dumbed down" about this ages-old solution to our new age problems.

As usual however, our coup got no play in the Courier, or any other media. One thing you can say about them. When they whore out to big money, they are loyal whores.

❖ *Jerry Hammond*

I had decided sometime in 1991 that I would try again for Governor and had let those intentions be known. Kentucky is a big state and I figured if I ran solid for the three years preceding the election, I could get to all the places necessary for a successful campaign. The powers-that-be decided to make that as difficult as possible with the passage of legislation in the 1992 Session that gave 2-for-1 public financing to candidates for Governor and Lt. Governor who could raise $300,000 of their own. This was very easy for the major party players who had the lists of special interest donors at their fingertips but it was an impossible threshold for a non-wealthy outsider to reach.

That package of legislation also decreed that a candidate could not actively campaign (raise or spend money) until they had selected a running mate.

The new law also said that the candidates for Governor and Lieutenant Governor must run as slate and not as individuals. I guess they thought I couldn't find someone courageous enough to hook up with me to form a slate. They couldn't have been more wrong. And I couldn't have been more lucky.

Jerry Wayne Hammond, originally of Buzzard Roost, Kentucky, over by Hemp Ridge in Shelby County was an ironworker by trade and an exceptional human being by way of hard work and intellect.

Jerry was reared in humble circumstances by a devout mother while his father served in WW II. He learned the Bible by heart and could quote Chapter and verse as he was often called on to do in the little one room church he attended four times during the week and twice on Sundays.

After high school, Jerry chose the Air Force and they were far the better for it. Jerry was trained in Intelligence and worked in the early forms of computers, which fascinated him for the rest of his days.

When Jerry was discharged, he returned home, married and had three daughters. He chose the profession of ironworker and joined the union and became a general foreman. (The guy who gets it done.) His talents were duly noted and he went to Frankfort as a liaison officer with the Kentucky Department of Labor and later the Director of the Labor Department's Division of Labor Standards.

Jerry learned the workings of state government firsthand for the next three years. He quit the Labor Cabinet in 1979 and went to work for the labor unions where he ultimately rose to be Executive Secretary of the Building and Construction Trade Council of Central Kentucky. It was in this capacity that Jerry defined his brilliance by his actions.

It was 1985 and then-Governor Martha Lane Collins was joining Governors in lots of other states in offering substantial tax credits and other incentives for corporations to locate within the state in the name of job creation. Governor Collins had her sights on Toyota and their desire to locate an automobile assembly plant in North America.

However, many folks, including Jerry, felt then and now that taxpayer's dollars should not be given to corporations, no matter what they promise to provide in return. In the case of Toyota, Kentucky said their offer was about $180 Million of incentives. Jerry figured it at about $306 Million.

Jerry was also upset because Toyota had never used union labor before. They were the richest corporation in the world, at that time, and here they were getting all that money from us and not using union labor. What was an ironworker from Buzzard Roost to do?

First, Jerry went to the Constitution of Kentucky for a solution and there it was. Section 3.... "and no grant of exclusive, separate public emoluments or privileges shall be made to any man or set of men, except in consideration of public services:"

That seemed clear enough to Jerry so he found the right plaintiff and they sued the Commonwealth to get their own $306 Million. At first Jerry's unions didn't want to get involved but, as Jerry developed his case, they came on board.

After years of wrangling, the case reached the Kentucky Supreme Court which ruled in favor of the Commonwealth in a 4-3 decision. In essence, they said that the Kentucky Constitution was not violated when the Commonwealth gave special breaks to a private corporation, in contrast to the specific wording of the Constitution, where the "ultimate objective of (the) bill was not only to alleviate unemployment but also to foster prosperity of people of state as whole."

There were several dissents, including that written by Justice Leibson, who said that "Pressure on the judiciary to find some way around the constitution in the name of political expediency has proved to be overwhelming." And further, "Here, Toyota gets a special privilege."

Judge Stephenson agreed. "...the transaction with Toyota is a gift."

Judge Vance joined in and caught the gist of it all when he wrote, "...this court has, I believe, eviscerated the Kentucky Constitution."

Jerry was not beaten however. When Toyota asked him what he was going to do then, he told them that he was never going to give up and he told them in a most unforgettable manner.

Throughout the months of negotiations, Jerry and representatives of his unions were meeting weekly with a Japanese spokesperson who was accompanied by an American lawyer. The lawyer did all the talking and the Japanese gentleman did not say a word.

Each session was the same. Everyone would arrive in the same room, sit across from each other at the same table and Jerry would try to negotiate a labor contract and the lawyer would say "No way." Nothing ever differed.

That didn't satisfy Jerry. He did a lot of research into the Japanese culture and, after the Supreme Court ruling, he scheduled one last session. Just before they went into the room, he told his union reps to do exactly what he did when he did it. They were a little puzzled but agreed to go along.

As usual everyone came into room and sat down. Jerry made one last attempt to talk union, which the lawyer cut short while the Japanese man was typically unresponsive.

When the lawyer asked Jerry what his plans were now that the Kentucky Courts had sided with Toyota, Jerry looked at the Japanese gentleman and then removed the tie from around his own neck and tied it around his head like a bandanna. Definitely surprised but determined to go along, the other union reps did the same.

Jerry then began chanting a Japanese phrase and the others joined in.

"Haka Maki. Haka Maki," they chanted and their voices got stronger with each rendition.

For the first time the Japanese fellow's face registered emotion. "Haka Maki" means "To the Death" and is uttered by those about to go to war where there will be no mercy. It was a favorite phrase of the Kamikaze.

The older man finally spoke. "What is it that you want?" And Jerry told him and he got it.

Jerry negotiated 10,000,000 (that's right, Ten Million) union hours in the construction of the Toyota plant in Georgetown. It remains the first and only time that the company has ever used union labor. Not bad for an ironworker from Buzzard Roost Kentucky.

Jerry and I had a mutual friend who knew I was looking for a running mate. He suggested Jerry and arranged for an introduction. I was immediately won over. Jerry was not.

For three weeks I tried to convince Jerry to run with me but he kept putting it off. He had had more politics than he could stomach for a while. But I wasn't about to give up. Here was a man's man. Strong, smart, dedicated and already successful in his fight for the working man and woman. My kind of running mate.

Finally I couldn't wait any longer. "Jerry," I told him, "This is what I want you to do. Pick out any place in Kentucky and we'll go there next Thursday. I want you to follow me around while I campaign so you can see how the people treat me. If you don't like what you see, I'll look for someone else to run."

Jerry agreed but didn't tell me where he wanted to go.

The Wednesday night before the Thursday venture, I got a call from a fellow who had just been arrested in Louisville that day. His arraignment was on Thursday morning and I agreed to represent him.

When I picked up Jerry that next morning, I explained the situation to him and he agreed to go to Louisville with me. Then we would go someplace else to test out my campaign potential.

We arrived at Louisville's Hall of Justice a little late and I rushed to find out the Courtroom where we needed to appear. When Jerry and I came to that room and entered, we found it was packed with defendants, clerks and attorneys. The attorneys, as is the fashion, were lined up along a wall, to be taken first by the Judge so they could go to other courtrooms if they needed. The Judge had not yet arrived.

As Jerry and I came through the door, a bailiff who was lining everyone up saw me and stated loudly across the room, "Well I'll be darned. It's Gatewood Galbraith. Gatewood, do you have a client here?"

I nodded.

"Well get over here and take this spot." (He indicated the front of the line of about 10 attorneys) "Men, move back there. Who's your client Gatewood?"

I told him my client's name and he went to a side door, opened it and spoke to the bailiff on the other side.

"Get Mr. So and So up first. He's Gatewood's client."

Just then the Judge entered the room and sat at the bench. He looked around the room and then saw me.

"Well I'll be," he said. "Gatewood Galbraith."

He stood up at his bench and spoke to the crowded Courtroom. "Ladies and Gentlemen," he got their attention then pointed to me. "This is Gatewood Galbraith and he's running for Governor. He's a fine man and I voted for him last time and I believe my entire family is going to vote for him this time. I invite you to do the same."

I didn't quite know what to say. Judges aren't supposed to publicly take sides in elections but this man's words were obviously heartfelt and I could only smile my gratitude.

"What can we do for you today, Mr. Galbraith?" the Judge inquired.

When I told him I was there for an arraignment the bailiff brought my client into the room.

"Your Honor," I began, "My client pleads not guilty to trafficking in LSD and marijuana and I ask for a reduction in his bond."

The Judge looked at my client with his shoulder length hair and raggedy clothes. Then he looked at the Clerk.

"He looks like an honest young man. I'll release him on his own recognizance if he promises to return for his next Court date."

"Certainly he will, Your Honor," I assured him.

"Good", said the Judge. Then he spoke to the bailiff. "There's no need for him to have to go back to the jail, is there? Then take that bracelet off his wrist and he can leave with Mr. Galbraith. Is that alright with you Sir?"

I quickly nodded yes and my client, Jerry and I walked out into the hallway. Frankly, I was stunned. I had some experience with Judges treating me nicely but this was heady stuff.

I made arrangements for my client to meet me on another date and turned to Jerry.

"Well Brother, that takes care of that. Thanks for coming along. Now tell me, where would you like to go in Kentucky to see how the people treat me?"

Jerry eyed me intently for a moment. "Gatewood," he said, "let's go back to my house and plan the campaign. I've seen all I need to see."

❖ *The 1995 Campaign*

And that was the start of the 1995 Governor's race for Jerry and me. (And his lovely wife Mary Lou, whose approval was absolutely necessary and whose assistance was absolutely invaluable.) They quickly became among my closest friends and I trusted their counsel on a wide variety of matters. In fact, as I said many times during that race, Jerry was the most qualified of all of us to be governor. Honest, Smart and Dedicated to the People. A Hell of a Man.

I also said many times throughout the campaign that one of the hardest parts of my job as a Gubenatorial candidate was figuring out when Jerry was wrong about anything. I believe those were the rarest of times.

We began the process of putting the campaign together, identifying the issues and our stands regarding same. It was amazing to us both that we agreed on so many things. Our material spelled it out, simple and brief.

"Freedom is the issue."

"Corruption is the problem."

"Galbraith and Hammond are the solution."

As to Freedom, we wrote that "Individual freedom and human dignity are the most important principals of self-government. All powers and policies of government must uplift and ennoble human existence-not put the people down or oppress them. The citizens of Kentucky need leaders with greater vision and a greater respect for the Constitution and the people's rights."

We also attacked Corruption because we agreed that, "it is systemic corruption that oppresses and impoverishes the people of Kentucky. State government must be reorganized and reordered to eliminate cronyism, favoritism, fraud, waste and secrecy. Creating a leaner, cleaner government will produce a fairer, lighter tax burden and more efficient and effective public service."

The pamphlet we produced also contained our stands on education, agriculture, Labor, crime, welfare and public health. We were the only slate to produce a written platform statement and the only ones to identify

Corruption as the main problem of Kentucky's state government. There was good reason for that. All of the other candidates were wading up to their eyeballs in the cesspool of corruption that pervaded Frankfort and passed as leadership by the Democratic Party. They weren't looking to change anything. They simply wanted to be the recipients of the payoffs of such a system. Actually everyone of them should have been the recipients of a stiff jail sentence. In fact, some of them were.

For many years, the Kentucky Legislature has been the epitome of corruption, favoritism and cronyism. Open vote buying was/is the norm and the Democrat Party held power with an iron fist. Nothing got through the legislature unless the proper payoff was made to the proper power-mongers. The Democrats controlled the Governor's office, the House and the Senate and they proved the adage, "Power corrupts and absolute power corrupts absolutely."

My candidacy in 1991 as a Democrat was a direct assault on this corruption and I had attacked it relentlessly. This was the reason they had tried to freeze me out of the Party, treating my candidacy as if it didn't exist. This was not only the strategy of the politicians but also of the Courier and the Herald which has led me to consider them just as much a part of the problem as the corrupt, low-life bribe- takers who ran the Commonwealth for their own benefit; the public be damned.

Finally, the stench emanating from Frankfort got so bad that the Federal government got involved, initiating an undercover investigation that resulted in the indictment and prosecution of 21 people, mostly officeholders and lobbyists. The offenses ranged from outright bribery, for miniscule sums, to lying to the federal investigators. Since the original investigation centered on the vote buying on the joint House and Senate Business Organizations and Professions Committee, its code name was BOPTROT.

The biggest fish caught was the Speaker of the House, Don Blandford, who accepted a $500 "golden handshake" in return for his influence on an upcoming piece of legislation. He was tried and convicted despite his assertion of the defense that what he did wasn't against the law.

That pretty well described(s) the attitude of the lawmakers in Frankfort, both then and now. They don't consider bribery and lying to investigators as criminal acts. They consider it a lifestyle. It had/has been in operation so long, it had been accepted as fact, even by those who would not take part in it. It was business as usual.

The revelation of this investigation, and its fallout, lasted for many months and did much to rekindle my fires for another campaign. But it was Jerry Hammond's addition to my ticket that really gave me hope. He recognized the same issues I did. He had watched the corruption up close and personal in his role as Labor's watchdog of the Legislature and he was as keen to clean house as I was.

Jerry's insight was such an asset. He taught me many things about the system including the fact that corruption was not always the laws they break but also the laws they make, especially in the name of Reform. He pointed out the excessive influence that a few lobbyists had in Frankfort and how they achieved passage of certain legislation with minimal bribes and maximum returns on their "investments."

Watching the legislative process, to Jerry, was like watching sausage being made. Once you saw it done, you very rarely wanted to see it happen again.

Jerry also taught me that the system itself, as it was being run then, corrupted many who sought office with good intentions. They found out that they had to play along to get along so they fell in step with the process of payoffs and promises. Power corrupts...

Jerry and I were glad to see all this Federal investigation come about and we shared the opinion of many that it didn't go far enough. Jerry was particularly saddened by the involvement of several legislators who he had believed were straight up and honest and everybody was amazed at how little money it took to buy a legislator. It was ridiculously low.

How low was the lowest payoff? I couldn't help making the comment that found itself included in Newsweek as quote of the week. "If I had known you could buy a Kentucky legislator for $200, marijuana would have been legal a long time ago."

Even Jerry had to chuckle at that but we were both deadly serious about bringing an end to the vote-buying on all levels. So instead of playing the regular political game of promising payoffs for support, Jerry and I prided ourselves on making only two pledges in return for the citizen's vote.

"We pledge to resurrect the Democrat Party to once again become the voice of the people."

And, "We pledge to restore liberty and choice by taking the government out of your bedroom, your bloodstream, your bladder, your brain, your business, your back-pocket, your bingo halls and your Internet bulletin boards."

Win or lose, Jerry and I were going to do this campaign our way which meant trying to educate the people even while we were trying to win the nomination. We sought out places and events to get the word out.

Jerry and I filed our papers in July of '94. We joined three other slates seeking the Democrat's nomination. Jerry was the class of the crowd.

Our opposition consisted of the Lt. Governor Paul Patton and his running mate, a Louisville surgeon named Steve Henry; Senate President "Eck" Rose and his partner Denise Angel and Secretary of State Bob Babbage and his sidekick Tommy Thompson, a tire salesman from Western Kentucky.

Paul Patton had made a lot of money in Eastern Kentucky coal and had been running for Governor since the middle '80s. He had been County Judge Executive of Pike County, the Chairman of the Democrat's Party and had run a "shadow" campaign for Lt. Governor in 1987. He followed that up by running for and winning that office in '91. He was ruthless and anti-labor which meant he had the support of big capital for his efforts.

"Eck" Rose was President of the Senate and had fallen victim to the self-aggrandizement of many legislators that leads them to believe that the whole state knows who they are just because they are big shots in Frankfort. "Eck" had a pocket full of favors owed to him by other legislators but that will never be enough to carry the state.

Our third opponent was Secretary of State Bob Babbage. How to describe Bob? Uhmmm.. Well, his lack of political principal and backbone led me early on to nickname him "Gumby" after the plastic cartoon character. Let's just leave it at that. (You will never know the lines I deleted here just before publication, Bob.)

Prior to our announcement as candidates, Jerry had resigned as Executive Secretary of the Building and Construction Trades Council. He was so very disappointed with the rest of the union leadership, especially those who had been persuaded to back Patton because of God knows what. Here was a scab coal operator who had fought strikes at his coal mines with armed guards and scab labor, yet other the union leaders organized for him and supported him.

Once again, the union leadership sold the membership down the river. It's an oft-told tale but true. I don't know what Patton could have promised the leadership but I know he never delivered anything to the union membership throughout his tenure as Governor. A mouth full of promises and a hand full of nothing.

The campaign began in earnest in Fall of '94. The first forum to invite all of the candidates to speak was the Kentucky Association of Counties, meeting in Paducah. It would also be the first time Jerry had seen me speak at one of these public events and he was apprehensive about it. KACO was comprised of county officials who had been wooed over the years by Patton when he was County Judge Executive. They were squarely on his side and Jerry did not expect us to get a favorable reception from them.

The convention hall was crowded with about 600 people and the four Gubernatorial candidates sat on a platform in the front. Paul and "Eck" spoke first. They delivered stock speeches with nothing new to say. I still had no idea what I was going to say when it came my turn to take the podium.

I looked out over the crowd and then the spirit took me over. I began to speak.

"Well, I haven't appeared in front of a crowd this large since they called a meeting of the creditors in my bankruptcy." The crowd appeared shocked for a moment, then erupted in wild applause.

"Now Folks, I've heard these other candidates speak at various functions and they are full of promises about how they re going to fix this problem and find a solution for that one. But there is one word which I never hear them use when they are discussing Kentucky's problems. One word which never passes their lips.

Ladies and gentlemen, that word is Corruption.

It is Corruption which has impoverished our state and keeps it ranked low in all of the major indexes of quality of life. It is corruption which drains our Treasury and our ability to adequately fund education, water and sewage treatment, County Health Departments and basic infrastructure. If corruption hadn't run rampant in Frankfort for the past decades, in the form of bribery, sweetheart deals and cronyism, we would have the funding for the basic services down to the county level.

To watch these men react, you would think they had never even heard of corruption before. But I must remind you that Mr. Rose has been up there for 16 years in a leadership position, Mr. Babbage has been there for 8 years in a Constitutional office and Mr. Patton has been there for 4 years including another 4 where he presided over the demise of the Democrat's Party.

And it was on these people's official watch that we experienced BOPTROT, whereby 21 of our brethren were led from the Capitol in chains and leg irons for selling out the interests of the people for a few, very few, pieces of gold.

So there's only two ways that you can look at my three opponents and their relationship with corruption.

Either they knew about this corruption all along and were willing participants in the system that operated on it, or they didn't actually know what was going on which makes them all Too Damn Dumb To Be Governor!

And by the way. They say they have solutions now but where have they been these past several years? Couldn't they have revealed them to us while they were collecting public paychecks for the past 4 years?

Some things they have talked about as their solutions for Kentucky's problems are to put more criminal laws on the people, increase their prison sentences for victimless crimes, add more police, increase surveillance and the need for more taxes to fund more prisons. This would draw precious resources from our already scant education and health budgets.

Well, I have a novel solution for many of Kentucky's problems. Instead of bringing dogs into our schools to sniff our children, instead of having helicopters hover over our fields and gardens like we are an occupied territory instead of the Land of the Brave and the Home of the Free, instead of trying to regulate everybody's lives from cradle to grave, let's try the Solution of More Freedom to the People, not less!

That's Right! Let's instill a policy of respect for the integrity and rights of the individual instead of the present 'us vs. them' mentality that pervades government. We can begin that process from the ground up by enacting the first pledge that Jerry and I make to you.

That is to ' resurrect the Democrat party to once again become the voice of the people.'

As you folks know, the Democrats' Party is on a resuscitator, it's suicide having been presided over by Dr. Graddy Stumbo, the Jack Kovorkian of the Democrat Party. (Well, we lost the First District and the Second District Congressional seats last November, so I'm not telling you anything you didn't know.)

So Jerry and I will return the Party to the people and away from its dominance by the elite special interests.

The second pledge we make is to restore liberty and choice by taking the government out of your bedroom, your bloodstream, your bladder, your brain, your business, your billfold, your bingo halls and your Internet bulletin boards and put it back in a little box where it belongs.

We don't want a leaner and meaner government. We want a leaner and cleaner government. A government that keeps basic law and order in the public streets but keeps out of the private lives of citizens in their homes.

We also want to halt the Corporate Welfare giveaway that is now the cornerstone of this state's economic development policy. Giving our tax dollars and tax credits to rich, out-of-state corporations for the alleged creation of jobs is insanity.

The Chairman of the National Council on Economic Development says that this is a program that is devouring us. The Council of Governors passed a resolution stating, 'We must quit trying to outbid each other for these large, rich, out-of-state corporations.'

So we want to quit practicing Aid to Dependent Corporations and begin offering incentives to existent Kentucky corporations for implementing state of the art environmental safeguards to clean up their act for the benefit of everyone.

That way, instead of being one of 39 or 40 other states out here trying to give away the most free land, water and money, we will be the number one state committed to clean air, clean water, quality of life, dignity of the individual and the right to self determination.

I would like to attract tourists to the Commonwealth and believe we can do so by designating Highway 80, running east-west in Southern Kentucky as a tourist corridor and have visitors driving east-west rather than north-south. They stay longer and spend more money that way. And that road runs from several world-class waterways in the west, Kentucky Lake and Lake Barkley, to another in the east, Lake Cumberland.

Building on the presence of that world-class system of waterways already in place, I propose a dam on the Kentucky River near Frankfort that would create another lake about 117 miles long which I would name Commonwealth Dam and Commonwealth Lake. This would be longer than Cumberland Lake but slightly more narrow.

This lake would reach from Frankfort to the mouth of the Red River at the Gorge without raising that river itself. In other words it would protect the Gorge and also the palisades. It would solve Central and most of Eastern Kentucky's water problems for all time and open up lots of Eastern Kentucky to development. If we put a moratorium on industrial development and allowed only commercial and residential building within a mile of its shore, we can insure its cleanliness and give several generations of developers new land on which to operate and take some of the pressure off Fayette, Jessamine and other counties whose land is being developed at such breakneck speed.

Finally, this lake would intercept much of the Ohio Armada which descends on Cumberland each year in increasing numbers.

No doubt this would be a grand venture but Kentucky needs to start coming up with some big ideas to address our chronic problems. This proposal needs to be seriously considered by whoever wins the office. Kentucky needs this kind of thinking.

In addition to our investment in our environmental infrastructure, let's also invest in our educational infrastructure. We propose a program we call The Commonwealth Incentive, whereby every citizen who receives a high school diploma or GED in Kentucky is entitled to an educational voucher good for tuition, books and supplies at institutions of further learning in Kentucky up to a lifetime total of $5,000.

This is not cash up front and is only spent when the individual personally makes a commitment to further their education. It is good for UK, community colleges, barber and beauty schools, truck driving classes and worker retraining.

The money is spent here in Kentucky and Kentucky workers and their employers benefit. Best of all, our state can afford it if the projections for a budget surplus, made by Mr. Rose, are accurate.

Are Jerry and I perfect? No way! Do Jerry and I have all the answers? Absolutely not! But we pledge that all of our mistakes will be honest mistakes.

As to the question of whether I am too much of an outsider to interface with the day-to-day workings of state government, I can proudly reply that Jerry is my interface, given his career working in and with state government.

He and I share the firm belief that Kentucky's solutions lie in the words of Thomas Jefferson and Abraham Lincoln, not in the importation of Japanese business methods and East German-like police control over the people.

And it does not help that new projects go only to the special interests. When Jerry and I go to other parts of the state, say the western part, the folks tell us that they can't get a project there. And we go to southern Kentucky, the folks tell us they can't get a project there and the same thing in northern Kentucky.

Well I've got a message for you folks. You're all getting screwed!

No projects get funded out of Frankfort unless you satisfy the pay-off system of these other candidates. The only other way is to change the system.

Speaking of changing the system, I want to take this opportunity to congratulate Governor Jones on his formation of the Kentucky Hemp Council to study hemp's potential as a cash crop in Kentucky. That took great courage even if the council was sabotaged by its chairman, Mr. Billie Joe Miles, who is the largest retailer and wholesaler of farm chemicals in the state.

I know you have heard me speak about hemp over the past many years and I hope you support my effort to return it as a cash crop.

But if you did not know me or what I stand for, and if I only had thirty seconds to get your vote, I would have only one question to ask you.

And if you answer this question one way, I've got your vote, no matter what else you think about me.

And if you answer this question the other way, I don't think you understand the question.

The question is, 'Did our forefathers' generation hit the beaches of Normandy and Iwo Jima so that we would have to pee in a cup to hold a job in America?'

The introduction of the police state methods into American culture is fatal to our freedom. The solutions to our problems lie in the words of Thomas Jefferson and Abraham Lincoln not Mr. Yamamoto or Helmut Schmidt.

And let's get this straight. I'm not a racist and I'm not xenophobic. I'm a Nationalist.

I'll trade with other countries, I'll have lunch with them and I'll play golf with them. But until they adopt a Constitution and Bill of Rights that gives their own citizens the rights and freedoms we enjoy, they are not our political peers.

If we abandon our principals of individual freedom and dignity, than our liberty and right to self-determination will abandon us. Our standard of living will fall and our jobs will evaporate as our children and grandchildren are thrown open to competition in the workplace with Four Billion other people on the planet, many of whom will work all day for a bowl of rice and a mat to sleep on.

That is not my vision for Kentucky and its citizens. My vision is rooted in the traditions of our Founding Fathers.

As to the size of government, Thomas Jefferson said, 'The least government is the best government.'

As to the role of government, Abraham Lincoln said, 'Prohibition strikes at the very heart of the principles on which this country was founded.'

And as far as having to pee in a cup to hold a job, I look to the words of General George Patton. 'Screw you Nazis!'

For a moment everything was very still in the room, like the audience had to take a second to understand what I had said. Then they exploded with applause and cheers that went on full two minutes. Many of them stood on chairs and waved their programs. If the election had been then and there, Jerry and I were the winners.

Then it was Babbage's turn to speak and he rose slowly and staggered to the podium. His face was white and he stood there for several moments before he clutched his throat and tried to speak. Nothing came out.

It was as if the audience's reaction to me had sucked all the air out of the room. Or maybe he just recognized himself from my description of the corruption he had been immersed in. He tried again to speak and this time managed to say the word "water". Everyone looked at him and waited. There was a water pitcher sitting right beside him but he made no move for it. He seemed paralyzed with fright or angst or both and we all just sat and watched him for about thirty seconds and I could not stand it any longer. I got up from the end of the table and gave Bob my glass of water. I was the only one who moved to help.

Bob took the water glass and downed it in one gulp. Finally he got it out.

"It's always tough to follow the animal act," he squawked. I stood up and raised my hands over my head like I had just been named the champion of a contest. Then I took several bows. The crowd gave me another ovation and Bob's goose was cooked from the git-go. It was a good line, the only one of his campaign, but badly delivered. He never recovered.

That speech became my stock delivery and I never missed a chance to put it on my opponents. After the third time I hit them with it at a forum, Babbage refused to get on the same stage with me.

After "Eck" heard it for the fifth or sixth time, he wouldn't appear with me either. It got kind of lonely with just me and Paul there but I enjoyed watching him start to squirm as my speech unfolded and I got to the good part about his being too corrupt or damn dumb to be Governor. To his credit he continued to make the appearances and sit through my speech and I returned the favor to him. Obviously, the guy was shameless.

Meanwhile the Republican's Primary featured Larry Forgy, a longtime Party leader who had been Vice President of Business Affairs and a Board of Trustees Member at the University of Kentucky and who had served on Kentucky's Council of Higher Education. Larry's campaign centered on attacking the corruption and insider dealings fostered by the Democrats, especially in the Legislature. We were singing the same song and you can bet that Patton and his cronies didn't like to hear it from any angle.

The Republicans were becoming active in other elections around the Commonwealth, most notably on the Congressional level. In what would be memorialized as a Republican Revolution in November 1994, the Democrats lost the First and Second Congressional Districts in Far Western Kentucky. The Democrats had held the First District seat for 125 years and the Second District had never had a Republican occupant before.

They surely deserved to lose these seats. The Democrat's leadership was arrogant, corrupt and had abandoned the people. The Republicans had a message of smaller government and less taxes. It resounded well in the conservative, though Democrat, western part of the state, even though the Republicans who were elected and went to Washington D.C. promptly forgot their pledges and sold out to the big money interests waiting for them.

The thing I remember most about this part of the campaign happened in Owensboro during a rally to defend tobacco and smokers' rights. This was the largest legal cash crop in Kentucky and it had come under heavy attack from the anti-smokers. This rally drew candidates running for a variety of offices including Congress in November of '94 and Governor in May '95.

I was standing behind the stage waiting for my turn to speak after Ron Lewis, a Republican novice who had never held office before. When he finished, he came down the steps and was met by a reporter.

"So let me get this straight, Mr. Lewis," he said. "You totally agree with Gatewood Galbraith, is that right?"

Ron went pale. "What do you mean?" his voice wavered.

"Well, you just gave them the same speech Gatewood has been giving them since he ran for Agriculture in '83," the reporter replied.

That pleased me and it pleased me even more when Ron won that seat in '94 with that speech. I was less pleased however, when he sold out just like the rest of them when he got there.

❖ *G.A.T.T. and the Militia*

Bill Clinton had won the White House in 1992 with the overt issue of the economy and the covert issues of sex, drugs and rock and roll. In 1994, the Republican Revolution occurred, where more than 30 Senators were replaced through retirement or loss of election and the majority were replaced by Republicans. They won with a message of smaller government, less taxes and term limits.

This vast turnover also created the largest "lame-duck" Senate in memory and set the stage for the purchase of America by the petrochemical-pharmaceutical-military-industrial-transnational-corporate-fascist-elitist-sons-of-bitches through the passage of GATT, the General Agreement on Trades and Tariffs, which I had burned in effigy in 1990. Senators who were leaving their posts and didn't have to answer to the voters anymore sold America and its people down the river.

GATT was the blueprint for retooling America's policies from Fair Trade to Free Trade. With its passage by our 1994 Senate, America no longer stands for Human Rights on an international scale. Our trade relations with each of the other nations no longer depends on how they treat their citizens or whether they get paid a living wage or whether they get chained to a machine until their work is done. Only money matters any more under this policy. Human Beings do not.

The formal passage of GATT also gave rise to protests by other groups, several of whom had contacted me after I burned it in effigy at Fancy Farm in 1990. These various groups went by just as many different names but they all had one thing in common. They feared the emerging totalitarian nature of the government and did not want to stand idly by and watch it take over.

Several of these groups styled themselves as the "militia", which is defined by Webster's Dictionary as "1. A body of citizens enrolled for military service, called out periodically for drill but serving full time only in emergencies. 2. A body of citizen soldiers as distinguished from professional soldiers. 3. All able-bodied males eligible by law for military service." The media spokespeople for the corporate takeover of America immediately attempted to cast anyone associated with the "militia" as fringe elements in this society.

The mass murder of a hundred people by the Federal government in Waco in early 1993 had brought howls of protest from many groups and individuals who recognized that the government had run berserk in Texas and that it presented a growing danger to every citizen and their civil rights.

Many conservative groups, including religious fundamentalists and gun owners, perceived Waco as a direct attack on their belief systems and they began to organize to meet this threat to America by its own government agents.

In meetings all around America, these citizens voiced their concerns and when some of them styled themselves as militias early on, the media picked up on it and liberally applied it to many disgruntled Americans, especially gun owners and collectors, who hold the Second Amendment as serious stuff.

These were the people who had sought me out at Fancy Farm in 1990 after my comments on the New World Order and GATT. And it was these people who I sought out in 1994, a year after Waco, when I decided to build a coalition of all the groups dissatisfied with the direction of our country and the people in charge of it. It was time to merge the efforts of all those citizens in danger from their own government. It was time to marry up Marijuana and the Militia.

I began to attend various meetings around the state, most notably among the gun owners. A vastly energetic activist from Western Kentucky, Norman Davis, had begun a group called Kentuckians for the Right to Bear Arms (KRBA) and had active memberships in 70 of Kentucky's 120 counties. I appeared in front of these groups at every opportunity, seeking their support and volunteerism.

For the first few minutes of each appearance they would look at each other with amazement that a "hippie" would be trying to identify with them by talking about marijuana. Then they began to listen to what I was saying.

I would explain my view of the New World Order and global economy and how it had been engineered by the synthetic manufacturers, who had displaced the farmers from producing the necessities of society; fiber, fuel, medicine and food. Then, when I explained cannabis hemp as petroleum and to what lengths the government had gone to vilify the plant in other capacities, to keep the farmers out of the fuel market, you could see the light bulbs come on over their heads.

They had no problem imagining their government doing that to the people and all of a sudden we weren't just a bunch of "hippies" anymore. We were another group of Americans caught in their own government's line of fire.

Then I would tell them this. "Look, I know that you and I don't agree on everything. As a matter of fact, we might mightily disagree on two or three issues like education, abortion or homosexuals. But we can't let our disagreement on two or three issues divide us and keep us from coming together on the 10 or 12 bedrock issues which bind us together as Americans; issues like preserving the Bill of Rights and using the Constitution as the blueprint for solving this nation's problems.

It is readily apparent to many of us who the real villains are today...The Renos, the Bill Bennetts, the gun control, one-world nuts who would sell their birthrights for the promise of security. We must defeat these people politically and we can do it by acting in unison at the polls. Please give me and Jerry your support and get your friends out too."

Not everyone jumped on board right away and some never did. Sometime I believed that there were as many government agents at these meetings as there were regular citizens. Also, these groups tended to attract some folks who were, how shall I put this, Miswired? However, that's the price of freedom of assembly and speech and I tried mightily to respect their views as citizens.

Or, as I put it when a reporter asked me if the militia movement had attracted a certain fringe element, "Of course, but so do the Catholics and the Baptists."

Many attendees at these meetings had military experience and they were generally the quiet, even-tempered ones. They had some background in duty, respect for order and common sense. They felt that Waco was a wake up call and they had been trained to be alert to dangers to America. They were also smart enough to know it might come from their own government officials.

There were also angry citizens, many of them with a real beef with "the government." And then there were others, the ones whose deep and abiding distrust of various government officials had turned them to a hatred of their government itself, which kept them in a constant state of indigestion. These guys made every disparaging remark they could about our system and how it was letting us down but I never saw this last group lift a finger to make it a better system. Those I kept a wary eye on.

There were a select few who knew how the system works and how to get results from it. The best of these was/is Norman Davis.

❖ *Me & Norman Davis*

I truly believe it is an accurate statement that, at some point in the past, someone acting in a governmental capacity pissed Norman Davis off. For every governmental official who has had the pleasure to deal with Norman since then, I feel your pain.

I like Norman Davis. Hell, I love Norman Davis, warts and all. He is the orneriest, savviest, don't-give-an-inch unpaid citizen watchdog I have ever met.

He knows more about the Legislature, the legislators and the legislation each session then most of their own leaders. And he's probably done more to keep taxes lower in this state than any other living citizen has.

Norman sniffs out and attacks legislation that imperils the Constitution and the taxpayer. Over-broad government, hidden taxes and regulatory tyranny are delicacies on which he dines with gusto. He is an analyst, a strategist and a patriot whose batteries never seem to run low.

Well, there was the matter of him dying on us a couple of times, but they shocked him back to life and he works just fine now. (I believe he went to hell and the Devil said "Hell No" and sent him back. So do his enemies.)

Norman caught on quickly to my explanation of the Synthetic Subversion and gave us his support during the '95 race. We welcomed his assistance along with his 3,000 email contacts and his alerting the KRBA membership in seventy counties.

Jerry especially appreciated Norman's computer capacities because this was right up Jerry's alley. He was the most adept computer operator I had met up to then and understood their utility in political campaigns, from networking and communication to designing literature and building web sites. In fact, Jerry built a web site for me in Fall of '94 that still stands today and I am just as proud of it now as then. It's at gatewood.com and you should visit it sometime.

Especially interesting are the articles Shadow of the Swastika and The Science and Truth Hearings. Forward the link to your friends. Get involved.

❖ *The Last Free Man*

I recall too that, about this time, I began referring to myself as The Last Free Man in America. It sounds great and after listening for years to elected officials defer to the puppeteers who pull their strings on every decision, I came to the conclusion that every one of them are fettered by special interests and payoffs and I was the only one who wouldn't be thus controlled. Thus the Last Free Man.

More recently, when asked by people how I have the temerity to call myself The Last Free Man in America, I explain, "It's a challenge, not a title. If you can be more free, then go ahead. It's up to you. If it fits, wear it. I'll be glad to share the challenge with you. Just do something to deserve it and you'll help us all."

❖ Practicing Law - 1995

Meanwhile, I had to practice law throughout the campaign. It was a little frantic at times but the Courts were generally quite accommodating. Some things could not be put off however and a speedy trial is the right of all Americans. That was the reason I had to defend a client in a jury trial on charges of Murder, Arson and nine counts of Wanton Endangerment, six weeks before the election.

My client was not a very popular fellow in the small town where he lived. He was charged with setting a fire in his apartment house that killed his wife and endangered the other occupants, including his and her three children. The townsfolk were right upset and the first time I came into town to act as his attorney, one of the waitresses at the local coffee shop refused to serve me.

When we finally arranged to have a $250,000 piece of property posted, by a family friend, as bond, the Clerk refused to accept it until I threatened take her to Court for obstruction of justice.

On the first day of trial, the Courtroom was packed. I felt that we had seated a fair jury but that was the last good feeling I had that day. Witness after witness took the stand and said negative things about my client. They had seen him at the scene, not trying to help his wife or children in any way, they said under oath. I was able to get each of them to admit that they had had prior problems with the Defendant but I could see a trend developing. The prosecution couldn't find anyone who had actually seen my client set the fire, but if they could say enough bad things about him, it would certainly register on the jury.

The lowest point for us was when two friends of the deceased testified that he had confessed to them that he had set the fire. That was the headline on the front page of the Herald Leader the next morning. "Galbraith's Client Confessed, Say Two Witnesses."

Beginning the next day, the prosecution introduced two "expert" arson investigators who testified that the fire had been started by someone and it was definitely arson. On cross-examination, they would not reveal who had paid for their testimony but it was obvious to everyone that they worked for the insurance companies who would not have to pay out on its policies if arson was proved. Once that got established, I ate their lunch.

Then I put my client on the stand. I thought he came across as honest and believable. The reporter for the Herald didn't see it that way however, and the front page headline on the next day read "Galbraith's Client's Story Riddled With Inconsistencies."

By the end of trial the second day I felt like I had been beaten with a stick all over my back and legs. (This was the trial where I learned to take two aspirin the morning of each trial because it is going to wear you out if you stay on edge every second of the way.) I made my way back to my house and tried to rest but I couldn't. Surely I had to prepare for the next day.

For the umpteenth time I got the five pounds of records which covered the investigation of the case and began going over each page of it again. About two hours later I was almost finished when I noticed a small, hand-written phone number sitting by itself at the top of a page filled with typed material. It was almost as much of a smudge as it was a recognizable number so I had never noticed it before. "What the hell," I thought. "What is there to lose?"

It was 10:30 in the evening and the message on the other end said that the number had been changed. It gave me a new one, which I called. A very pleasant female voice greeted me.

I introduced myself and explained the trial and where I had discovered the number. I asked the lady how it might have gotten there.

"Well it must have been because my roommate and I were the first two people on the scene," she offered.

I couldn't believe my ears. I was completely unaware of these witnesses.

"That's right," she continued, "we had an apartment right across the lawn from the fire and we ran outside when we saw what was going on. We saw T. standing outside their bedroom window yelling for his wife to throw the babies out, which she did. As soon as they were out, T tried to climb back into the window to get his wife out but the heat was too intense. He almost caught on fire himself. We told the police all this and were really surprised when nobody got hold of us after the first day. Do you need us to testify?"

"You bet," I said and made arrangements to meet them the next morning. Imagine the surprise in the courtroom when these two young ladies, with no axe to grind against anyone connected with the case, exonerated my client by substantiating his testimony and blowing out the opinion of the Herald Leader newspaper. They responded in their usual sophomoric fashion the next day when they announced the verdict of the jury on page 24 of section B. "Jessamine Man Acquitted of All Charges."

Throughout this time I was still seeing Willie on a frequent basis. I would catch up with him when he was playing in the area and he always seemed glad to see me. He had become like an older brother to me and I welcomed his advice.

When I asked him to do another benefit for me, his response was immediate and sincere. "Of course." I recall that evening on his bus because he showed me a Billboard Chart which named the top album sellers of all time. Not surprisingly, the Beatles were number one and Pink Floyd was second. Willie was 25th and listed as selling more than 33 million albums.

"Willie," I said. "I've got good news and bad news for you." He grinned in anticipation. "The bad news is that you are still behind the Beatles. The good news is that you are still ahead of Johnny Rotten and the Sex Pistols."

Willie agreed to appear at the Kentucky Theatre for Jerry and me on Monday, April 17th. That turned out to be the night that KET picked to hold its statewide debate between the candidates, from eight until nine o'clock. To accommodate that, we scheduled our show to begin at 9:30 p.m.

The debate went well and I rushed to get to the Kentucky Theatre. When I got there the place was full and everyone was in a party mood. The place seats about 900 folks and there is not a bad seat in the house.

9:30 came and went. All the guests were having a great time and no one complained that the show hadn't started. Jerry and I were starting to get a little worried. Where was Willie?

10:00 o'clock came and went. We tried to get Willie on his cell phone and couldn't. Still no one in the audience complained. Finally, about 10:15 I took the stage and apologized for the delay. I said that I had the greatest faith in Willie and if he said he would be there, I was sure he would show up.

Just as I started to exit the stage, my lady friend came running in. "Willie's here," she exclaimed. "He just drove up!"

I looked to the back of the hall and there came Willie, guitar in hand, working his way through the crowd. He got up on the stage and hugged me then launched into his signature opening number, "Whiskey River Take My Mind."

Sweeter music had never reached my ears. (Later I found out that Willie had finished recording a song earlier that evening in Nashville and had jumped in a rental car to make the drive to Lexington with his road manager who was too tired to drive. So Willie let him sleep and he drove to Lexington himself, finding Main Street and coming to a screeching halt in front of the Theater after a hectic 4-hour drive.)

Willie played for two and one-half hours. He was fantastic. Just as soon as he finished one of his classics, he started another. Several times I figured he had exhausted his hit list, only to be reintroduced to another one. Willie wore that audience out.

When the concert ended about 12:30, Willie went to the front of the stage and greeted every member of the audience and autographed everything they handed him. Some of them had three or four items. I bet he signed his name at least 1500 times but he never faltered and I watched in awe as he related to everyone who came up to him. His technique for doing this was/is simple but brilliant and I have described it before but it bears repeating.

When you are talking to Willie in a crowd, he is looking at you. He doesn't talk to you while looking at someone else. He looks directly at you and you actually feel his interest in what you have to say. It's like a sunbeam has been directed onto you and you feel bathed in his light. He greets you, listens to you and responds. During that time, it's just you and him, no matter how large the crowd you stand among.

When it's time to move on the next fan, he brings closure to your conversation so that you don't feel like he has abandoned you for another person. You know you've been blessed and understand that he is going to direct his light onto another fortunate human being. Willie's one of a kind.

But Damnit, he hasn't jumped all over some of the sure-fire, can't miss country song hooks I've furnished him over the years. Jewels like, "I'm Tryin' Cryin' But I'm Thinkin' Drinkin.'" (Starin' at life but it ain't blinkin'. I'm tryin' cryin' but I'm thinkin' drinkin'.) Now what self-respecting country music star could pass that one up?

Or how about "Those Razor's Edges I Used To Walk Look Like Four Lane Highways to Me Now." Huh? Great, Huh?

How about this for a torch song, Willie? "She Loved Me Now and Then, I Loved Her Then And Now." These good one's don't come to me that often Willie. You ought to jump on them when you can.

And finally, my real pride and joy. "It Don't Pay To Be Bashful in Nashville."

(Oh, it don't pay to be bashful in Nashville, But nothin' cures your blues like a gig for cash will, Well maybe just an ounce of real good grass will, Let you skip that bus trip back to Asheville.) Last chance Willie. When everybody sees them, "the crowd will go wild."

Primary Election Day, May 23, 1995 finally came. The turnout was moderate and Jerry and I ended up with 29,039 votes or 8.7 %. We were very disappointed, of course, but recognized the dynamics of what happened. We wuz robbed!

That's right. From the very start it was apparent that Mr. Patton had the insider "grease" flowing. He had a made a study of the payoff systems around the Commonwealth and had primed them perfectly. Lots of folks jumped on his bandwagon because they knew they would dine well at the trough if Patton won.

However, even that was not enough for Paul.

In direct violation of new election laws passed in 1994 to curb political corruption, Lt. Governor Patton had several of his Executive Branch cronies work directly on his campaign while on state time. They tried to cover their trail by claiming otherwise but the evidence was enough to get them indicted the following year by the newly-elected Attorney General Ben Chandler.

This battle between Patton and Chandler went on for over 7 years and Patton tried every way in the world to get Chandler to drop the charges, but he wouldn't. As it turned out, Patton pardoned his buddies just before he left office in 2003, after his second term as Governor. But I'm getting ahead of myself.

Suffice it to say that I don't believe that Paul Patton ever won a "clean" election, where the votes were honest and no illegal money changed hands. He is not the kind of person to leave such things to chance. When he can buy the outcome, he will. That's one of the reasons his administrations were such disasters for Kentucky. He thought money justifies anything.

As we all know by now, however, "Silent Retribution is Forever Balancing the Divine Scales of Justice." Sooner or later, Paul would have to pay the price for his skulduggery. That time to pay came years later, in his second term, but it was still fun to watch as he came crumbling down. We'll get to those details later.

At the end of this Primary however, Paul was the Democrat's nominee. His opponent in the Fall General Election would be Larry Forgy who had survived his own donnybrook in the Republican Primary.

It would be one hell of an interesting race.

❖ *Reaffirming My Oath*

So, back to work practicing law. God I'm blessed to do this for a living. When you don't have to punch a time clock it's so much easier to express and activate yourself in a political direction. Time is a person's most valuable resource and I have always wanted to control as much of my own time as possible.

And, of course, I immediately began looking for ways to continue getting the word out to Kentucky. I ain't never giving up!

Let's look at it this way. Let's say that you have discovered the cure for cancer. You know that it cures many forms of cancer and relieves the suffering of cancer patients. Would you shut up about it?

If the powers-that-be tried to shut you up about it, would you turn your back on your knowledge and quit telling people about it? I don't think so. You, like me, would feel compelled to educate your fellow being about it. I certainly do.

That compulsion to educate fit nicely with the offers and opportunities that came my way three weeks after the Primary.

❖ *The Fourth of July Parade*

WVLK radio, the top rated AM station in Central Kentucky had just hired a top-notch radio personality from the New York market named Tom Martin. Tom had graduated from Morehead University and was looking to return to his home state.

He and I met and hit it off and he asked if I would like to be a regular guest commentator. I jumped at the chance, not only for the exposure my issues might get, but also because Tom had constructed a really dynamite show with a very hip and intelligent format.

On about the fourth or fifth show, Tom read a news item that I couldn't believe was true. It seemed that the Mayor of Lexington and her trusty sidekicks had been planning the city's 4th of July celebration and parade when they came upon what they thought was a swell idea. Instead of just celebrating the "birthday" of the United States of America, they hit upon the theme of celebrating that and the birth of the United Nations at the same time and in an equal manner.

The announced theme of the Parade was "Independence Day: The U.S. and the U.N. for a Better World." Additionally, they wanted the U.N. to be the Grand Parade Marshall for the event and, since they couldn't actually find someone that looked like the U.N., they decided that a U.N. float would lead the parade.

My blood ran cold. July 4 is the date reserved for celebrating the birth of this truly extraordinary country and the U.N. had nothing to do with it. Their charter was signed on June 26, 1945 and they came into existence on October 24, which is celebrated as United Nations Day. They could have a parade on that or any other day as far as I was concerned but I was dead set against them trying to salt our parade with their propaganda.

Besides, I was aware of both a 101 year old WWI veteran and a Bataan Death March survivor who would be honored to lead the parade. They were never asked before the U.N. float was decided upon.

Now let's get one thing straight. I'm not totally against the U.N. I feel they could do a good job addressing natural disaster relief on a worldwide basis and there is a need for a forum to discuss worldwide issues.

However, I draw the line on their attempts to violate the sovereignty of any nation, particularly mine.

When U.N. officials attempt to gain police or regulatory powers within the borders of the U.S., that is an assault on our Constitutional rights of sovereignty and my own right to self-determination. I haven't had a chance to vote on the U.N. officials making the rules and frankly I don't trust them worth squat when it comes to preserving my individual freedoms. I see what a lot of their member-nations do to their own citizens and I don't want them to have any power over me.

Well, when Tom read the news on his radio program, I publicly vowed that I would protest the parade theme. I didn't have anything particular in mind except that I would speak out against it as an example of misuse of tax dollars and a really bad call on the part of city leaders.

When the 4th of July came, I still didn't have a plan in mind. Jerry and I and several friends went downtown and I took a position behind the reviewing stand, which had been placed in front of the Courthouse on Main Street. I stood on the steps of the Courthouse and began talking to the crowd waiting for the parade.

Dozens of folks gathered around including supporters of the U.N. who mistakenly asserted that the U.N. is trying to establish democracies around the world. It was very good give-and-take in the American tradition.

As scheduled, the parade began one-half mile from where the reviewing stand sat. When they came into our view they were about one block away. There was the Mayor leading the parade and behind her were 8 mounted police officers and behind them was the U.N. Float. Big as Dallas.

The Mayor reached the reviewing stand where every elected official in the county had gathered. She passed by it. However, just before the mounted police came to it, they fanned out to my side of the street and formed a wall of horseflesh between the parade and me.

It was obvious as hell that they had been ordered to keep an eye on me and to keep me from interfering with the event. That really ticked me off. I had not planned any disruptive activity, only to verbally express my disdain for the people responsible for this kind of fuzzy thinking.

With the realization that they had gone this far to try to intimidate me with an overwhelming police presence, that old familiar feeling came washing through me. It's that feeling I get when I take the speaker's podium anywhere without knowing what I'm going to say when I get there. It's an internal release that I actually feel, where I give over what happens to a spirit within me that I trust to guard and protect me. I believe it's my guardian angel.

One thing for sure. I'll be damned if I was going to be intimidated. I stepped quickly to the wall of mounted police and ducked under the belly of one of the horses. I immediately went to the center of Main Street, twenty feet from where the reviewing stand began and found myself right in front of the U.N. float. It came to a stop, as did I. For a frozen three seconds we faced each other, then "the crowd went wild" and the police went to work.

Two officers came running to me and took me by the arms. "Gatewood, get out of the street," said one of them who I knew from Court.

"Nothing doing," I replied. "This U.N. float is not leading the parade while I'm a free man."

The officer shook his head as he proceeded to handcuff me. "Gatewood, you are one crazy son-of-a-bitch."

Simultaneous with their cuffing me, a half-naked, young, longhaired man ran into the street and lay down between the float and me. I had never seen him before and had no idea what he was doing but I liked his spirit. More police took him by the hair and arms and dragged him off the street.

Then began one of the proudest moments of my life. Next to the birth of my three daughters and my marriage to their mother, it ranks right there at the top.

The two police officers who were arresting me turned me around to take me to their squad cars and marched me straight up the middle of Main Street and right in front of the reviewing stand. By God, I was leading the Parade!

It was true. I got to lead the 4th of July parade in 1995 in Lexington, Kentucky. It was a two mile long parade and had more than 75,000 spectators and never mind that I was under arrest, wearing handcuffs and being led off to jail.

As we passed the stand, I really let the city officials have it. I don't remember everything I said, but I expressed my views in no uncertain terms. They could only stare back in vacuous wonder.

Friend Jerry had his movie camera out and captured the scene for posterity. There I am, leading the parade up Main Street in handcuffs. A perfect example of the Law of Unintended Consequences. If the city leaders had not tried to disrupt my freedom of expression, it would have been limited only to words. As it was, when they tried to intimidate me, I had no choice but to go that extra mile.

(Note for future reference. I don't like it when people try to intimidate me.)

The arresting officers treated me nicely and they had no reason not to. I was driven to the jail, fingerprinted and invited to a cup of coffee by the Sgt. in Command. I took him up on it.

Jerry posted my $2,000 at 10% bond for me within minutes and I was released to find a gaggle of reporters waiting for me at the door.

"What were you charged with," they wanted to know.

"My papers say Disorderly Conduct and Blocking a Public Highway," I said.

"Are you going to plead guilty to either of those charges?" one asked.

"Hell no," I replied. "Your news film will show that I wasn't disorderly, only that I refused to move when an officer told me to. As to the blocking of a public highway, I believe that its status as an open public highway was altered to allow the parade to take place. I don't think they can prove either charge."

(The County must have agreed with me. The next day they served me with a third charge. Interfering with a Procession.)

Then they asked me what I was trying to prove and I had to explain again that I am a Nationalist and very protective of the sovereignty of the United States. I am not willing to abdicate any of it to another entity, especially one that I cannot hold accountable And I especially am not willing to share any credit with the U.N. for this nation's Independence, so let's not confuse the kids.

Finally they departed and I set about trying to find out what happened to my unknown confederate who was arrested with me. His name was John Dougherty and his bond was the same as mine. His friends got that done and I met him when he got out.

"John, my friend," I greeted him. "What the hell were you doing? You could have gotten hurt laying in front of that float."

His reply endeared him to me forever. "I know, Gatewood. But I wanted to make sure that they had to run over me first before they could run over you."

(Later on, when I have been introduced to audiences as the man who lay down in the middle of Main Street to stop the parade, I set the listeners straight. "Look, I stood in the middle of Main to stop the parade.

I only lay down for two reasons and stopping parades isn't one of them.")

"GALBRAITH ARRESTED" screamed the headlines in the next morning's papers replete with a big color photograph of me being led off in cuffs. And then the reverberations began.

Calls of congratulations came in from all over the country, dozens of them. Gun rights groups, militia groups, anti-U.N. groups, other nationalists and lots of Republicans who actually know what the designation "conservative" means.

They all appreciated the size, scope and message of my actions and that it was a one-man action. I immediately got put on the mailing lists of lots of folks I had never heard of before and some that I had including the FBI, the CIA, the NSA, the BATF and several others of the alphabet soup gang.

That suited me. I'll take the heat. The Last Free Man in America can't back down. It's his job to make the right statement on behalf of all the freedom lovers in this country and stopping a parade is a hell of a lot better than stopping a bullet to make your point.

As expected, the newspaper's editorials came after me with great abandon, ignoring my stated positions and touting theirs on the U.N. All warm, fuzzy, one-worlder stuff. (I don't believe any of the editors on the Herald or the Courier has any military training. They need to pipe some testosterone into the water coolers to give these folks a hint of what a stiff resolve might be.)

My actions were headline stuff for three days and then the media interest waned a bit. I agreed to represent my co-defendant along with myself and we asked for a jury trial in the matter. That proceeded smoothly enough until I subpoenaed both the Mayor and the Chief of Police. Then things started to snap, crackle and pop.

The County moved to quash the subpoenas and the Court asked me what was pertinent about their testimony.

I answered thusly. "Well, I want the Chief of Police to testify as to who told him to put a wall of mounted police between the parade and me in an attempt to curb my freedom of speech through intimidation. And then I want the Mayor's version of that. Plus, I am interested in listening to her defend the U.N. for an hour or so."

I am convinced that did the trick. A week later, they offered to drop all charges against both of us if we agreed not to sue for false arrest and the deprivation of our civil liberties through intimidation. All of our points having been made, we agreed.

❖ *My Comedy Career*

Several months later I received an offer, which I found fascinating. The Comedy Club of Louisville invited me to guest host their acts for a week. A modest fee was arranged and I set about to discover if I was really a stand-up comedian in political garb or vice versa.

As usual, I wanted to do something a little different than the other guys so I thought about it and this is what I came up with. But I've got to warn you, some of it is a little racy, so for you folks who are reading this book to your children at bedtime, you might want to skip this part.

"Good evening Ladies and Gentlemen. I'm Gatewood Galbraith, the Last Free Man in America. I'm your emcee tonight. I've run for Commissioner of Agriculture once and Governor twice so I guess that qualifies me to introduce you, the public, to another bunch of comedians.

Say, do you like this hat? Willie Nelson gave me this hat. They used to call it a ten-gallon hat, but I've discovered that you can only hide 7-1/2 ounces in it.

As you may know, if I had won the governor's race, the first thing I would do is ground all of those military helicopters hovering over the fields and gardens of the people of Kentucky. This is America, not Afghanistan and we are not an occupied territory and it's time to stop treating our citizens like we are one.

We are already becoming a Police state you know. You can leave here, get in your car and drive away; and they can stop you for any reason or no reason, make you get out of your car, bring a dog up to sniff you, your car and all of your belongings, take blood out of your arm, make you pee in a bottle and stick their hands where the sun don't shine if they care to.

That, Ladies and Gentlemen, is a Police State.

Do you think John Wayne would have put up with that? Huh? Do you?

Ol' John's riding his horse down the trail and they drop a log in front of him. 'Get off that horse,' they say. 'We're going to take blood out of your arm, you have to pee in this bucket and we are going to stick our hands down your pants.'

I think John Wayne would have said, 'I'm afraid not Pilgrim. This is where I draw my line in the sand.'

And this is where I draw my line in the sand, Folks. I will not live in a Police state. You and I need to resist that attitude all the way.

However, as a matter of fact, I am for taking marijuana away from the young teenagers and I believe we ought to give it to the old folks in the retirement homes. Not only would it increase their appetites and put a smile on their faces, but think of the increased visitation by the young folks...Hey, let's go see Dad!

I guess I've reached middle age myself. I'm pissed off when I'm searching for a good cigar and all I can find is good pot.

Well, I see where they just made sodomy legal in Kentucky. How about that?

Now you can't raise your voice to your wife but you can have anal intercourse with a complete stranger. And you can put an infected penis in your mouth, but you can't smoke an herbal gift from God to relieve your pain and suffering.

What's my position on gays in the military? Hey, I want them there. I want that guy next to me in the foxhole saying, 'Don't you worry, Dear. I won't let them hurt you.'

Used to be you could only get blown out of your foxhole.

Now this is my first time on a comedy stage, not counting my political speeches and I've noticed that a lot of comedy is based on putting other people down. So I made up my mind that what I am going to try to do is lift people up, enlighten and educate them with my time at the microphone. Give them power, insight and strength. I want it so that when you leave here you might say, 'You know, that fellow wasn't funny at all, but I do feel a damn sight better about myself.'

So what I want to educate you about is your power under the Constitution of the United States of America. You have immense power as a citizen if you only know it. And becoming aware of it will make you a better parent too. I'll show you what I mean with my training program.

I call it my 'Just Say No Officer, you can't search the damn car' plan.

That's right. Say you've been pulled over and one ornery State Trooper has you get out of your car. Now he asks you if he can search your car.

'No Officer, you can't search the car.' (We'll leave out the damn here because you aren't an attorney).

'Why not,' he will ask?

'Because I said so,' you should say, trying to sound just like your parents. 'And the Constitution says I can be free from an unreasonable search.'

Now by this time, the Officer has made up his mind that you are more than the average, know-nothing dolt he usually pulls over. You are one of those smart-ass dolts, he sometimes happens across, who's been listening to that guy Gatewood Galbraith, and boy is he going to teach you a lesson.

'Well, I'll just bring in a dog,' he will threaten and you should respond, 'Well, you just do that Mister', especially if you don't have anything in the car.

Just think of all the good smoke the rest of us have, going by on the highway, while you have this guy on a wild goose chase. We appreciate you keeping him there as long as possible.

And remember this. If you can't face down a 6 foot 4 inch, heavily armed, pissed off State Trooper along side a highway, you don't stand a chance against a ticked-off 4 year old in Toys R Us."

It was a fun week and I met some outstanding comics. And now I can really appreciate the grind involved in traveling the U.S., doing one, two and three nights of stand-up comedy, then moving on. My hat's off to you guys. But remember, it only holds 7-1/2 ounces.

Meanwhile Willie and I had been talking and I encouraged him to locate his next Farm Aid concert in Kentucky. His people got in touch with the proper people and the 1995 Farm Aid benefit was scheduled for October 1 in Cardinal Stadium in Louisville. I am especially proud to report that this Kentucky venue, one of the largest ever to host a Farm Aid, sold out quicker than any other show they have ever held. More than 60,000 seats went like that! Way to go Kentucky!

❖ *Woody & Me and "Hempsters" the Movie*

By this time, my appearances on Tom Martin's show had gained somewhat of a following. Tom's show had such an intelligence and format that we talked about nearly everything. As you might imagine, cannabis was a frequent topic and one day we covered a story about a California man who had mailed several pounds of marijuana to a hospital to illustrate its use as medicine. That sparked a conversation about its different uses and I spontaneously vowed to plant 5,000 hemp plants to show its viability as an industrial/textile crop.

As this was late in the year, I had to wait until the next Spring to put my plan into action. However, before I got too far into it, I got a call from some folks who asked if I minded stepping aside and letting a fellow named Woody Harrelson plant a few seeds to illustrate the point that cannabis/hemp is not supposed to be treated the same as cannabis/ marijuana under the letter of the law.

That sounded fine to me. I've always felt that I didn't HAVE to be the one who scores the winning touchdown…I just want to be on the winning team. If anyone else can come along and advance these issues further than I can, God Bless 'Em! I'll push them or pull them or just get out of the way.

So the next year Woody came in and planted 4 seeds in Eastern Kentucky and was duly arrested for it. (Four years later, after various arguments had been waged in Kentucky's higher courts, they refused to legally differentiate between cannabis for industrial purposes and cannabis for medical purposes because of the changes having been wrought in Kentucky's statute by the aforementioned Bill Lear. But Woody was found not guilty by a jury of good ole-fashioned, God-fearing Eastern Kentuckians. Don't you just love juries? I know I do.

Woody's activities were covered by various media including a film crew out of Dallas, which was interested in documenting the efforts of several activists working to change the laws regarding cannabis/hemp.

However, Woody's "people" were also anxious not to allow the issue of "hemp" to be talked about in the same breath as "marijuana". They thought they would/could differentiate it in the minds of the public so that they could garner support for this plant as an industrial/ textile crop and not have to answer any attacks on it as a "drug."

In this they were sadly mistaken. The powers-that-be will not cooperate by addressing this issue in a factual or scientific manner. You must remember that it was they who began the attack on this plant because they need it suppressed in every aspect. The admission that it may have value in any respect is a direct attack on their attempt to subvert all natural products in favor of their synthetic replacements. They will not allow any differentiations to take place.

The Dallas film crew covering Woody's adventures had never heard of me. They had done their shooting and were going back to Texas when a bystander asked if they had talked to "Gatewood". They said no and were quickly informed that there was this guy who might have some information on the matter. They called me and asked if I was available for an interview. The answer was yes.

Michael Henning and Mark Birnbaum, Dallas filmmakers extraordinaire, came to my house for a ten-minute interview and left when their film ran out two hours later. They couldn't get enough.

For several months thereafter they arranged to film several other of my events and later presented me with a 5 minute 30 second film called "Gatewood for Governor," filmed around my leading a demonstration in downtown Atlanta.

I generally do not watch myself on film but I have shown this film around the country on many occasions and it always sponsors thought and conversation among the people who watch it. Isn't that the goal of all films?

Meanwhile the filmmakers continued to collect footage from around the country from other activists and began to develop the film *HEMPSTERS: Plant the Seed.* This turned into a six-year project that eventually included Willie Nelson, Merle Haggard, Woody Harrelson, Julia "Butterfly" Hill, Craig Lee, Alex Whiteplume and a cast of thousands. It is the best film rendition, that I've seen, of what this movement is mostly about. Passion for the Truth as a beacon for decision-making in our personal and collective lives.

I'll update you on it about a hundred pages from now.

Meanwhile, I was trying to stay active and involved. I was a regular speaker at the "militia" meetings and actually was able to define many common interests among the diverse individuals who attended them. My talks centered on the Constitution and how it applied to all of us, even those who used their freedoms to act in manners which may be repugnant to the rest of us. Even the most intolerant of the militia had to tolerate that out of respect for the Constitution.

❖ *Me & Mom*

1996 held two more highlights that stand out in my mind. The first had to do with my mother.

I haven't spent anywhere near the time and space in this book that I ought to have telling you about my family and especially my mother.

After the family's financial fortunes went south in the mid '60s, Mom began teaching school again after 25 years as a housewife. She went back to UK to get her teaching degree and began teaching 3rd and 4th grade at a local parochial school. She also began walking 3 to 4 miles a day back and forth to school.

To put it bluntly, Mom became a hell of a walker. When she retired from teaching in 1983, she continued to walk every day, rain or shine. When the city began a 4th of July 10K race (6.2 miles) in 1988, she entered at age 75. When she reached seventy-nine, she requested the race organizers to begin a new age category of eighty. When she reached 84, they began a new category for 85 and over. Each time Mom would be the first, if not the only, racer in that age category, so it would be fair to say that Mom won her race, in her age category, more consecutive times that any one else ever did.

She had to drop the race after she got a hip replacement in 1999. But she still swims for an hour every morning at a pool near her home.

After her retirement, Mom also volunteered her services daily to agencies affiliated with the United Way. Seven days a week for the past 25 years, she leaves her house every morning to go do good for other people.

She's extremely modest about it but it doesn't go unnoticed by others and Dollie is the only two-time winner of the Lexington's Outstanding Volunteer Award and was one of President Bush's Thousand Points of Light.

In '96, she also was chosen to carry the Olympic Torch for a half-mile through Northern Kentucky on its way to Atlanta. Today, at the publishing of this book, Dollie Galbraith is 91 years old and still volunteering every day. What a Gal!!!!!!

❖ *Another Revolution, Another Hero*

1996 was also a landmark year for me, us, them and everyone else in America. In this year, the voice of change became a roar and the people of California, exercising their right of self-determination, passed Proposition 215 which allowed them to grow and possess marijuana for its use as medicine.

What a victory for We, the People! For the first time in the history of this country, a state, using its powers of referendum, passed a law refuting the federal government's position of criminalizing marijuana and everyone associated with it. The people specifically rejected the government's view, fueled by big money from the special interests, that marijuana has no value as a medicine and passed a law which allows anyone with a recommendation from a doctor to grow and possess marijuana for their own use. And if they are too disabled to grow it for themselves, a caretaker may do it for them.

Smaller government, less intrusion, relief of suffering; that Folks is "compassionate conservatism."

The success of Proposition 215 was the result of efforts on behalf of tens of thousands of everyday people but it originated as the brainchild of another genius of this generation.

Dennis Peron is not a big man physically but his heart is as big as the world is wide and his dedication to relieving pain and suffering among the people is even larger than life.

Dennis began his public life by being arrested for selling marijuana in San Francisco's underground. As a talented activist even then, he rose to the top of his craft and was eventually busted for operating the "Big Top" supermarket out of an abandoned grocery where the discriminating marijuana smoker could choose from over thirty bushel baskets filled to the brim with fine buds.

During this time, Dennis became aware of marijuana's medical properties, especially suitable among the gay community where AIDS was coming on strong. Because AIDS is a "wasting" disease, where nausea and suppression of appetite leads to insufficient nourishment and eventually to death, the effect of marijuana in stimulating appetite has been a life-saver.

In the early '90s, Dennis's partner contacted AIDS and was in very bad shape. One night the police busted down his door, arrested Dennis, dragged his friend from his deathbed and threw him down the stairs. It was a sight that Dennis will never forget. He swore then that he would never rest until marijuana was available as a legal medicine in this country. And he hasn't.

California's referendum law allows any citizen to begin the process by writing the law they want and then acquiring the necessary number of signatures on a Petition to have it placed on the ballot for the voters to accept or reject it.

This law differs from that of other states allowing referendums because, in California, an individual citizen chooses the language of the law, while other states will allow the citizens to vote on a law only if the legislature chooses the language, i.e. Kentucky. These are the states that don't trust the people.

Dennis wrote what became Proposition 215, which essentially read

d) Section 11357, relating to the possession of marijuana, and Section 11358, relating to the cultivation of marijuana, shall not apply to a patient, or to a patient's primary caregiver, who possesses or cultivates marijuana for the personal medical purposes of the patient upon the written or oral recommendation or approval of a physician.

(e) For the purposes of this section, "primary caregiver" means the individual designated by the person exempted under this section who has consistently assumed responsibility for the housing, health, or safety of that person.

He began organizing to get the required number of signatures and I offered to come west and speak on its behalf around California. Dennis told me thanks but it wouldn't be necessary and it wasn't. He got the signatures in time and when it was set for a vote in the November 1996 elections, I arranged to be there.

Even before the referendum itself, Dennis and other activists had formed Cannabis Buyers' Clubs throughout the state. If a person had a disease or illness for which marijuana was indicated as therapeutic, and a doctor recommended marijuana as a medicine, then that patient could register at one of the Buyer's Clubs and purchase the marijuana necessary to their treatment.

The San Francisco Buyer's Club was the largest of these outlets because of its location among Frisco's large gay community. Marijuana is the best treatment for AIDS because of its relief from chronic pain and its stimulation of appetite. This particular Club was the home base for Dennis and his efforts.

When I first got to the Club, I was amazed. It took up three floors of an old warehouse and had two health bars, hundreds of chairs and sofas and thousands of paper doves hanging from strings tied to the rafters. They were made of every color imaginable and each had the name of one of the Club members on it. Twelve thousand in all!

I was extremely pleased that so many of the Club members recognized me and knew me by name. Many of them mentioned that they had been following my efforts in High Times and from what Dennis and Jack Herer had told them.

Their graciousness almost overwhelmed me. They were the ones who were in various stages of sickness and death yet they were the ones encouraging me not to give up the fight.

Over the next two days, I literally spoke to hundreds of people whose life was being saved or extended by smoking marijuana. There was not one iota of insincerity or, for that matter, self-pity, in anyone I saw. They were all benefiting from the courage and insight of Dennis Peron, whom they had nicknamed "Earth Angel."

Another California hero I visited was/is Dr. Tod Mikuryia. Dr. Tod was one of the Doctors who testified at my Science and Truth Hearings in Lexington in 1991. He deserves a tremendous amount of credit for overcoming prejudices and lies to get the science and truth of the matter into the sunlight. He has been unrelenting in his reliance on the truth winning out and has struggled everyday for the last 40 years to see it happen.

On the day of the election, we all gathered in the headquarters at the Club. Dennis was there and also Jack Herer, Ed Rosenthal, Dr. Tod, Steve Kubby and a host of other activists. When the results came in, the people had spoken. Proposition 215 had passed 53% to 47%. "And the crowd went wild!"

Immediately the ghouls in the federal government went to work to overturn the people's will. The particularly noxious William Bennett, "Drug Czar", chastised the people and vowed to never allow the law to take effect. The head of the Drug Enforcement Administration, Thomas Constantine, chimed in with the same tune. (BTW, the DEA is the most corrupt government agency ever devised. Their rip off of the taxpayer is outrageous, as is their battle to set aside the will of the people and stand guard over the monopolies of the pharmaceutical industries).

Immediately they threatened any doctor who would recommend marijuana to a patient with the loss of their license to practice. They blurted out the same old lies about marijuana having no proven medical utility and they doubled their efforts to have the major TV networks spread their lies by broadcasting, for free, their anti-marijuana propaganda. These networks do it because they are paid immense amounts of money by the pharmaceutical companies to run ads for their synthetic medicines. They are the puppets of their major advertisers and all you have to do is watch TV for an hour and tell me how many drug commercials were presented to you. They are well-paid whores, but whores nonetheless.

I am reminded of the story of the Iditarod Trail in Alaska. Each year they hold a race there to commemorate the epic story of when Nome, Alaska was hit with an outbreak of Diphtheria in 1925. The whole town was sick, isolated and in the middle of a storm, when certain dog sledders in Anchorage decided to make a run through terrible conditions to get medicine to the people. After working their way through 1150 miles of pure hell, they got to the town and saved many of its residents.

I look at Bennett, DuPont and others who try to keep marijuana illegal and unavailable to the sick and dying as bush-whackers along-side the Iditerod trail, trying to keep the medicine from reaching the townsfolk.

I hate them and all they stand for. I believe anyone who would intentionally stand in the way of relieving another's pain and suffering is evil, especially if they are doing it for money. They ought to be in prison. Or worse.

Proposition 215 was also a landmark illustration of our country's separation of powers and system of checks and balances. It highlights the concept of "State's Rights", whereby each state retains the right to have its own set of laws on any particular subject and it is not obliged to enforce any federal statute.

Therefore, while the Federals may have laws against marijuana, the states may devise their own statutes and enforce them. If the Feds want to enforce their own laws, they must use their own resources. That keeps them somewhat in line.

The success in California spurred the imagination and efforts of the rest of us and Petitions began in several other states. Within the next four years, eight other states passed similar referendums, mostly in the west. Each time the Feds have tried to influence the vote, using our tax dollars. These special interests have tried to thwart the will of the people at the voting booth using our tax dollars.

We ought to put these assholes in jail, making the proper use of our tax dollars.

So 1996 ended on a very high note for me. At last, We, the People, had spoken. And in the language I had been listening for during the last 20 years

❖ *Me & Tobacco & Death*

While I was in San Francisco I had Dr. Tod examine me. His diagnosis of emphysema led him to prescribe marijuana for me. I still carry that recommendation with me but I have never had to rely on it. The black market in Kentucky will sell me marijuana whether the Dr. recommends it or not.

The diagnosis of emphysema was no big shock to me as I had realized for some time that my cigarette smoking over the years had taken its toll. I have to laugh at the irony that marijuana cured my asthma so well that I could smoke tobacco without going into paroxysms. I had experimented with tobacco as a teen but began smoking heavily in my early twenties. I gave it up twice, for four years each time, but had taken it back up from '94 to '96 and I could really tell its effects this time. It began to interfere with my public speaking and that was that. I can give up anything if it interferes with my ability to make a speech.

Lots of Folks look at emphysema, also called Chronic Pulmonary Obstruction Disease, as a death sentence. There is no known cure and it is progressive. Eventually the patient simply runs out of the ability to breathe sufficient oxygen to stay alive.

I look at the diagnosis as a reminder to appreciate every day, and the people in it, to the maximum. Let's face it. Life itself is a terminal disease and it's how you face up to it that defines your quality of life while you have it. In fact, death makes life meaningful.

Besides, with my philosophy of personal responsibility, if there is any blame about my situation, I must bear it. My Mom told me cigarettes were bad for me when I first tried them but I didn't listen. I should have known better and I probably did, but I didn't act on it. That fits my definition of dumbness; knowing something is the right thing to do for yourself but not applying your knowledge.

This background led to the formulation of my response to the question put forth during one of my campaigns. "Gatewood," they asked, "how do you propose to pay for the medical care of all the Baby Boomers as they get to be eighty and ninety years old?"

I responded. "Well, the first thing I would do is get off the ass of all the tobacco companies in the world." They were shocked and their faces showed it.

"That's right. Hey, Benjamin Franklin said 'nine out of ten deaths are suicide' and that was before they invented pre-rolled cigarettes. The fact is that cigarette smoking remains the most individualized, voluntary form of suicide left to most folks and they should be allowed to take themselves out by their own choices long before they reach eighty or ninety and we have to care for them. Let's face it. We don't want a lot of folks running around with healthy hearts and lungs and totally out of it with Alzheimer's disease.

And one more thing. We need individualized, voluntary forms of suicide available to us because the opposite of that situation is collective, mandatory suicide and none of us want to see that." I believe those folks are still pondering the logic of it, but it's clear to me. Get off the people's backs and quit trying to save them from themselves.

My response to my own situation has been to smoke marijuana and exercise like hell. (The fitness bug is like the flu bug. It causes sweat and muscle ache.)

I remember well the day I gave up tobacco for the third time in early 1996. I didn't feel well and I was coughing up crap. "That's it," I resolved to myself. No more. I'm an idiot. (Always a good thing to remind one's self occasionally).

Not only are my lungs shot but so is my stamina. I need to do something about that. Then I got down on the floor and did five pushups. One set of five pushups. It was a start.

Within a week, I was doing three sets of ten pushups a day. As with most everything else, the real secret was in re-learning to breathe properly.

Than I began walking outdoors. I had been a member of several gyms in the past twenty years but I was never happy with the used and recirculated air that comes from being indoors. It just doesn't feel fresh.

At this time, my office was located at the corner of South Limestone and Waller Avenue. I began walking from there over to Woodland Park and back, a distance of about two miles and doing a set of pushups every little while. Within a year I had added two miles to my walk and was doing seven sets of thirty pushups each. It made me feel a hell of a lot better and death doesn't seem so close when I can take a lung full of fresh air and appreciate the moment.

(Several years later I peaked out at 4 miles a day and four sets of ninety pushups. Now that was almost like work and I don't like to be dominated by anything, including my own internal work ethic, so I've taken a one year vacation from heavy exercise and I feel right good about it. We'll see I reckon.)

❖ *Me & the U.N. & the Militia*

As 1997 began, I had no plans to run for another office especially as a Democrat. The leaders of that Party considered me a loose cannon, a position I could understand since I was against their plan to loot the Treasury and make payoffs to their political cronies.

Yet, it was apparent to me from the start that Governor Paul Patton had a penchant for corruption and small ideas. As with his fore-bearers, he did not consider the system of payoffs and quid pro quo to be corruption. He considered it to be a lifestyle. I watched him spend the $350 Million of our tax dollars (a "budget surplus") he had promised to certain legislative leaders in 1995 for their support in his run for Governor. He had no vision and no ethics from the get-go and, as far as I could see, he hadn't developed any in his first two years in office.

His economic development plan for Kentucky was insane. Give away free land, free buildings, free money, cheap labor and tons of tax breaks to corporations to locate here and provide some jobs. And there is no telling of the number and size of the kickbacks involved in those negotiations. It must have been a pretty penny.

Between his economic insanity and his arrogance, Paul had compiled quite an enemies list after two years. Conservatives, veterans, coal miners, gun owners and others kept a watchful eye on his shenanigans, especially when he called a special session to shred Kentucky's Worker's Compensation Statute and leave Kentucky's injured workers in a hell of a mess.

By law, in special session, Kentucky's Legislature can only consider legislation regarding the subject matter set by the Governor. However, this particular Legislature was called on to perform an additional task by another party while they were in this session and they responded with what might be their finest hour in my lifetime. Here's how it happened.

The 1994 Republican Revolution had succeeded because they promised to downsize government through attrition and privatization. As a result, in 1996, the Tennessee Valley Authority, TVA, announced that they were divesting themselves of all non-power producing properties, which included a piece of land in Western Kentucky called the Land Between the Lakes.

In the 1930s, the Federal Government formed the TVA to construct dams in Tennessee and Kentucky for the purpose of flood control and the production of electricity. They dammed several rivers in the southwest part of Kentucky and formed huge lakes including Lake Barkley and Kentucky Lake. (Kentucky has four of the ten largest man-made lakes in the world).

These two lakes circled a landmass of about 170,000 acres which was owned by TVA and which they never let be developed. In fact, when they acquired it under eminent domain, they promised that it would always be open to the public for primitive recreation, camping and the visitation to the gravesites of their ancestors by folks who had to move when the lakes came in.

When TVA announced they were going to divest themselves of this property because it was not part of the production of power, they also said they were going to give it over to the United Nations for their use as a "Biosphere."

The establishment of a biosphere by the United Nations means that they are given eternal ownership of a piece of land where they prohibit and regulate the human presence by whatever means necessary.

Each biosphere has a "core" area where no human beings are allowed. Period. Surrounding the core is a buffer zone where some activity is allowed such as limited farming and some recreation.

The big point is that the land becomes owned by the United Nations and their rules apply, not the laws of the country wherein the biosphere is located. So when the TVA said that they were going to make the Land Between the Lakes a U.N. biosphere and that neither the Constitution of the United States nor the Constitution of Kentucky would apply there, Norman Davis and I went on the warpath.

We investigated the biospheres in other places, 67 in all at that time, and they were as bad as we thought. We found most of our preliminary information on the Internet including color-coded maps, produced by the U.N., on their plans to regulate land and its development in the United States and beyond.

Norman and I are aware that Kentucky's Constitution contains a provision that says that land within Kentucky cannot be bought or sold to another government without the consent of the Legislature. Immediately

Norman and I collected the proper information, wrote a letter to each of the Legislators explaining the situation and laid it on their desks during the Governor's Special Session.

The response was overwhelming. Immediately a Resolution was drafted opposing the transfer of the Land Between the Lakes and it passed both the House and Senate unanimously. Furthermore, they sent a certified copy of the Resolution to President William Jefferson Clinton, who proceeded to throw a "hissy fit."

Old Bill is all for this U.N. crap and this was the first time any state had objected to the placement of a biosphere in their territory. He certainly wasn't happy but both Norman and I were ecstatic. For once in my life, Kentucky's legislature had "done me proud". God Bless Norman too.

This effort to remove Kentucky land and citizens from the protections of the Constitution agitated a lot more folks and attendance at meetings of Kentuckians for the Right to Bear Arms and other conservative groups increased. Clinton was in his second term as President and was promoting issues which frightened lots of Americans. Gun control and gay "rights" don't play very well in Kentucky and dissatisfaction with the state of affairs was rampant at these meetings.

I kept making the point that we had to find common ground with lots of other groups with similar concerns if we hoped to make a difference. I told everyone there that it makes no difference to me if a person is male or female, young or old, rich or poor, black white, yellow or red, gay or straight as long as they are citizens of the United States and will help me protect our common rights of individual freedom, privacy and sovereignty.

A minority of the attendees at these meetings couldn't come to grips with the need to form coalitions. They were/are the dogmatic kind and distrustful of any form of government or people who believe that government can be minimized and harnessed to provide basic services to the people.

By this time, Kentucky had emerged as the state where the "militia" was most active and noticeable. Statewide meetings and weekend retreats of armed men dressed in camouflage received media attention and "the liberals and gun-control nuts went wild." They couldn't believe that some people would actively resist their own government and the do-gooder programs they wanted to inflict on the people. Of course, most of them had never met a government program they didn't like.

Publicly I defended the militia and Jerry opined that it might hurt me vote-wise but more important to me was preserving the position that the people have the right to resist an oppressive government and one of those times might be coming on in the United States. (This was especially true since the Great Liar Clinton was again in the White House, Janet Reno had revealed her true fascist nature and the Democrats were going full-tilt boogie after guns.)

(The Great Liar Clinton was later succeeded by the Great Liar Bush who, ironically, won because of the backlash of voting by the country's gun owners.)

This was especially true in my mind because, under Clinton, the number of arrests for marijuana possession soared. Here that S.O.B. had smoked marijuana continuously in college and as Governor of Arkansas and yet he supported putting everyone else in jail for it because he wanted the backing of the pharmaceutical Nazis who would give him the big bucks. What an Ass!

(I don't know if there is a Hell or not, but if there is, I take some comfort in knowing that certain folks are going to be buried hotter and deeper than I am, with William Jefferson Clinton being one of them.)

Sixth Grade Class

Galbraith Family - Easter 1959

Stylin' - 1971

My Hero - Willie

It couldn't get any better

My Hero - Jerry

My Daughters - Molly, Abby, & Summer

My Hero - Jack

My Hero - Dennis

November 1996 - Proposition 215 Headquarters

Dennis Peron - "Earth Angel" to millions

My Superhero Mom

July 4, 1998 - 10K race

Yum!

Kathy Lyons - My Lt. Governor Running Mate, 1999

Willie would be proud

Working hard for your vote - Congress 2002

Machines of freedom's highway

My Heroes - Lynne Maner and Dana Beal

A true genius for this generation - Jack Herer

Marc Emery
Another genius and his efforts

Playboy Mansion 2006 - Mark Perkins and Ray Benson

❖ *Me & My Family*

John Lennon wrote that "Life is what goes on while you are busy making other plans" and my life is no exception to that. While my professional and political life were fairly public, my private side held the most joy and happiness for me.

My oldest daughter Summer graduated from high school at 16, as did her two younger sisters later. Susan and I had started them out in Montessori School, then put them in public schools after six, five and three years respectively. When they entered public school, they were advanced a year or two, so they graduated at a younger age. I know it wasn't easy for them to start college at 16 but they worked through it and each of them has made the Dean's List on several occasions while holding down their own jobs.

Now all three of them are beautiful, intelligent young women and I have to be the luckiest Dad in the world. No wonder I'm always smiling. I'll be smiling a hell of a lot more when they graduate and there are no more tuition payments. Whee!

Now is also a good time to mention brothers and sisters again. My oldest sister Judy passed on this last year, but all things considered, we have been an extremely lucky group. Except for Dad, we were all in reasonably good health. His health had deteriorated as his drinking had increased and, when he lost the ability to care for himself, we had to enter him into a nursing home in 1980 where he spent 17 years, until his death in '97. Dad was a fine man, kind and gentle until the very end but he, like many of us, couldn't beat the bottle.

Alcohol is addictive and a poison to boot. Much of my criminal defense case load is alcohol-related and I had my own time frame where it was problem, so you could say I know about alcohol's ability to destroy from a first, second and third-hand perspective. This is the reason I say that if I could wave my hands and replace all alcohol products with cannabis, I would do it in a heartbeat. Crime would go down immediately as would the cost of health care while happiness would increase. Sounds like a good trade to me.

Beginning in 1985, my family started planning their vacations together at a beach somewhere in the South every two years. All seven of we siblings, our children and Mom started out on Florida's Gulf Coast and have since moved to North Carolina's Outer Banks. We rent two or three beach houses with 20 to 25 bedrooms and get together for a week of sun tanning, sand castles, card games, (there's a game of hearts going on 20 hours a day), the settling of old arguments and the beginnings of new ones. We generally have 25 to 30 members of the family there plus at least two or three others who come along for the adventure. It's always a hell of a good time for everyone. Another good reason for smiling.

All of my Brother and Sisters are well-balanced, successful human beings, hard-working and practical. I know they have to put up with hearing "Say, are you related to that fellow Gatewood?" every time they give the name Galbraith. But they do so with humor and patience. Ain't I the luckiest guy around?

❖ *Me & Kathy Lyons*

In 1997, after much consideration, and in time to qualify as an Independent candidate for the 1999 Governor's race, I changed my registration to Independent. Kentucky's laws say that a person can only run for an office under a Party banner if they voted for that Party's candidate in the last general election preceding the targeted election. I hadn't made up my mind to run in '99, but I wanted to keep my options open.

It was quite apparent that neither party held the answers to reforming the corruption that had institutionalized itself in Frankfort over the past 30 years. Both major parties had been bought out, both on the Federal and State level, from the top down. "They" were moving to take control of our political apparatus to forestall any citizen's revolt against their coup.

"They" have engineered the introduction of huge amounts of foreign capital into our politician's bank accounts and call the shots accordingly. "They" had succeeded in passing the GATT Treaty and were already in the process of moving tens of thousands of jobs overseas, decimating Kentucky's manufacturing base and destroying our middle class, all with the obvious approval of our state's elected leaders, Republican and Democrat alike.

The day I registered as an Independent was a red-letter day for me. I actually felt physically relieved. No more Party bullshit! No more "Our guy may be a S.O.B. but at least he's our S.O. B. so we've got to elect him" crap.

And, no more May Primaries!

Hot Dog! No more Primaries! I could run now as an Independent in the Fall 1999 General Election if I qualified by securing 5,000 signatures of registered Kentucky voters on a Petition and could find another Kentuckian to run with me. Most of early 1998 was spent considering my options.

I had been "iced" by the Democrats who had taken me out at the Primary level. My messages were based in true conservatism but only Democrats had been given the opportunity to cast a vote for or against my platform. The only way I could get to a Fall General Election was to by-pass the Primary as an Independent. "Just how hard would it be to get 5,000 signatures," I wondered?

"And how hard will it be to find a running mate," I wondered again?

I went to Jerry with the proposition that we give it another try but he declined with grace unless I simply couldn't find anyone else to do it. What a diplomat!

He knew that was a challenge to me and that I now had to prove to him that there was another person in Kentucky who would have something to do with me.

I looked high and low around the Commonwealth for the right person They had to be registered Independent already and able to handle their own in public. They had to have a thick skin and a sense of humor. And we had to be in agreement on the various issues.

I searched the Second Amendment groups from Eastern Kentucky to the Knob Creek Machine Gun Shoot held in Bullitt County where you can rent a .50 caliber machine gun and rip hell out of an old car in the middle of a shooting field. I suggest that everyone visit Knob Creek and watch one of those things being fired. See what it does to what it hits, to fully appreciate the courage it must have taken for our forefathers and grandfathers to hit the beaches of Normandy and Iwo Jima and advance right into the teeth of one of these killing machines.

I looked into the other parties, the Libertarians, the Greens, the Natural Law bunch, the Constitutional Party and the Patriot Party. All of the prospects there demanded some allegiance to their own platforms and I just didn't believe that any Party had the answers, so I decided to take my time and let fate take its course.

Along about June of '98, I became aware of a woman near Murray, Kentucky who had a public reputation as an activist and environmentalist. A no-nonsense, straight-talking lady who also had a permit to carry a concealed and deadly weapon. What a find!

I contacted Kathy Lyons by telephone and told her of my interest in her political future. She was appropriately cautious but intrigued nonetheless. We arranged for me to visit her and her husband in late July.

As I drove up to their farm house just outside Murray, Kathy and her husband Wallace stepped out onto the front porch and I liked what I saw right away. They were up-front and friendly and Kathy had on a go-to-hell-hat if there ever was one. Now I like people who wear go-to-hell hats because I've worn several myself. These are hats that you get attached to and it doesn't matter how ugly other people think they are, by God, you're going to wear it and if they don't like it they can go to hell. It takes a certain kind of person to wear one. My kind of person.

It didn't take me long to discover that Kathy was spirited, opinionated, smart and principled. We didn't agree on everything, but we shared common ground in our faith in the Constitution and Bill of Rights, on fighting corruption, seeking a smaller government with less taxes, preserving the Second Amendment and stopping all arrests for marijuana so we could get it to sick and dying Kentuckians immediately. That's a lot of common ground so, when I left the next day, I was pretty sure that Kathy would accept my invitation and the challenge that went with it. A week later, she told me to deal her in.

Hot damn, she had it all. A female, from Western Kentucky, who had never been arrested. She brought real balance to the ticket!

Under Kentucky law, we couldn't begin to collect the 5,000 signatures necessary to get on the ballot until that year began so the winter of '98 and the early Spring of '99 were spent putting our platform together.

On February 23, 1999 Kathy and I announced our intentions to run and the beginning of our Petition effort at a news conference in the Capitol Rotunda in Frankfort. I was tickled to death at how she handled the media.

From then on it all seems to be a blur to me now. I had no idea on how much effort it takes to get 5,000 individuals to sign their name, address and birth date or Social Security Number on a Petition. Jerry put it into perspective for me as usual. " 5,000 doesn't sound like a whole of people Gatewood, but if you invite them all over for breakfast, you'll find that's a heck of a lot of eggs to scramble one at a time."

I gave out Petitions to friends, family, acquaintances and even enemies who I hoped would get over it. I hit all the crowds I could find, armed with several clipboards and dangling ballpoint pens tied on with hemp twine.

The bars were a favorite target, especially later in the evening. While I don't drink, I was/am interested in getting the young vote educated and involved. I also hit lines outside of movie theaters, outdoor concerts, art fairs and any other bunch of three or more people which I, as an inveterate politician, call a crowd.

The response was quite gratifying. Lots of everyday folks were disturbed with what was going on in both Frankfort and Washington and they shared my view that neither of the two major Parties could offer a solution since they were the problem.

From a tactical standpoint, we figured it made good sense to submit an excess of signatures so we set our goal for 7,000. This would discourage any challenges to our qualifications and show strong support for our effort.

Continuing our tactical approach, I went to see Willie again. I found him in Atlanta on April 20 and laid out our plans to him. Frankly, I was more than a little nervous. Willie had treated me like a younger brother up to now and had gone way out of his way for me twice. I thought that I might be going to the well once too often. But, I reasoned, if I was going to go all out to win this thing and actually bring relief to the sick and dying, I had to play every card.

Willie considered my proposal, then cast those famous eyes on me and that famous face broke into that famous, infectious smile and he said, "OK." Man, what a guy!

Then I asked him how much he thought we should charge for this one and he laughed again. "Gatewood, let's do this one for free." And we did. We set the date for early September and I reserved the Red Mile Harness Track for the show.

❖ *Me & Kathy and the Reform Party*

Meanwhile, the Democrats and the Republicans held their May Primaries and there were no surprises. The incumbent, Democrat Paul Patton, was unopposed and the Republicans, conceding defeat already, chose an unknown lady from south central Kentucky, Ms. Peppy Martin, to carry their banner. It was a low point for the Republican Party and illustrated the inherent weakness in allowing one person to serve two consecutive 4-year terms.

By early June we had about 6,000 signatures on the Petitions. I was fairly satisfied but did not know how much of a challenge either of the Parties would mount to their authenticity. We would need another 1500 for me to feel safe.

One day I got a call from Jerry. He had spoken to one of the leaders of the Reform Party of Kentucky who had expressed an interest in the possibility that Kathy and I run for Governor/Lt. Governor under their banner.

Because their founder Ross Perot had run for President in 1996 and had received more than 6% of the vote in Kentucky, their Party automatically qualified for "ballot access" in elections within the Commonwealth. That meant that we didn't need the signatures and couldn't be challenged on our qualifications if we took their nomination.

Kathy and I were intrigued. We examined the National Reform Party Platform and found ourselves in basic agreement with its principles. It was America First and sought to protect American jobs and families. I did not particularly like Mr. Perot and thought he was pretty "far-out" with some of his domestic issues. But the fact remained that he was willing to put his money where his mouth was and offer We, the People, an alternative to the thoroughly compromised U.S Congress and two major Parties.

Mr. Perot and his Party opposed the sell-out of Americans by the passage of G.A.T.T. by the largest lame-duck Congress in history in 1994. By that Treaty, America no longer stood for Human Rights on the international scene. By that Treaty, America forsook the workers of the world and threw our own young citizens open to competition with workers half way around the world who will work all day for a bowl of rice and a mat to sleep on. The only ones in favor to this arrangement were the large corporations who wanted access to semi-slave labor around the world so that they didn't have to pay American workers a living wage with even modest benefits. And, of course, they own Congress so they were the only ones who had to want it. Nobody else counts.

Mr. Perot ran twice for President, in 1992 and 1996, receiving 19% and 8% respectively. After his family was threatened by the hoodlums whose monopoly on power he challenged, he declined to offer himself as a candidate again but the Party sought to survive by seeking other candidates. Kathy and I were a catch for them as they were for us. It was a mutually beneficial arrangement.

Kathy and I were nominated by convention in Lexington in late June and announced publicly on July 1 in the Capitol Rotunda. The media was represented by the usual suspects asking the usual questions. There are a couple of good apples in that crowd but the correspondents for the Courier and the Herald are as much of the problem in Frankfort as the corrupt politicians. Arrogant, aloof and pushing the party line, they facilitate the cover-ups necessary to allow the special interests to thrive. And they severely limit any challenges to the way things are, by boycotting those voices that seek change.

And the need for an immediate change in the Frankfort leadership was obvious. Governor Patton had inherited a budget surplus of $350 Million dollars in his first term and had run through that like a drunken sailor, lavishing favors on his key supporters in the Legislature and his cronies throughout the state.

Road contracts, personal service contracts, state property rentals and more acted as methods of paying off those special interests that had given him all that money to run on. It had/has been going on for decades but Paul took it to new heights. In his first year as Governor, the amount of personal service contracts let by the state (where they contract out for a private service to perform state work) was approximately $200 Million. In his last year (jump ahead to 2003), that amount was over $800 Million. These were big issues to us but the media downplayed them and us every chance it got, so the public was largely unaware of the extent of the corruption.

So Kathy and I were off and running. The July 4th Parade was a grand experience and the reception from the crowd was really something. four years earlier I had led the Parade by the reviewing stand in handcuffs and under arrest. This year I was riding in a convertible and being treated like a hero by the crowd.

I have to admit, I liked the new version better.

We got the same kind of reception from the people at Fancy Farm in early August. Hot and crowded, noisy and vibrant, it's where to be if you are serious about politics and Kathy and I were quite serious. Bless her heart, she had an answer for every question they threw at her and got the better of them on their every attempt to make her look bad.

The most coverage I got during the entire race was for my response to a question by reporter Mark Hebert of a Louisville TV station. With his camera rolling, he walked up to me and asked, "Gatewood, when was the last time you smoked marijuana?"

I looked at him and replied with my own question. "Mark, when was the last time you took Viagra?"

He got a quizzical look on his face. "I don't take Viagra, Gatewood."

"Then how come you're such a big Prick all the time Mark," I responded?

Mark broke into a wide grin. "Hey, I hope I can use that one."

And it turns out he could, and did several times over. I'm convinced it got us more than a few votes in Louisville.

The event that got us the most votes however was easily the most memorable event of this campaign, the concert by Willie at the Red Mile Harness Track in Lexington in September.

When Willie had said he wanted to make it a free concert, that presented somewhat of a quandary since we didn't have the money to pay for putting it on. That problem was solved by working with the folks at the Red Mile. They could let me have the Paddock area, no charge, if they had the concessions and we could draw more than 2500 people. It was a hell of a deal.

I had $1000 to advertise with and the rest was word of mouth. On the day of the concert it was sunny and warm. In fact, the weather was perfect. Volunteers showed up out of nowhere and put up decorations and signage, hooked up computers to enroll more volunteers and to take contributions.

More than a few of the arrivals were flabbergasted to learn that they didn't even have to pay for parking. Dozens of people told me that it was a lifelong dream for them to see Willie and they couldn't believe it was free.

It all fell into place in the very last minutes before Willie took the stage. Which was great because 9000 people showed up to watch this true American hero put on a 2 and 1/2 hour show that had everyone rockin' from start to finish. His sister Bobby accompanied him and they sang every hit he ever had. By the time he was finished, both he and the crowd were worn out. It was perfect from start to finish and one of the most exciting days of my life. Lots of other people felt the same.

After that, the campaign hit full stride. Speeches here, speeches there. Kentucky's a hell of a big state when you go from one end to the other, especially twice in one day. Kathy did most of her work in far-western regions while I became a road warrior for a third time in quest of the Governor's Cup.

There's lots of time to think when you're on the road by yourself especially when an event is two hundred miles away and you go there, give a 10 minute presentation, and then drive back. Most of the time, I leave the radio off. I value the serenity, the relative quiet and the opportunity to think things through without a telephone ringing in my ear. That's quality time for a guy like me.

That method of travel changed quickly when a friend of mine hooked me up with the owner of a bus line, which catered to touring rock bands. He had a fine older bus, which had seen many miles, which he could rent to me cheap and even put a custom paint job on it for me. Hot Damn! You Bet!

I rode the bus with him the last three weeks of the campaign and we had a ball. We could pick up volunteers and workers by the dozens and the sight of that shiny big machine pulling into the town square by a Courthouse in Kentucky's rural areas was a news event in itself.

GATEWOOD FOR GOVERNOR was written on either side in 3-foot letters against a purple-violet background. The inside held couches, table and seats enough for 16 people in the front and another 12 in the back room. In between were a kitchen, a bathroom with a shower and 12 bunk beds. I'm sure that the bands who used the bus before we got it had fun in a larger variety of ways than us, but they couldn't have had more fun then we did. We were always broke but you could say we had a certain presence in the race.

Meanwhile, Patton was campaigning less than full steam; just enough to keep the campaign contributions flowing and his core group of Democrats interested in going to the polls. He was watching the numbers in the polls to make sure we didn't pull a Jesse Ventura on him. He had no worry from the Republican candidate whose own Party had fallen just short of denouncing her.

In fact, lots of folks thought that Kathy and I would receive a lot of Republican votes because it was apparent that their candidate had no chance of winning. Things looked so favorable for that prospect that both parties let it be known, statewide, that if Kathy and I even placed second in this race, we would have the minority Party's right to name appointees to dozens of Boards and Commissions throughout the state, replacing the Republican Party's right to do so. But they didn't really have to worry; not the way votes are counted in this state.

Finally, November 2 came and the polls opened. Turnout was light to moderate and Kathy and I worked all day in our respective hometowns. We got out the last of our bumper stickers and signs and then went to the Hyatt Regency in downtown Lexington to watch for the results.

The initial results, gathered from Fayette County looked promising but that was altered by the votes from the rural areas where Kathy and I had never gotten any coverage. There, the Party apparatus ground out the core vote, even in the face of a corrupt administration and obvious disregard for the condition of the working man and woman in Kentucky.

When it was all over but the shouting that night, I remember the final voting percentage as Patton 61.8%, Martin 22.9% and Galbraith/Lyons 15.3%. Denied again.

But there was some consolation. Next to Ross Perot and Jesse Ventura, Kathy and I had gotten a larger percentage of the vote than any other Reform Party candidate for any office, anywhere.

On a budget of less than $20,000, Kathy and I received 88,930 Votes. We were naturally disappointed to lose but we had no regrets. I was quite proud of Kathy and felt she did a hell of a job.

And, as it turned out, we, along with the rest of Kentucky's citizens, had been the victims of more of Paul Patton's method of winning elections, which seems to center on evading the laws that the rest of us live by.

The new election laws called for partial public financing of statewide campaigns in an attempt to curb the graft that occurs when candidates accepted contributions from people who later would look for special payoffs. These laws said that during the last 30 days of the campaign no contributions could be accepted.

Paul's own records showed that he received more than $600,000 after the deadline, so Kathy and I filed a complaint with the Registry of Election Finance which was supposed to oversee the campaign finances of each candidate. They accepted Paul's explanation that the money had been collected before the deadline, but they had just not gotten around to reporting it for that period.

And wouldn't you know it. The Registry said OK, even though his actions violated both the letter and the spirit of the law. But that had never stopped Paul before and, or course, it didn't hurt that his Party cronies controlled the Registry.

❖ *Notes on the 1999 Race*

Frankly, I needed some time to recover from this one. It was my first time in the General Election and I liked the feeling of offering my candidacy to all the voters of the state, Independent, Republican and Democrat. It was apparent however, that I would always lack the resources to fully fund a statewide race for any office. Kentucky is so large and diverse that it will always take a major amount of money to mount an effective campaign, especially for a third party and especially given the routine boycott of all third Party campaigns by the media.

And then let's get to the real meat of the matter. I do not trust the vote count given by the electronic voting machines in Kentucky's elections. Over the years I have had dozens of people say to me, "Gatewood, everybody in my family voted for you but you came out zero in our precinct. When we complained, they said 'Oh, you must have pressed the wrong button.' We didn't press the wrong button Sir."

So I've done a lot of reading on the electronic voting machines and I don't trust them as far as I can throw one. They can be programmed months in advance to produce specific results with no way of tracing an actual specific vote. There is no paper trail of a person's vote. It could end up counting for anybody. Personally, I don't trust the people who manufacture these machines.

They've given me no reason to.

The 15.3% that Kathy and I received was really phenomenal. We had no money, no organization to speak of, no way of getting to all of Kentucky and were boycotted by the media. When we were mentioned by the Herald or the Courier, it was always in a snooty or derogatory manner. Their treatment of us was illustrative of what is wrong with Kentucky and why we haven't been able to solve our chronic problems of poverty, illiteracy and poor health. Every time a possible solution presents itself, the media supports the status quo, which fights to resist anything that may upset their applecart.

And it's just not the Herald and Courier. I've seen lots of other editorials that attacked me as the messenger rather than examine whether what I say has merit or not. You would think that these writers would examine the accuracy of my information and attack that if I'm wrong but they don't. They lack the courage to take on the facts so they stand by while our elected leaders at all levels ignore science and truth while passing and enforcing laws which line their own pockets and those of their corporate owners. There's little wonder that less than 18% of the population reads newspapers.

I think it's because so few editors have any real world intelligence. Now days, most of them have come up through college, then go to work as employees for the paper. Many of them never have real jobs where they have to relate to real people. They are fitted to conform to their corporate boss's agendas and they are not promoted if they think for themselves. And the longer they stay in the position of editor, the more ignorant they become because they are afraid to even consider an alternative to their master's agenda. They simply stop thinking.

That's my view after I've seen them ignore the science and truth of marijuana as a medicine. They've called me a "deadbeat" and a "buffoon" and said I'm unworthy of consideration for anyone's vote. They say all these things about me but they never discuss the science, which shows marijuana relieving chronic pain and suffering of the people. That's why I hold the editors such as David Hawpe of the Courier, Tim Kelly of the Herald and Randy Patrick of the Jessamine Journal in such contempt. They are voluntarily ignorant impediments to getting medicine to the people who need it most. I'll see you in Hell, boys.

❖ *Update on Medical Cannabis*

After this race I truly had no plans to run for another office. I still wanted to get my message out and considered other ways of doing it. Lobbying the legislators and educating them seemed the most obvious strategy but most of them were just as recalcitrant, and cowardly, as the editors.

By this time, the scientific information on marijuana as a medicine had multiplied; proving beyond any reasonable doubt that it is the most effective medicine on earth. Because the DEA had blocked all research in the U.S. at the bidding of their masters, the pharmaceutical cartel, scientists in other countries took up the challenge. Their results made even bigger liars of our own government when they discovered that cannabis is even a better medicine than I had been telling folks for years.

Great Britain conducted two years of top-flight tests and concluded, among other things, that marijuana was a wonderful pain reliever and treatment for multiple sclerosis. They also developed a spray to be delivered under the tongue for those people who did not smoke it. They say it "transforms lives."

Canada also conducted tests and found out the truth about Cannabis as a medicine. They have since begun growing their own to distribute to their citizens.

How much more evidence do our policy-makers need?

None.

They simply haven't read the truth sitting right in front of them. They are too lazy or incompetent or they just don't care. Ain't it a shame?

❖ *Me & State Politics*

Between practicing law and compiling the more recent studies of cannabis I tried to stay busy and not despair over the status of politics in the Commonwealth.

With Paul in his second term, corruption was alive and well in Frankfort. The same good ole' boys were in line for the same payoffs but this time things were not as well funded as in the past.

Paul had blown all of the budget surplus and things had gotten a little tighter. Also, the Republicans were engineering their own uprising and managed to take over the State Senate where they elected one of their own, David Williams, to be President of the Senate. This was definitely a bone in the throat of the Democrats who saw their stranglehold on the state begin to unravel.

The Republicans had managed to take a majority in the Senate when two Democrats switched Party affiliations. You never heard such an uproar from the powers that be. They couldn't stand the prospect that Kentucky was in the process of becoming a two party state. But they needn't have worried too much.

The Republicans were/are just as corruptible as the Democrats.

The way I read it is this. The Republicans had reached their low point in the '99 Governor's race when Kathy and I had come close to knocking the entire Party off the ballot. This had scared the bejesus out of them so their top ghoul, Senator Mitch McConnell, went to work. He found a couple of Democrats who were being iced out by their own leadership and convinced them that they would be better off by switching parties. Hell, who could blame them?

I don't know what Mitch offered them to switch but it was worth it just to see the reaction of the Democrats. They were foaming at the mouth, especially when David Williams took over as President of the Senate and began treating the Democrats in the same fashion as they had treated the Republicans all those years. The Dems couldn't stand a taste of their own medicine.

(I told several Democrats that David Williams is the most arrogant, conceited and imperious piece of self-righteous fluff to occupy that chair since most of the last people who sat there, all Democrats. And I was right. There's not a nickel's worth of difference between them.)

❖ *Me & the 6th Congressional District*

The Spring of 2000 came and several things caught my attention. First was an invitation to join WVLK host, Dave "Kruiser" Krusenklaus, on his afternoon radio programs on Wednesdays of each week. We would cover the political news of the week and any other subject that came to mind. "Kruiser" is a top talent in the Lexington market and his show is top-rated, as is his station. I really enjoyed the give and take, as did the audience apparently. Over the next two years, we gained listeners at a steady clip.

The next thing that I found fascinating was the upcoming 6th District Congressional race. That seat, representing the people in 19 counties in Central Kentucky, had been used as a musical chair, for some years, by both parties. As soon as someone won it, they seemed to be drawn to run for another office.

The Republican nominee was the incumbent, "Ernie" Fletcher, who had won it in 1998. He had been preceded by "Scottie" Baesler, Democrat, in '92, '94 and '96 but "Scottie" had stepped down in '98 to run for U.S. Senate and lost.

In 2000, there was a huge push on by the Republicans to gain an advantage in the United States House, which was evenly split so they vowed to do whatever it took to hold their 6th District Kentucky seat. This included raising record amounts of money to spend and running incessant attack ads beginning earlier in the year than ever before. And the Democrats responded in kind.

The Democrats nominated Baesler in an attempt to win back what they considered to be their birthright. They also raised record amounts of money and began spending it on advertising just as mean-spirited and vicious as their Republican counterparts. As soon as the Primaries were finished, it began.

Ad after ad after ad on TV and radio. They consisted of sound bites and slogans, posturing and pontificating. After a while, it was simply ridiculous. It represented all that is wrong with American politics today.

Most of the real issues were never discussed; just a couple of hot button ones, including Social Security and Medicare. And, oh yes, another one that ended up beating the Democrats in the 6th District and nationwide, gun control.

It's hard for me to imagine why the Democrats shot themselves in the foot so badly by campaigning so hard against guns. I have no idea why they thought that was a winning issue. Bad advice, I reckon, which led to a failed strategy.

The public reaction was one of resigned disgust. Lots of folks criticized both candidates and parties for their tactics and decried the lack of discussion of many other issues. However, it was much like discussing the weather. Everybody talked about it, but nobody wanted to do anything about it.

After watching the nonsense for a while, I decided to give the voters an option to the "Republicrats", so I asked the Reform Party for their nomination for Congress. They liked the idea and gave me their nomination in late June.

Once again, I was in major race with no money but that has never been my prime concern. If it's true when people say that their vote is not for sale, then it should make no difference how much money a candidate spends; but it does.

Both the Republicans and the Democrats spent millions on that race, debasing each other, their Party and our political process in general. When I tried to interject some actual issues into the discussion, I was ignored again by both my opponents and the media. This was particularly pathetic on the part of the newspapers, because they were the biggest critics of the content and tone of the race; yet when I offered an alternative, they ignored me and the message. They have only themselves to blame for their loss of credibility with the public.

Once again I ran a person-to-person campaign, attending citizen's meetings and hitting as many groups as I could. I also began a new method of campaigning for me; standing on street corners with a big yellow sign asking people for their vote.

That's right. If the media wouldn't alert the people that I was in the race, I would educate them about it by playing in traffic.

The response was immediate and gratifying. I started out by standing at Nicholasville Road and Man o War and then moved to a different busy corner each morning and afternoon during rush hour. And right here, I want to offer my humble thanks to each and every one of you who honked and waved and flashed me a victory sign. For those few of you who flashed me another sign and sped away, I can only say, "So's your Mother."

Meanwhile, each of the other candidates tried their best to discredit their opponent and their Party. After a while, it became obvious why the voters should elect me.

"Ladies and gentlemen, I believe that both of my opponents are Honorable men and that what they are saying about each other is true, which makes them both unfit for office."

Meanwhile, there was also a Presidential election going on between a couple of men named Bush and Gore. After Clinton's eight years of duplicity, deceit and pondering over the definition of "is" and "sexual relations", a great many God-fearing, decent folk wanted the SOB out of office. So the Republicans decided it was their time and they set out to capture the Office of President.

Democrat Al Gore actually tried to distance himself from Clinton, which was a mistake, because Al didn't understand that America actually has a fond streak for con men and at least Clinton had a personality. Without a vivid persona, saddled with a self-destructive national Party platform of gun control, socialized medicine and advancing a gay agenda, Gore plodded through; hopeful the Party machine could turn out the vote. (The Democrat Party tried to help, mailing two and a half million voter registration cards to illegal aliens)

On the Republican side, George Bush, son of previous President, George Herbert Walker Bush, won the nomination over Bob Dole despite his criminal record and the crimes for which he had not been charged. (e.g. cocaine use).

(It's just a hunch, but I bet if a young black man in Houston, Texas, was found in possession of cocaine, he would have forever been barred from running for President. He would be a felon. I guess George Bush was just a lucky guy.)

So both of the major Parties had immense amounts of money to spend on both the local and national levels and the media was a willing partner in the feeding frenzy that passed for political discourse over the airways. It was an endless display of negativity and name-calling on all levels and left me with little wonder why so many eligible citizens refused to take part in the process by going to the polls. I was hoping my candidacy would invite their interest and their participation. And for quite a few of them, it did.

❖ *Me, T.J. & the Reform Party National Convention*

For the first time in my political career I actually had a campaign manager. His name was T.J. Litafik, a young Pike County man "et up" with politics since he learned how to smile and shake hands.

T.J. had managed Republican "Peppy" Martin's campaign for Governor in 1999 and had done an admirable job given lots of obstacles. He was knowledgeable, astute and tireless and it was his initiative that secured for me the most remarkable political appearance of my lifetime. I was invited to give the keynote address at the Reform Party National Convention in Long Beach.

Well, it didn't start out that way. First, T.J. contacted the leaders of the National Reform Party and reminded them that Kathy and I had received the largest voting percentage of any Reform Party candidate in the history of the Party except for Jesse Ventura and Ross Perot. That got the ear of several of the leaders but there were even more who were frightened by my stance on marijuana and there was no instant invitation to attend, much less address the crowd. But T.J. kept working on them.

Part of the problem was that there was a major split in the Party itself. Its founder, Texas billionaire H. Ross Perot, refused to run again for President so that nomination was wide-open.

Party regulars backed a man named Hagelin but coming on, from the outside, was another man seeking the Reform Party's backing, nationally known columnist and political commentator, Patrick Buchanan.

Supporters of each man were completely polarized and negotiation was out of the question. Both sides accused the other of trying to hijack and destroy the Party. The tone of the convention would be disputatious and acrimonious and both sides wanted to know where I stood before they would let me speak.

Normally, I would not submit for prior approval what I planned to say in a speech, but in this case I did. I worked for several days on my presentation and did my best to capture the possibilities presented by a viable

Third Party on the American political scene. When I faxed two of the leaders a copy, they replied that they would secure me an opportunity to address the crowd. They just weren't sure when it would be.

That was good enough for T.J. and me. We flew out to Long Beach to take our chances.

Once there, T.J. again worked on the leadership and by the time he was finished, I was timed to give the opening keynote address to the entire convention. Never underestimate an Eastern Kentucky politician.

❖ *The Speech*

On the opening day, there were several thousand people present from around the country. Most of them were not politicians, but everyday citizens trying to be a part of the solution to the political knots that the two major parties had tied the country in. They were looking for someone to make sense out of what America was becoming.

I stood behind the stage while several Party leaders made their way to the microphone and welcomed the conventioneers. When my time came, and I was introduced, the response was polite. Very few of the folks had ever heard of me and none of them knew what to expect. When I was finished, they all knew me and where I stood.

This is what I told them.

Good Evening Ladies and Gentlemen.

My name is Gatewood Galbraith and I am your Reform Party Candidate for United States Congress from the 6th District of Central Kentucky. Like almost everyone else here, I was once a member of one of the two so-called major parties. I ran twice for the Democrat's nomination for Governor of Kentucky, in 1991 and 1995, before that Party abandoned the farmers, the miners, the unions, the veterans and the working men and women of this great nation and joined with the Republicans to ignore the Constitution and to exploit the wealth and good will of the American people in the name of a New World Order and a global economy.

So in 1999 I joined the Reform Party and, as such, I am proud to offer my candidacy for Congress to the voters of Kentucky.

The issues on which I have conducted my campaign are straightforward. Both the Democrats and the Republicans have abandoned the Constitution and walked away from the principles and people who made them great in their mad rush to accept obscene amounts of money from the special interests, who seek to the purchase the birthright of present and future America. The Democrats have already been bribed to abolish Fair Trade and, in the name of Free Trade, abandon Human Rights, and open America's workers to competition with virtual slave labor around the world. At the same time, the Republicans, who engineered the Republican Revolution in 1994, were promptly compensated to forget their pledges of smaller government and less taxes.

So, in this day and age, where the Democrat and Republican Parties are no longer the voice of Main Street, but the puppets of Wall Street, it is natural that a Third Party should appear to champion the traditionally conservative proposition that the Constitution is the blueprint for the operation of the government of the United States; and that the Bill of Rights cannot be swept aside at the whim of transitory elected officials, administrators and bureaucrats in the name of protecting We, the people, from ourselves.

The Reform Party itself can survive and thrive, locally and nationally, by laying claim to those conservative principles and to that political territory abandoned by the other two parties. Our Reform Party candidate can win this Presidency by being the voice of the working men and women, the gun owners of America and 2nd Amendment proponents, the miners, the unions, the elderly, the Social Security and Medicare recipients, the military, the veterans and the taxpayers, all of whose interests are being short-changed while corporations are making record profits and our leaders spend America's tax dollars trying to play policemen to the rest of the world.

And let me take this opportunity to address the youth of this nation, in the hope that they will join us and lend energy to this effort to rediscover America and its greatness through a truly conservative philosophy of government. There is much confusion among the young about what being a conservative really means, and that suits many interests because one of the tools of the New World Order is the concept of "New Speak" where the definition of common terms becomes so altered no is really sure what they mean anymore. Over the past two decades they have misused the term conservative so much that everyone is confused about it. So my young friends, let me set the record straight. Newt Gingrich was not, and Mitch McConnell is not, a conservative. They are much closer to Aliens! Now Barry Goldwater was a conservative and he would have taken Newt and Mitch by the ear, led them behind the woodpile and thrashed them for trying to pass off this emerging police state and its bloated, increasingly private, prison system as a conservative law and order philosophy. And to the Republican Party and Governor Bush, let me say that a "compassionate conservatism" does not include jailing millions of people for victimless crimes or depriving our elders of their proper medication while giving away billions of tax dollars to corporate welfare.

Only a truly conservative candidate can insure that this is a campaign based on principles, not personalities; and I believe that those truly conservative principles include a smaller government, less taxes and a commitment to take government out of the bedrooms, bloodstreams, bladders, brains, and back-pockets of the American people and put it back in a little box where it belongs.

The core of the American Revolution, what made it such a critical event then and what makes it so critical to continue now, is that, for the first time, the benefits and results of the processes of government are to flow to the people, not some king or other privileged elite holding power! Right now, in this day and age, that proposition is being sorely tested by the huge strength and influence of the petrochemical-pharmaceutical-military-industrial-transnational-corporate elite who view the protections of the people by the Constitution and the Bill of Rights as impediments to the implementation of their New World Order and global economy, where the benefits flow not to the people, but to the corporate bottom line.

These dangers to the American way of life are obvious to a great number of Americans, so it is natural that we should organize in political opposition to their presence. Since our Third Party effort naturally attracts those disaffected from the present corruption of the Republicrats for a wide variety of reasons, we are certainly not going to be in agreement on every issue and we may be seriously apart on one or two issues. But we must not let our differences on these divide our efforts to come together, as Americans, under the great mantle of the Constitution. America itself is at stake and we must do all in our power to find our common ground within this election, to unite as defenders of the Constitution and the Bill of Rights so that indeed, this great nation, of, by and for the people, shall not perish from this earth.

God Bless You

Well, there it was. Everything I had learned in my 29-year study of this nation, its politics and its people was laid out for all to see. I had identified the problems and proposed some solutions. What else could a poor man be asked to do?

The crowd's response to the speech was fantastic. After the first three sentences everyone was on their feet and most of them remained there until after I was finished. At the end, I got a three-minute standing ovation. It was the best speech I had ever given. And the right time to give it.

However, my plea for the unification of the party went unheeded by the leaders. The floor fight and the behind-the-scenes wrangling over who would receive the Party's nomination went on full tilt. The Party itself was in deep trouble.

❖ *Me, Pat Buchanan, States Rights, Marijuana & Third Parties*

It was a three-day convention with get-togethers and parties aplenty scheduled each evening. On the first evening, after my speech, T.J. and I got invited to take a cruise on a party yacht with a hundred other people and Mr. Buchanan.

Pat Buchanan is a tough talking, inside-the-DC-beltway, Irish Catholic Conservative who was seeking the Reform Party nomination on a platform of America First. His view was that we needed to clean up the personal corruption in Washington among our leaders and to solve America's problems before we tried to build a world-wide empire against the advice of our Founding Fathers and in the face global dynamics which militated against our trying to "play policeman to the rest of the world."

Mr. Buchanan had taken a lot of heat from lots of corners for his anti-abortion stand and other conservative domestic policies. He was criticized for many things but never his intelligence or his loyalty to his principals. He is a world class researcher and wordsmith who deserved the nomination because he had outworked everyone else to get it.

I sought him out on the boat and got ten minutes of his time. I chose my words carefully and outlined to him my own views of the Reform Party and how it could achieve success.

I explained to him the platform on which I had been campaigning and how it had been received in the '99 Governor's race. Essentially I told him that the Reform Party could survive and thrive if it became the strongest Party for the gun owners and for medical marijuana under the concept of State's Rights, whereby the Federal system must keep its mitts off the laws and desires of the people as expressed in their states laws.

State's Rights are an inherent part of our division of powers and checks and balances. They are Constitutionally based and true Conservatives pay them a proper homage. They were misused during segregation, cited as the rights of the people of various states to discriminate against minorities but the concept itself is a great safeguard against

Federal fascism and it must be utilized to give the people a right to be self-determinative on a local level.

As expressed to Pat, my views were that the Democrats had insulted and frightened most of the gun owners of America and that the Republicans were compromised on the issue themselves. I thought the Reform Party could embrace the issue, support the 2nd Amendment and reap millions of votes. As a matter of fact, I had received the endorsement of the Gun Owners of America, the nation's strongest voice for our 2nd Amendment rights and I thought it boded well for the national party campaign.

Similarly, if Mr. Buchanan would support those states who had passed referendums allowing medical marijuana, citing State's rights as a basis for doing so, he would be supporting basic Constitutional checks and balances and relieving the pain and suffering of millions of Americans who might be grateful enough to give him and the Reform Party their vote.

I thought it was a hell of a suggestion but it was apparent that his advisers had warned him about the guy who supported "marijuana." He was pleasant enough but somewhat distant and apparently my words had no effect on his strategy after he won the nomination.

In fact, after he won the nomination two days later and went on to score less than 1% of the national vote in November, I had to wonder whether he had any strategy to begin with.

The outcome of my own race for Congress was demonstrably better, though still short of victory. I got 32,436 votes within the 19 county District for 12%. I had been outspent by more than 300 to 1 and outvoted 9 to 1. I had fallen short again but it was clear that our message had a lot of support.

The Reform Party never recovered from the rout of its candidate, Mr. Buchanan, losing ballot access in scores of states. But that was a minor election story to the media, given the fiasco that developed between Mr. Gore and Mr. Bush.

Allegedly, the popular vote was so close that the whole election came to hinge on the outcome of a disputed count of votes in a small area of Florida which would define who had won that state's electoral votes and therefore the Presidency. You never heard such whoopin' and hollorin' in your life, from both Parties. And in the end, the United States Supreme Court declared Mr. Bush the winner, even though he allegedly received less of the popular vote than Mr. Gore.

Mr. Gore and the Democrats had only themselves to blame. If Al had won any of the three states of Kentucky, Arkansas or Tennessee, he would not have to win Florida and he would be President. He lost all three of those states however, because of his Party's desire to disarm America. They scared the gun vote and lost the race. You will notice that, since then, the Democrats don't talk about gun control anymore. It's rightly perceived as a losing issue. And it should be.

(By the way, when people come up to me now and say, "I wasted my vote by voting for you," I reply, "So did everyone who voted for Gore." Then we all laugh.)

Even more laughable are those people saying that Independent and Third Party candidates should not run because they affect the outcome between the two major parties. They got mad at Ralph Nader because, they say, he took away votes from Al Gore, especially in Florida, and cost the Democrats the election.

Hey, let me tell you Folks the same thing that I'm sure that Ralph would tell you. None of you own my vote and none of you can expect my vote just because you are running against another jerk. I'm not voting AGAINST one jerk any longer. (That's just your way of getting me to vote FOR another jerk). No way Jose. I'm voting for people who most represent what I'm all about. It might not be Ralph, or it may be but the way I see it, there is no such thing as a "wasted" vote.

When enough votes are tabulated by a Third Party or Independent candidate, one of the major parties will incorporate his/her issues into their general platform, and the mechanism for non-military institutional change will have completed another turn.

❖ *Me, the Radio Show and Practicing Law*

So there I was again. Now 0 for 5 but just as optimistic as ever. Daily, people of all walks of life would approach and thank me for giving them an alternative, a real voice on the ballot.

And a real voice on the radio. After more than a year of Wednesdays on WVLK with "Kruiser", that station approached me about my own show. They were interested in a regular weekday gig, but I couldn't handle it because my law practice would be disrupted. We finally settled on a two-hour show on Saturday afternoons from 12 'til 2. And it first aired on April 21 of 2001. Even though it ran for a year and a half, we never did decide on a name for it. I guess there's no need to now.

It was a fun show and I did anything I wanted to. WVLK was great about artistic license and remote broadcasting. (Which means that as long as I had a telephone, I could call it in from damn near anywhere, and did.)

I broadcast from my daughter's college dorm phone on the date of her graduation from Hood College, Maryland, and from a mountaintop in West Virginia that winter when I got delayed out on the road. The pay-phone was out in the middle of nowhere, off the rural interstate, and while I was sitting in my car, motor running and the phone cord barely reaching through the window to my ear, a deer ran right in front of my car and, a minute later, two hunters came running along the same path.

But the remote I remember most was when I broadcast the show while leading a Cannabis Liberation March down the Main Street of Paducah, Kentucky. We had to run commercials when we hit those parts of town where the cellular phones would break up and the battery went dead twice on me but lots of folks tell me it was their favorite show of all.

We talked about anything and took a lot of calls about everything. My favorite topic was medical marijuana and I disseminated a hell of a lot of information about it on that show. I have never forgotten, and will never forget, that the goal I have set for myself in this life is to relieve pain and suffering by educating people about God's medical herbs. And I especially admired the irony that one of the leading sponsors of the program was JOINTRITIS Rub for arthritis relief.

I wasn't paid for these shows but I traded off my time for advertising on the station so my practice kept ticking right along. One of my cases stuck with me a little longer than the others because it illustrates just how deranged, ironic and surreal the "War on Drugs" has become.

A lady from Louisville called me. Her son had been in jail for 4 months awaiting trial on an Indictment charging two counts of Trafficking in Dilaudid (a powerful narcotic) and Persistent Felon Offender First Degree (PFO 1st). That means he had been convicted twice before for felonies. The transactions were clearly recorded on video and audio and he was looking at 10 years in the big house. Bond $75,000. Unfortunate circumstances for him all the way around.

I told her I didn't know what the heck I could possibly do but she persisted and finally I agreed to take a look at the case. I went to see her son in the Jefferson County Detention Center and he was a mess. Another addict going cold turkey in the suburbs of Hell.

His story however, fanned my own flames. Yes, he was a long-time addict and had gotten in trouble for dealing in the past. He was twice convicted, but after his second charge, he had gotten a job and cleaned up as much as he could. He was maintaining his habit with one pill a day so he didn't need to deal to afford his monkey. He was just trying to get along and stay out of trouble.

Then one day his dealer says, "I want you to sell one of these pills to a girl friend of mine." When my client protested, his dealer said, "If you don't sell this pill to this girl, I'm going to cut you off and not sell you anymore."

My client wrestled with his dilemma only a little while. The nature of addiction is that you will do anything to maintain your habit and he was no exception. So his dealer set up the transaction.

The dealer drove over to my client's apartment with his pill to sell. He then drove my client to a parking lot where his "girl friend" and two of her friends climbed into the car with them. The dealer handed my client the pill, he handed it to the girl, the girl gave him the money and my client gave it to the dealer. Done Deal.

For the next six weeks, the "girl friend" pestered my client to sell her another pill. He refused. Once again, his dealer said that if he didn't do the deal, he was getting cut off from his source. Once again my client agreed and the dealer gave him the pill to sell, only this time the dealer did not go along when my client met with the girl and her two "friends." My client then took the money back to the dealer.

Well, who woulda' thunk it? Don' t you know that the "girl friend" and her two "friends" were all cops, wired to the bone for the best hi-tech recordings of the nasty little dealings. A classic set-up from the "git go". And while I have never actually done it before, this must be as close to "shooting fish in a barrel" as you can get.

So they came and arrested him several months later and put him in the hoosegow. The Judge was not sympathetic, given that he had a two-time loser, with the latest charges "on tape", so the bond wouldn't be lowered. He was grist for the mill and grist he would remain.

We made several motions to get his bond lowered and finally the Court allowed us to post a property bond of about $75,000. At least he was out of jail to await his fate.

The next thing we did was to investigate our defenses. One thing was clear to me. This was Entrapment, pure and simple. That defense says:

1. " A person is not guilty of an offense arising out of proscribed conduct when:

(a) He was induced or encouraged to engage in that conduct by a public servant or by a person acting in cooperation with a public servant seeking to obtain evidence against him for the purpose of criminal prosecution; and

(b) At the time of the inducement or encouragement, he was not otherwise disposed to engage in such conduct.

The defense does not apply if the agent merely affords the Defendant an opportunity to commit the offense.

But it appeared to me that the defense was available to us. Hell, the Police had one of their agents, the dealer, threaten my client with the hell of drug withdrawal unless he committed a crime and then that same agent of the Police furnished the drug, the automobile and the Buyer and the money. (Along with some convenient witnesses.) What a pile of manure!

I'll tell you what happened. The cops needed some busts to justify their obese budget so they yanked the leash of one of their drug-dealing pet lizards to furnish them with a fall guy and then that lizard set up one of his customers by threatening him with the agony of withdrawal if he didn't follow instructions.

Now you might not think much of "drug addicts", but a lot of them came across their addictions accidentally, i.e. being introduced to heavy drugs because of medicine for injuries and finding them impossible to give up without help. And there is no help in many areas. So they are left to fend for themselves in a Black Market that is as much of a creation of the police as it is of the citizens.

Large and small cities alike have their network of informants and snitches, locating and finding drug dealers and users and turning them into the police so they won't get busted or do time for their own criminal behavior. Many times they are major drug dealers themselves, allowed to operate as long as they furnish others to be arrested and run through the People Processing Industry.

The People Processing Industry (PPI) is the third major component of our modern-day Gross National Product. (GNP) In the beginning, our nation's wealth was measured by its volume of manufacturing and services in a year. How many dollars were generated by the manufacturing of goods (products) and the providing of services (legal, professional, lawn mowing etc.) to the people combined?

Now, the PPI is a completely different market that is not involved in manufacturing goods or providing services to the market. The PPI is designed solely to force-process people through a system that strips them of their liberty and dignity by making criminals of them for an increasingly wide scope of basic behaviors. Processing more people has become the aim of large corporations who now control the operations of prison systems in the U.S. and the more prisoners they can fill their beds with, the more dividends they earn. No wonder these interests contribute so much to the War on Drugs. They make huge profits.

The money earned by private interests, by forcing more and more people through the penal system, is blood money, based on the pain and suffering of literally millions of citizens. They are involved in a modern version of slavery and the private prisons they own should be shut down or they should be locked up in them themselves. Now that would be an appropriate use for that space.

So, in the case of my Louisville client, the PPI was hard at work, using the police and the taxpayers money to manufacture a crime that would not otherwise have happened, so that they could justify their budget and create profits for the owners of the prison system.

I guess taking away ten years of a person's life is a small price to pay for a larger corporate dividend. Especially if he is just a "druggie."

Well, suffice it to say, I was really ticked off. This was just the kind of crap I have been fighting against all of these years. I asserted the entrapment defense and demanded a trial by jury.

Then I demanded that the Commonwealth produce the dealer who had set my client up. They refused saying they didn't know where he was. "Didn't know where he was?!!!!!" A major drug dealer, the pet lizard snitch of several officers and they didn't know where he was. I was getting madder by the minute.

So they couldn't get him to trial, huh?

My client went to work and found out that the dealer was now living in New Albany, Indiana, across the river from Louisville. I fixed up a subpoena directing him to attend the trial and then my client called him and told him he wanted to buy another pill, so the dealer came back into Kentucky and my client served him with the subpoena.

That was a sweet moment and finally gave us some leverage, a commodity in which we were solely lacking up to this point.

Came the day of trial and the dealer did not show up. The record reflected that we had served him and we asserted that he was a "material" witness, which meant he had direct knowledge of, and indeed was present at, one of the transactions for which my client was charged. We had the Constitutional Right to demand his attendance at the trial. No material witness, no trial.

The Asst. Commonwealth Attorney and the police were fit to be tied. They had all this video and audiotape of which they were so proud and they couldn't get it off the ground. They asked for and got a continuance.

Then they filed a Motion to dismiss the first charge, where the dealer was present and they only wanted to try my client on the second charge, where the dealer wasn't a witness. But I argued that the dealer was necessary to give information on how the police were first introduced to my client and what he had said about cutting him off from his own pill if he did not sell to the girl.

The Judge agreed that the dealer was a material witness and we had three different trial dates over the next year that came and went because the police would not produce the dealer.

Then the Commonwealth made us an offer, which we could hardly refuse. If my client would enter a plea to an amended charge of Criminal Facilitation, they would dismiss the PFO 1st and recommend probation.

Hell Yes! You Bet!

They did and we did and my client walked out of the Courtroom, battered and bruised but Free! And with a mighty happy Momma.

But this whole scene was squalid, immoral and classically un-American. This citizen, whatever his human condition, was set up by the police and their drug- dealing agent. Ten years of his freedom was on the verge of being squandered in the name of making the police look good and like they were actually doing something about the illicit drug market in their city. They are doing something about it all right. I estimate they are responsible for at least half the drugs on the street, letting their CIs (Confidential Informants) operate freely while their "chumps" get fed into the PPI. Like shooting fish in a barrel.

My client in this case needed treatment, not prison. Or a prescription for the drug to which he was addicted. He shouldn't be relegated to dealing with the Black Market for his "fix." And everybody looks at this problem and says that can't be the solution, to feed an addict's habit indefinitely. And everyone knows that these people can't kick their the addiction without extensive in-patient treatment at a terrific cost in professional therapy.

There is, however, an alternative; a natural medicine obtained from the bark of a tree growing in South Africa called the Iboga tree. For many "addicts", hooked on heroin, cocaine, crack, painkilling pills, oxycontin, methamphetamine and other addictive substances, a one-time treatment with this natural substance will eliminate their physical craving for their drug. It literally cleanses and "resets" the body's receptor cells, so that they have no memory of craving the drug.

This doesn't mean they will never use again. Most of these addictions are the result of about 80% physical craving and 20% lifestyle and who you hang around with. If you hang around other users, you are quite likely to begin again because you have never gotten rid of the user mindset. Ibogaine cannot make you change your living habits. It will, however, eliminate your body's physical cravings.

This is huge. No other substance is known to have this effect. It should be a terrific tool for treating addicts and offers a wonderful alternative to jailing the addicts. It should also be a hell of a lot cheaper.

So let's see. It's cheaper, it's effective and it's natural. No wonder it's illegal in three countries with the United States being one of them. There's just too much money in jailing our citizens instead of curing them. Sound familiar?

So if you have a family member who needs help with an addiction, for goodness sake, get on the internet and look up Ibogaine. Or try ibeginagain.org. Or call cures-not-wars at (212) 677-7180. It can turn your life around.

❖ *Me & Marc Emery*

So the summer of 2001 came and went and I was already feeling antsy, that I wasn't doing enough to deliver cannabis as a medicine to the people. I was speaking to a group occasionally, but after the thrills and chills of electioneering, I felt like I was operating on about four of my eight cylinders. I can see why old politicians and actors have a tough time hanging it up toward the end. You get addicted to the attention, the applause, the focus of so many people who are looking at you. It's like their eyes are sending tiny rays of attention at you and when there are thousands of them feeding into you at one time, you can actually feel its impact on your own body. It's like a "rush" and your body starts to crave it after a while. Oops, I'd better hush up. The FDA will try to regulate it if they get wind of its physiological implications.

During this time, I became aware of a vast change afoot in the political climate in Canada regarding cannabis. I had heard they might be considering a change in the cannabis laws and then I read a Time Magazine article regarding an exceptional individual named Marc Emery who was leading the movement out of Vancouver, British Columbia (Canada's Pacific coast).

Matching my friend Dennis Peron in courage and action, Marc was encouraging Canadians to grow cannabis for medical purposes and to supply the patients in the U.S. with the finest medicine available. According to Time, who dubbed Marc the "Prince of Pot", there were between 20,000 and 25,000 indoor growing operations in British Columbia alone and their monetary impact was already bigger than any other industry in the Province, including mining and lumber. No doubt, Marc was revered in many quarters and hated in others.

Several lower Canadian Courts had agreed with Marc and his supporters that the use of cannabis was outside of the power of Parliament to criminalize. This caused the Drug Nazis in the U.S. to go ballistic. The U.S. government, especially the DEA, heavily criticized the Canadian decisions and expressly threatened to slow commerce between the countries at the borders if Canada didn't treat cannabis as a criminal matter.

Simultaneously, the U.S. did put trade embargoes on certain Canadian goods, most notably beef, and refused to let Canadian businesses have any part in "rebuilding" Iraq after the war. (Canada need not have worried about that. It all went to Dick Cheney and Haliburton anyway.) Ostensibly this was done for other reasons but the main thrust was to keep Canada from legalizing cannabis.

With this background in mind, I had to go to Canada and meet this man who talked his talk and walked his walk.

I had never been to Vancouver before though I had tried to cross the border when I was hitch hiking across the country in '68 and was refused entry. This time I flew in with my friend, Mark Perkins, and we were treated like the rest of the tourists.

Vancouver is a bustling seaport, resting in a harbor protected by Vancouver Island, which intercepts most of the storms flying in off the North Pacific Ocean. Like most other harbor ports, it has a varied cross-section of population and cultural influences, including Chinese and Asian.

We arrived late in the evening and met with Marc the next morning. Marc knew of my background and activism and greeted my friend and me warmly. We spent most of that day together and Marc showed us around.

We visited some indoor growing operations (climate doesn't matter when you grow indoors) and some outdoor ones and were impressed with everything we saw. The reason for this was that they had used some of the best seeds in the world originally procured from Amsterdam and later harvested from seed crops in Vancouver.

Marc had started selling these improved seeds worldwide from his Vancouver location and at present is the largest seed dealer in the world. He advertises everywhere. This has its drawbacks in that he is viewed as an international drug trafficker by the DEA and Interpol. If he leaves the country, he will be arrested and put in prison for a very long time. So he stays in Canada.

In keeping with his views, Marc also started a string of "head" shops where Canadians can buy rolling paper, pipes and other "paraphernalia" useful in smoking cannabis, plus coffee, books and clothes.

For the longest time, the Canadian police took pleasure in raiding these shops, seizing the merchandise and trying to charge Marc, but he is one tough cookie.

After fighting them in Court after Court, Marc decided to get to brass knuckle politics so he changed his company to a political party, the British Columbia Marijuana Party and changed his shops into individual political headquarters. They ran candidates in the 37 "shires" (political jurisdictions) and got an average of 7.5% of the vote their first time out. That's a pretty good showing from someone who knows. And I love their slogan. "Overgrow the Government!"

This man, Marc Emery, is a true activist and patriot (of the Canadian variety), which is pretty damn good and he is no quitter.

He began an Internet television station POT-TV.com and a slick and informative international magazine called "Cannabis Culture." Like Jack Herer and Dennis Peron, he fits Einstein's definition of genius, "One percent inspiration and ninety-nine percent perspiration."

Marc is one of those people who, when he finds the truth, feels compelled to put it into action, especially if it will help other people. He did so with cannabis. Then, two years ago, he found out about Iboga.

Immediately Marc educated himself through the Internet and speaking to those in the know. Then he went to work exploring Ibogaine's therapeutic impact on drug addiction by witnessing patients as they went through the treatment process. His observations were based on 22 people going through 35 treatments (some folks needed a second treatment.) His conclusion: that this is a viable treatment for those who really want to kick their habit. And it is a definite alternative to wasting billions of dollars on a "War on Drugs" where the only goal is putting drug addicts in prisons that cost many more billions to construct and operate.

So Marc Emery is definitely a genuine hero to me, putting his own safety and freedom on the line for those who have little or no voice. When we left Vancouver to come back home, I told him that I would help him in any way possible. That offer is still open, Marc.

BTW, more recently, Canada seemingly has caved in to pressure from the U.S., and its highest Court ruled that Parliament can criminalize cannabis. Shortly thereafter, Marc Emery was arrested for smoking cannabis in public with a group of students in one of Canada's more remote areas. The local authorities tried to hold him without bond and he spent at least one night in jail. While there, he penned this letter to his supporters. I'll let his own words speak for him:

Thu Mar 25 2004 04:42 PM

We Shall Be Released

I am released from jail after 72 hours in Saskatoon lock-up and remand centre.

I used the term 'We Shall be Released' in spirit of the folk gospel song because this is a harsh place, Saskatchewan, in the grip of an evil tyranny by the government and policing forces in all Saskatchewan, and there are many victims here, I am merely the most known of many victims of vicious marijuana prohibition.

It is a shame and disgrace that Saskatchewan is part of Canada, a condemnation of Canada, the province of Saskatchewan and the city of Saskatoon. The police in this province are implicated in many police scandals involving death, framing accused persons, concocting evidence, in addition to extremely punitive sentencing.

I was released on an outrageously high bail of $3,500! I am officially accused of passing two lit joints, thus I am charged with trafficking, which carries a 7-year maximum. The crown is seeking SIX MONTHS INCARCERATION on this charge, of passing two joints! I had in my possession 2.3 grams of pot.

In addition to $3,500 bail (in cash!), I cannot POSSESS MARIJUANA or HAND OUT MARIJUANA until my VERDICT, up to 3 or 4 months away! Wow! In addition, I MUST SUBMIT to any WARRANTLESS SEARCH OF MY PERSON, MY HOME!, MY CAR, at any time by any police officer. If I break these conditions, I will be remanded in custody until trial in Saskatoon. Wow!

Further, the crown here wanted a curfew, restrictions on my ability to travel and lecture and participate in the federal election. The crown also asked that I not be in any building where marijuana smoking may be going on. These conditions were rejected by the court.

In jail and remand, I could not eat any food as it was all garbage and contained meat, which I cannot and will not eat, so I lost weight (although I look much trimmer), though, strangely, I was never hungry. My ankles are bruised an ugly blue from leg irons being put on them several times during the ordeal. I was conveyed back & forth each day in a stuffed, very claustrophobic and nerve wracking police van, crammed full with 12-14 prisoners.

There are many violent offenders, drug addicts and addicts to alcohol in the Saskatoon Remand Centre. I was always treated well by all other inmates, and the police or guards did not discriminate against me (any different from the systemic abuse all prisoners endure), but three days, $3,500 bail, searches on my home, person, car for the next 3 months (without warning), prohibition of any contact with marijuana, going 3 days without food, ALL FOR LIGHTING AND PASSING TWO JOINTS!

Ironically, a fan, Justin McGowan, sunk me when he testified to police, in admiration of me, that I passed out two joints, which brought about the trafficking charge and the avalanche of bad news. Even then, it is shocking and outrageous.

But then, that's why I headed this thread WE SHALL BE RELEASED because the suffering of the cannabis culture here is great, and remedy is desperately needed, and I shall be here often to rally the marijuana community in this forsaken province. I am full of sorrow for the people here. They suffer a reign of evil by Bible thumping prohibitionists and corrupt police and sadistic prosecutors. I am merely a victim of their obscenities but unlike those here, I garner attention, unlike so many others here who languish in obscurity, and no one hears their crying or pain.

Thank you to all who called the detention centers and jail, but the sad truth is, the system here is cruel and punishments meted out cavalierly to those that these laws are surely designed to punish.

I read the Bible here intensely, not for redemption, but because I know now the Bible condemns all this unChristian behavior. These people are Philistines who mis-use the Bible as their bedrock to inflict pain and punishment on the vulnerable, the poor, the young, the drug addicted, and other marginalized persons. There are many natives in jail. All the natives I spoke to who were drug addicted or alcohol addicted had no father growing up, though they never said this information in any sentiment or cloying way. They were always surprised when I asked each one about their childhood, but I have learned from my patients at Iboga Therapy House that all drug addicts suffer awful and permanently scarring childhood trauma in their delicate youth, and they spend all their life struggling with this. The system metes out punishment in a most bitter, anonymous way, to individuals (though they are hardly regarded an individual persons) who are never even responsible for the conditions of their psyche they now endure.

They are not all good people, but surely they will only get worse, and more desperate, warehoused and disrespected like this. It is a depressing situation. A few inmates were very happy to know 'a famous person' and confided many things to me, and their brief trust made me feel blessed, that I have love of friends, family, others, and can take comfort in that while many here languish in despair that I know will be difficult for them to escape and survive.

I am going out to eat with Cheryl, who was great throughout this ordeal, though I am sad now again to think of those people back in detention.

I am to come back to Saskatoon next week on Wednesday for my 'set trial date', and I want to hold a rally at the court house, as I will do every time I have to come back here. I will redouble my efforts to motivate activists here and across Canada, as I have seen the enemy, and it is everywhere in Canada, more so worse here in Saskatchewan. There will be no retreats nor lack of will, there is only honour and greater glory in doing what must be done to correct this awful situation.

I was delighted to find I enjoyed reading the Bible and studying it, and I am keen to read all of it and read Chris Bennett's work, 'Sex, Drugs, Violence & The Bible' and learn more.

I will comment more later, but do not relent in your activism. I am released, but like you, and all others in the cannabis culture, here in Canada, the USA and the world, I am not free. We are stripped of our birthright, to freely enjoy God's intended gifts, and an abomination is loose amongst us, driving many of us to despair, so we have this mission before us that will never end.

Thanks for all your thoughts, words, actions on my behalf. I am, as always in these times when I have been arrested (twenty arrests, 14 jailings, 5 raids now for cannabis), grateful and secure in the knowledge that people love and care for me, and I am humbled by your tribute to me. I remain unbowed, vigorous to the cause, of which I will always put forth my best efforts on our behalf, and I am enriched by this experience.

WE SHALL BE RELEASED.

God Bless You Marc Emery. May you slay many fascist Philistines with the jawbone of the creature of truth. I hold you in the highest regard, as do millions of others on both sides of the border. Stay safe.

❖ *Me & State Politics - 2002*

2001 was a relatively quiet year for me and there was little to indicate that 2002 would be any different although it did start off with a major embarrassment for every Kentuckian. It seems that the Republicans had taken over the majority in the State Senate and were finally beginning to give as good as they got for all those years when the Democrats dominated everything. Well, what they got was a complete stalemate in the Legislature when it met in its full session in early '02.

When the Legislature meets in a full session every two years, their only mandated official duty is to pass a Bi-Annual Budget, a two year plan for the operation of the Commonwealth's business. Early on, the 2002 Legislature got to name calling, and finger pointing, by each Party and their "leaders" (sic). And the main sticking point was that the Republicans accused the Democrats of feathering their own re-election nests by continuing to fund state election candidates with public dollars.

Originally designed to remove special interest contributions from dominating state elections and the politics that followed, "Campaign Financing" was a heated topic and one that the Republicans chose well to use on the Democrats.

With Kentucky in a constant revenue crisis, the majority of citizens could only consider as indefensible, the use of their dollars to fund a politician's campaign.

The Republicans insisted that the '02 Budget not include such campaign financing and the Democrats argued that it should be funded. In the public arena, the Republicans beat them to death with it.

The upshot of all this Party maneuvering was that Kentucky failed to pass a Budget to fund the state's operations.

Talk about embarrassment.

We had the only state Legislature that was unable to do its only job, which was to pass a Budget. They went through the full 60-day legislative session and couldn't agree.

Other states faced the same budget crisis and met it by negotiation and compromise, facing the tough questions of raising taxes and cutting services. Every one of them passed a budget. Kentucky couldn't get past its institutional corruption and get the job done.

Governor Paul Patton enacted his own spending program to fund basic services and everyone, including you legislators, wondered aloud if this was legal. Of course it isn't, you screwballs, but that's never stopped you before.

The fact is that your incompetence in 2002 set a precedent for ignoring the express mandates of our very own State Constitution to feed your own political faces. It also set a precedent for future Legislatures to duck their responsibilities.

The solution to this is simple. The Governor should call the Legislators into a "Special Session", without pay, and make them stay in Frankfort until they pass a Budget. If they can't accomplish the only job they were elected to do, they sure as hell don't deserve to be paid. (Jerry told me that the reason they passed laws making government more expensive when it was shut down, was to keep the people from shutting it down forever.)

❖ *Me & Local Politics*

I knew there was a Mayor's race coming up in Lexington, in May, and I discussed it occasionally on my radio show. The apparent lineup of candidates included an alleged "conservative", Scott Crosbie, and two alleged "liberals", past Vice Mayor Teresa Isaac and local businessman Jim Gray. And while the office of Lexington Mayor is officially and historically a non-partisan office, both major parties got involved in this one in a big way.

Crosbie had started out his career as a Democrat and got elected to the City Council as an at-large Council member. He then switched his registration to Republican and got a quasi-endorsement for Mayor from the Republican Party chief ghoul, Mitch McConnell, plus a hell of a lot of money to run.

The Democrats countered with Jim Gray, a political neophyte, whose family owned a successful construction firm with its headquarters in downtown Lexington. He had money of his own but the Democrats helped him out plenty.

The dark horse of the field was Teresa Isaac, a divorced mother of three who had held the Vice-mayor position from 1993 until 1999. She was the most non-partisan of all and received no money from any Party. Her support was strictly from among the people and she deserved it because of her one-on-one work with individuals and neighborhood associations. She had little or no money.

According to the polls in early 2002, Gray was a narrow leader over Crosbie with Isaac trailing, but within sight of the guys.

Since my radio show was a perfect vehicle for stirring up rumors and speculation, I did my best to brew up an interesting mix.

Naturally, I considered running myself. I had done very well in Fayette County in my Congressional race and had received a lot of encouragement from my friends, so I made public the fact that I was considering a run and made an appearance or two. "And the crowd went wild."

I believed that there were two main issues in this race. The first was that the office was in danger of becoming hostage to partisan politics which spells disaster for the policy of even-handed delivery of municipal services to the City of Lexington and Fayette County. I pushed that issue every chance I got and it was being discussed in other forums so I felt like my brief public presence had some effect.

The second issue was far more apparent to the voters and probably their main concern. The Kentucky American Water Company, serving Fayette and surrounding counties, was being sold to a foreign conglomerate called RWE, headquartered in Germany. Its ownership is a well-kept secret. Allegedly, 35% of the company is owned by a consortium of German Mayors but the ownership of the other 65% is lost in a blur of interlocking international corporations whose ownership is a complete mystery. The "Kentucky" "American" Water Company was in grave danger of becoming neither, so various forces emerged to oppose the proposed sale and to urge that the city itself purchase the company.

The lines on this issue were drawn early. I was, and am, in favor of the city purchasing the company by eminent domain. This is the power of the state to take private property for public use with payment of compensation to the owner and the city's purchase of the Water Company certainly fits that description. The company is a basic public utility, occupying a monopoly position in the delivery of water to everyone in Fayette and several surrounding counties. Its rates are regulated by the Public Service Commission (PSC) and it is guaranteed at least a 9% return on it's money.

Ostensibly, the PSC would continue to look after the consumer's interest after the sale to RWE. After all, it originally approved of the sale over the objections of the public. However, I believe that the Commission acted without the knowledge about, or in consideration of, the changes in its jurisdiction and authority enacted by the international treaty known as GATT (The General Agreement on Trade and Tariffs.)

This treaty effectively subjects local economies to international control through enforcement by the World Trade Organization (WTO) which has the power to forestall local development if it affects the profit margins of an international corporation. (Yes Virginia, there is a beast of globalism running amuck and it is set to gobble us all up). Add this to the fact that Kentucky voters approved a (probably illegal) referendum in 2002, which stripped Kentucky's Constitution of a provision which subjected local businesses, owned by foreign entities, to local control, and you have the

WTO setting and enforcing local rate hikes for our water. I'll be damned if I will let that happen.

Teresa was also and always in favor of local ownership. After all, 95% of cities the size of Lexington own their own water systems so it seems to make sense everywhere else. Why not here?

Gray was non-committal on the issue during the campaign. It was maybe this and maybe that.

Scott Crosbie, on the other hand, was widely perceived as supporting the sale to RWE and its backers were his backers. The money flowed freely and the race was on. The guys ran ads, one after the other, day after day. To their credit, each of the three candidates faced each other in numerous "debates", so the public got a good view of them.

The top two finishers in the May Primary faced off in the November election. The betting money was on Gray to edge Crosbie with Teresa being an also-ran. The polls indicated this near the election by showing Gray with 31%, Crosbie at 30%, Teresa with 26% and 14% undecided.

I decided not to run however for a couple of reasons. The first was that Teresa was doing a great job of representing local control of water as a main issue.

The second reason I chose not to run was that I came to believe I could accomplish some of my agenda without having to actually win the office. If one of the candidates would promise me to closely examine my issue of stopping arrests for misdemeanor marijuana possession in Fayette County, I would withdraw my candidacy and support that person.

I went to Jim Gray first. I explained my position to him. I wanted the Lexington Fayette Urban County Government (LFUCG) to stop arrests for minor cannabis possessions and just give them a ticket. Make them appear in Court and pay a fine, yes, but don't take trained police officers off the street and waste their time booking in marijuana smokers. It's terribly inefficient and a hindrance to effective law enforcement.

This approach has proven to be a winner in other college towns, including Ann Arbor, Michigan, home of the University of Michigan, where a ticket and a $5 fine was assessed for possession. I think the amount has risen recently but the principle is the same. Efficient law enforcement.

Jim looked at me askance. "Gatewood," he said sincerely, "my people won't let me do that." And I knew he was being honest with me. The Democrats were calling the shots with him and they would never agree to it. Nor would the Republicans who backed Crosbie. Indeed, only a non-partisan could make a deal like this without having to clear it with a bunch of Party hacks. I went to see Teresa.

I explained my position to her and she expressed a legitimate interest in the idea. The first thing she asked me was if it was being done in other cities. I described its success in other locales and she said she would give it full consideration if she won the office.

That was good enough for me. In and of itself, it wasn't enough, but in conjunction with our agreement about the water company issue, I had a candidate I could relate to. I told her I would give her my full support.

The other big reason I decided not to run was that I would have to give up my radio show. I had gotten pretty used to it and it seems a few listeners had too. Besides, it would be more fun giving "them" hell than having to put up with them while actually holding office.

So I started working the crowd on Teresa's behalf. My stock line in the matter was this: "When you talk with Teresa, you will be talking with the Mayor.

She won't have to run across the street and ask a group of businessmen in a corporate boardroom what the position of the Mayor is on the matter. She is her own person, un-beholden to the Party machines." The people seemed to like that.

By the time the Primary date rolled around, everybody was glad to see it end. The airwaves had been dominated by the campaigns and my show was no exception. On the last Saturday before the Tuesday event, I laid it on the line and gave Teresa my unqualified support and asked my friends and listeners to please do the same.

And, can you imagine? When the smoke had cleared and the last vote was counted, Teresa led the field with 34%, Scott had 33% and Gray came in third with just less than 33%. We had pulled a major upset and proved that local control of the Water Company was a winning issue.

❖ *Me and the Militia Again*

While that race was going on, another important issue was beginning to boil. My friend Charlie Puckett, one of the leaders of the Kentucky State Militia, was being charged, by the Federal Bureau of Alcohol, Tobacco and Firearms (BATF), with being a Felon in Possession of Firearms

A mechanic by trade, (and a damned good one if you believe his customers), Charlie was energetically involved in the militia "movement", attending meetings statewide and standing strong for "America First." He was a ready spokesperson for the militia and appeared on talk shows around the world. He was a strong voice on behalf of the Second Amendment.

Several years earlier, Charlie had called me and asked my legal opinion about his ability to own a firearm. It seems Charlie had been convicted of a criminal offense in West Virginia when he was 19, but he wasn't sure if it was a felony or not. Kentucky had just passed a Carry Concealed Weapon Permit System, which allowed permittees to carry a deadly weapon concealed on or about their person. Statistically, violent crimes go down in every jurisdiction where this is allowed. (Criminals are afraid to try victimizing people they think may be armed.)

Charlie wanted to know if he could get a permit. He explained that he would have to take training from a certified instructor and, under state law, get clearance from the FBI. I told him that, if he was a felon, he wasn't supposed to own a weapon. But if the FBI, after a mandatory background check, cleared him for a permit, it must be all right.

Charlie took his training, applied for his permit and the Commonwealth issued it. He owned several firearms thereafter, always believing he was in compliance with the law.

In November of 2001, Charlie, whose stand for the Militia had obviously attracted attention, was approached by officers with the BATF and asked if he owned a firearm. Charlie readily admitted to it and cited his state permit as permission to do so. The BATF agent did nothing at the time.

In February of '02, thirty heavily-armed federal agents converged on Charlie, with weapons drawn, as he and a companion came out of a motel in a heavily- populated commercial district in Lexington. They later said they wanted to catch him "off-guard" and in no position to resist.

That was ludicrous. All they had to do was give Charlie or me a call and we would have arranged to meet them anywhere. As it was, if they thought he might resist, why had they chosen a heavily populated area to approach him?

The Federal system allows their prosecutors to move that certain people be held without the benefit of bond if they represent a danger to others or are likely to commit further crimes or to flee. They asked for a hearing to argue that Charlie should remain in jail without bond.

The Militia and its members had been taking broadsides from the media, especially the newspapers and their editors, for several years. The word itself was being misused to describe anyone with anti-government inclinations and a healthy respect for gun ownership. The media had great success in subjecting the concept of what the militia actually is to New Speak; vilifying what should be honored, obfuscating what should be taught in every school as true history.

This was most apparent when the word Militia was being used during the hearing on Charlie Puckett's bond. The Federal Government put on ATB agent Mr. Rob Young as their only witness, to testify that Charlie constituted such a threat that he should be held without bond while he was being prosecuted. He cited Charlie's status as a Commander in the Kentucky State Militia, the fact that he associated with known Militia members, the content of communications of other Militia members, the content of other Militia web sites and statements from Charlie himself indicating that he believed that, if the government had ceased representing the people, it should be replaced.

Agent Young's testimony went on for 45 minutes or so. By the end of it, he had painted a dire picture of the Militia and all of its members. He had nothing good to say about them.

Then it got to be my turn.

"Agent Young," I began, " do you mean to tell me and the Court that you consider the Militia to be a direct threat to our very system of Government?"

"Yes I do," he replied.

"Do you believe that they are operating under a delusion and cannot be trusted to have the best interests of this country at heart?" He agreed.

"Is it your belief that the word of an individual member of the Militia cannot be trusted because of their status as a Militia member." He agreed again.

"Would you be suspect of the word of a Militia member, even if it was under oath, because of these delusions?" He nodded again in agreement.

"Then I guess, Agent Young, that we cannot believe a word you have said here today, eh?" He acted like he hadn't heard me correctly.

"What do you mean?" he asked in disbelief.

"I mean that you are a member of the Militia and because of that we cannot believe a word you've said here today."

He looked at me like I had started speaking in tongues.

"I am not a member of the Militia," his voice took on a stern note.

I got a little stern myself. "Oh yes you are, Sir. Mr. Marshall, would you please hand this paper to the witness?" I gave one copy to the prosecutor and handed the other to the Marshall, who took it to Agent Young in the witness box.

"Now Agent Young, I want you to identify to the Court what you hold in your hand and then I want you to read it aloud to everyone."

Agent Young looked in disbelief at what he held. "Do I have to," he inquired of the Judge Magistrate?

The Magistrate looked at me. "What is it," he inquired?

"It's the copy of a Federal Statute, Your Honor. I should think it would be allowable."

He nodded toward the witness. "Go ahead," he directed.

Agent Young had a hard time getting started but it was a short statute and eventually he got through it. This is what he read:

10 USCS [Armed Forces]
"311. MILITIA: COMPOSITION AND CLASSES

(a) The militia of the United States consists of all able-bodied males at least 17 years of age and, except as provided in section 313 of title 32, under 45 years of age [which deals with membership in the National Guard] who are, or who have made a declaration of intention to become, citizens of the United States and of female citizens of the United States who are members of the National Guard.

(b) The classes of the militia are--

(1) the organized militia, which consists of the National Guard and the Naval Militia; and

(2) the unorganized militia, which consists of the members of the militia who are not members of the National Guard or the Naval Militia."

When he finished, I began again. "So Agent Young, are you an able-bodied male and a citizen of the Unite States?" I waited for him to reply. He acted a little like I had insulted him.

"Of course," he responded unhappily.

"And are you between the ages of 17 and 45?" I was really beginning to enjoy myself. Agent Young was not enjoying any of it.

"Of course," he replied.

"Then sir, you are a full-fledged member of the Militia and by your own reckoning, your word is not to be trusted." I sank the blade as deep as I could.

The agent's voice rose and he began to wave the statute around. "I don't believe this," his voice was cracking now.

"Well let me ask you this, Agent Young. Who is more delusional here? My client, who gratefully accepts the mantle of Militia member cast upon him by our very own government, or you, who, under oath and holding it in your hand, denies that a Federal statute creating the Militia actually exists?"

He was speechless, but I didn't let up. I turned and indicated the audience, which consisted of 8-10 ATF agents in full regalia. "And how do you feel, Agent Young about the Militia now that you realize that you have been running around for these past several years with a gang of heavily-armed Militia members? Your colleagues." He remained silent, but you could see him trying to rally. I didn't give him the chance.

"And now Agent Young, I would ask you to read this, section 219 of the Kentucky Constitution, that says that 'all able-bodied male residents of the state between the ages of 18 and 45' are members of the Kentucky State Militia. I didn't wait for him to read it. He didn't offer to.

"And how do you feel about it all now, Agent Young, that you know that the Judge Magistrate hearing the case here today probably fits into the description of the statute and is also a member of the Militia?"

I smiled broadly at the Judge and he smiled back. He certainly had enough grace not to deny it.

Finally I asked Agent Young. "And tell me Sir, who first said the words that when a government ceases to represent the interest of the people, it should be replaced? Thomas Jefferson or Charlie Puckett?" He didn't respond but he didn't have to. My point was made.

After I was finished with Agent Young, the Judge Magistrate had a few questions for me, especially about the number and nature of the weapons seized from Charlie's home after his arrest.

I pointed out that millions of Americans had weapons collections and some of them were bigger than others. "But Mr. Galbraith," he looked at me inquiringly, "Thirty-five thousand rounds of ammo?"

I said the first thing that came to mind. "Well Judge, you don't want to run out at the wrong time."

He considered that for a brief second. "Of course not."

Then he let Charlie out on his own recognizance.

Charlie's total legal picture was far less rosy however. The Federal Grand Jury had returned an 11 Count Indictment against him. They included 3 Counts of Felon Possessing a Firearm, 3 Counts of a Felon Possessing Ammunition, 2 Counts of Possessing Destructive Devices, 1 Count of Possession of a Device to convert a semi-automatic into a fully-automatic weapon, 1 Count of coercing a Witness and I Count of forfeiture of all items seized.

Several of these Counts were quite serious and the total time he was looking at, if convicted of them all, was over 30 years. Pretty hefty for a guy who thought he had been cleared by the law to possess firearms and that he was operating within its limits.

As Charlie and I began to go over the evidence against him and consider his defenses, I was fairly optimistic. He had a CCDW Permit from the state which, by law, was subject to a FBI clearance. And he had no intent to break the law. That would have to be a factor, don't you think? And one illegal object left on his property wasn't his. So we prepared to go to trial. And lots of people around the Commonwealth took great interest in the process.

Then, once again, I came face-to-face with the Federal system. Let me tell you something. There's a hell of a lot of Federal law out there that I haven't read. Okay, I haven't really read any of it. And that can be a problem because, if you don't know it, the prosecutors will eat you up. Those guys get paid a lot of money to sit around and read up on how to screw with defense attorneys and their plans. So I figured I ought to get some help on the technical end of it and I went to a young man whose work in the Federal Courtroom I had previously noticed.

Pat Nash had been in practice about 6 years. For two years before that he was the Law Clerk for the Chief District Judge of the Eastern District of Kentucky, Henry Wilhoit. He knew the rules and a lot of the applicable case law. Most importantly, he knew where to look to find what we needed to know. And he knew what he was talking about, which always leaves a favorable impression on me.

Pat and I got together and I immediately knew I had made the right decision. He looked at me after we had gone over what I considered to be our defenses and said, "Gatewood, I don't know that we can use any of them." I admit I blinked.

"Do you mean that his CCDW Permit, his okay by the FBI and his lack of intent to break the law can't be used as defenses at his trial?"

Pat nodded. "You generally don't need intent in the Federal system, Gatewood. Here, truly, ignorance of the law is no excuse. And besides, Charlie tells us that he doesn't have anything in writing from the FBI clearing him, only that he asked an FBI agent if he could own a gun and the agent told him it was all right."

"But we can subpoena that agent, can't we?" That seemed fair enough.

"Not unless the FBI tells us we can," he replied. "We must get clearance with their main office before any agent testifies, active or retired. And besides," he added, "did you notice that the application that Kentucky uses to get a permit doesn't ask whether you have ever been convicted of a felony?"

He handed me a copy of an application we had gotten in discovery that morning. It did not ask if the applicant had ever been convicted of a felony. I began to get a sinking feeling.

I called Charlie and asked him about it. He said that an FBI Agent friend of his told him it was all right and he gave me his name.

I called the FBI and asked for information on the procedure to get the agent to testify. I was told that the agent would not be available to testify. The sinking feeling got more pronounced.

So Pat and I filed the appropriate pre-trial motions to argue that Charlie's planned defenses were appropriate for trial and a hearing was scheduled.

We got killed.

Pat was excellent, I thought. He articulated our case law and responded to the challenges of the Judge and prosecutor but, in the end, we got killed.

The judge ruled that it was no defense to any charge that Charlie had the permission of the Commonwealth to own a firearm. The Commonwealth couldn't override the U.S.

It was no defense that Charlie thought he was obeying the law. He did not need to intend to break the law to be guilty of it.

And thirdly, he needed to show that a Federal agency had Okayed his firearm ownership, and since that Federal agent would not be available, we couldn't tell the jury about him. How do you like them apples?

Well, I didn't like them worth a damn. It put Charley in a hell of a spot. Going to trial now would be like heading down to the OK Corral with the Earp boys but no ammunition. We got to work to make a deal.

We weren't entirely without leverage. We had a shot at winning on the charge of possession of the metal piece that could change the nature of a semi-automatic into what they claimed would be a fully automatic weapon. That did include the element of intent. If he didn't know it was there, that would be proper defense. However, we could win that one and still lose Charlie a lot of time.

During these negotiations, Charlie received an anonymous note stuck on his front door that claimed that he was the target of an assassination plot. Everyone involved in this case, on all sides, was naturally nervous to begin with, but Charlie took this threat quite seriously and did what he thought best. He went underground.

Immediately he became the object of an intense manhunt that stretched over several states. Surveillance was cast on his associates and I'm sure that wiretaps were rampant. The thing about this written threat was that it could be coming from anyone, including agent provocateurs, or any of several interest groups, intent on sparking a confrontation between the Government and the Militia.

Charlie's wife presented the note to me and I gave it to the Feds. It looked legitimate enough and certainly must have seemed so to Charlie. He wasn't one to scare easily so I knew he took it seriously.

Meanwhile, there was nothing we could do but wait. Several months went by, as did our scheduled trial date, and still no Charlie. Actually, I thought the Feds were better than that.

Than one day a fellow called and said Charlie had contacted him and wanted to turn himself in. It was quickly arranged and a very nervous Probation Officer met with Charlie to accompany him to the U. S. Marshall's Office. I felt that it was probably the safest place he could be.

The negotiations to resolve the matter began in earnest again. In the end, Charlie pled guilty to a total of 3 Counts with sentencing guidelines of between 30 and 37 months. At the sentencing, he was given 30 months with credit for time already served. Part of the deal was that he would not be charged with "Bail Jumping." The source of the letter was never discovered.

As of the writing of these passages, Charlie is in a halfway house awaiting release. He plans to avoid the public eye, stay home and spend as much time as he can with his devoted wife, Devona, and return to his niche as "one hell of a mechanic."

Speaking of mechanics, no history of me would be complete without an acknowledgement of my love for my T-Bird, a silver '88 that has found its own way home more often than I care to remember. In my political quests, I've driven thousands of miles late at night, so tired I could hardly stay awake. Thank God Providence has prevailed. But there's been some wear and tear on my baby.

The body is dented in several places and there are some minor rust spots. The paint is flaking on the front underside, the dashboard is cracking and I've managed to lose all four of my hubcaps over the years, one at a time. It looks like it has been run hard and put up wet and you can bet it has.

But the great part is that I bought it from my friend Jerry Hammond in 1994 for $3500 when it had 74,000 miles on it. In the past 10 years, I have added 450,000 to 500,000 miles to that total. That's right. It's no misprint. This baby has over 550,000 miles on it and still gets 23 mpg. And no car payments! Whee!

Finally, it has one other feature now, and I can't figure out whether it's an asset or not. It has kept me from getting emotionally involved with any other woman over the past several years. When I ask if I can drive them home, they get a glimpse of my chariot and politely decline. That's alright. I understand that. However, if they say they will ride in it, then we are already too close. In a way, it's my own "emotional curb feeler", and has probably saved me another house.

❖ *Me, Ernie & Congress Again*

Though I hadn't been a candidate in any of the May primaries (where Teresa and Scott Crosbie had qualified to run against each other in November for Mayor), another result had really piqued my interest and sparked discussions on my radio show.

In the '02 6th District Congressional Primary, the Republican incumbent, Ernie Fletcher, was naturally unopposed. The real shame of the matter was that the Democrats didn't run anyone at all. Not one Democrat took to the field of political battle to argue the issues, to keep the opposition honest, to represent the people vs. the corporations.

Nope. They hid and they ruminated and commiserated and said it was just no use. They believed Ernie had this race cold and they knew he was loading up to run for Governor in 2003. They didn't want to spend any money they didn't have (Paul had broken the Party and their Bank) so they gave Ernie a free pass. I thought it was a major sign that the Democrats were on their way out as a force in Kentucky's political arena.

On July 2nd a coalition of Churches held a "Patriotic Rally" at a local minor league baseball field, home of the Lexington Legends. Well, a bad case of fundamentalism overcame several of the organizer/preachers and pretty soon, everyone but them and their followers were being damned. Not by them, because they're Christians, but by the Lord himself.

By the time that the shouts of Amen had faded away, they had consigned to Hell all liberals, homosexuals, cross-dressers, Hollywood stars, rock musicians and the United States Supreme Court.

That is a pretty impressive list, I must say. If all those people would just vote for a Democrat, they could unseat Ernie in 2002. But they hadn't even mustered a candidate. Was the Democrat Party trying to tell me something?

The news editorials following the Rally were full of shock and outrage. They were damn near overcome by such an excessive display of fundamentalism and political incorrectness. That was followed by a wave of letters to the editors expressing dismay at the growing power of the "Christian Right." And I wondered aloud on my show if they were dismayed enough to vote.

I thought hard about it for several weeks and considered the challenge. An Independent effort might actually pick up those voters who recognized the need to keep Church and State separate. And, if being condemned to Hell by the opposition didn't motivate the folks to vote against it, then maybe they deserved to get a little taste of the flames anyway.

I examined my options. The chemical mix in this race would be different than any other. I was a true Independent for the first time and the Democrats didn't have a dog in the fight. The display by Ernie and his supporters of clergy-politics had frightened a great number of people. And I didn't have anything to lose. Except my radio show. Which truly was a heartfelt loss.

To get on the ballot as an Independent for U.S. Congress, a candidate must submit the signatures of 400 registered voters from the District where they reside. Having secured 5000 signatures in 1999, I considered this a minor matter, as it turned out to be. From the time I decided to run and picked up the Petition, it took me 8 days to get about 600 signatures. It took me even less time to line up the bus for one last go-round.

I was only a little surprised by the entry into the race of another candidate, representing the Libertarian Party, Mark Gailey. He presented his 400 signatures and got on the ballot too. He pretty much stuck to his Party's dogma... no government, a return to the gold standard and abolishing the IRS. I figured he would muster only a few, die-hard, anti-government votes. I figured that right.

I had my last radio show on August 10 of 2002. It had been a real treat, lasting about 16 months and I'll always be grateful to WVLK for the opportunity.

Of course I spent the last two hours politickin' like hell. I endorsed Teresa Isaac for Mayor and the purchase of the Water Company by the Urban County Council.

I endorsed me over Ernie and asked all of the Democrats to join the effort. They had nothing to lose by it either. They had already conceded.

I turned in the signatures on August 12 and held a news conference in the Capitol Rotunda. Only a few of the news media bothered to show up. This was going to be an uphill battle all the way. And it was going to get steeper with the media every day from there on out.

Within days it was apparent that my campaign was going to be the subject of a total boycott by the newspapers and almost all of the TV news. I had developed positions on serious issues, at odds with my opponent, but when I held news conferences at the Government Center in Lexington, on those breaking issues, only one news outlet showed up and that was WVLK. They are, by far, the most complete and balanced news source in Central Kentucky. They let each side of every issue have its say on their airwaves. They might not agree, but they will let their listeners hear it. That's Class! And the American way.

And let me take this moment to pay homage to Central Kentucky's Talk Show diva, Sue Wiley. Sue has had me on her TV and radio talk shows 20 times over the years and she has gone for the jugular each and every time. And she tells me she loves me each and every time. And I believe her each and every time. I feel like a male praying mantis after each of her shows but I keep coming back for more. And I Love You too, Sue. I do.

Another serious matter was to contact a constituency and see if I could raise any money to pay for advertising. If I could pay for it, they couldn't refuse it.

The most obvious target group for money was the Kentucky Academy of Trial Attorneys, KATA, who had already been targeted by Ernie, but not for the same reasons.

One of the issues in this race concerned the ability of juries to award large sums of money to the victims of medical malpractice and intentional injury. The doctors, of whom Ernie was one, complained bitterly about the high cost of medical malpractice insurance and said it drove them from the practice of medicine. They wanted to limit the amount of damages you could collect for mental pain and suffering (say, if they cut off the wrong leg) and for punitive damages. (Say, if they did it on purpose).

It made/makes no difference to the Docs and their PR machine that the total of all the medical malpractice awards made against them for their incompetence constitutes only 1 % of their expense overhead. They were crying ruination and getting the support of the Republican Party.

As one might imagine, KATA opposes limits on the awards a jury might give for pain and suffering and for outrageous and/or intentional injury. Sure, some of them make large sums of money by securing same for their clients but it is those big punitive awards that keep big companies, such as Ford, from continuing to build death traps (read Pintos with gas tanks in the rear) even after they know it will kill dozens of people. (And you can bet Jack in the Box no longer serves poisoned hamburgers.)

So I sent the members of KATA a fundraising letter pointing out that I naturally favored their side of the issue because it represented the best chance for individual justice in any given matter. Open access to the Courts and the ability of juries to administer justice is the backbone of our Constitutional system.

The letter was great and the response was dismal. From a mailing of 700 letters, I got 8 responses and let me thank those folks right here. The rest of you'all are some mealy-mouthed so-and-sos who deserve everything the Republicans throw at you. Unfortunately, your clients are also suffering from your inaction and smug Party politics. (Hey, most of you are Democrats. Haven't you noticed you're getting killed at the polls and in the media? Maybe you ought to look outside the Dems for help. They ain't doin' squat.)

So there I stood, in a Congressional Race with no money and boycotted by the media. Then it struck me. If I was going to stand alone and gain no attention from the media, than I might as well stand in traffic. Again.

So I got a big yellow sign that read VOTE GATEWOOD FOR CONGRESS in large, black letters and went to stand on every major street intersection in the 16 County District, most of them in Lexington.

The response was immediate and extraordinary. The honks and whistles, the "Give-em-hells" and thumbs up gestures were music to my ears and candy for my eyes. Sometimes on a busy corner, I would see the drivers in 10-12 straight cars and trucks flash me the V sign or the heads-up signal. I thanked them with a wave and a grin, trying to make eye contact to show my appreciation.

I needed all the positive input I could get. It starts to get to your back and legs, after 2 or 3 hours on the concrete, holding a big plastic sign that catches every breeze. Sometimes I would have vivid flashbacks of standing along side the road when I was hitchhiking to nowhere, 35 years earlier. The irony was not lost on me but, at least this time, I had a destination in mind. The U.S. Congress.

Too, I was in better physical shape now than when I was 21 years old. I had kept up my physical regimen for several years in row but standing out there in the weather, with a sore lower back and legs feeling like lead, reminded me that I still wasn't as young as I used to be. (In fact, I had participated for several years in Lexington's July 4th 10 K race, 6.2 miles, and had tried to better my time each year, though my pace was a "Passionate

Mosey." I retired after the '02 race when I was passed midway through by a little fat girl talking on a cell phone. Talk about a wake-up call).

The biggest issue in this race that I saw was the lack of intent on Ernie's part to keep the job once he got it again. Everyone knew that Ernie was going after the Governor's office in the 2003 election, which meant he had to resign the Congressional seat if he won it. Since he was looking to leave it, and the Democrats had not run anyone for it, I told the truth. I was the only one who wanted the job!

And Ernie wasn't much of a Congressman to begin with. He took his orders from the office of Senator Mitch McConnell and I sometimes wonder if Ernie has ever had an original thought of his own. So I had this to say about him.

"I know that my opponent has been a Baptist preacher, an engineer, a pilot, a doctor and now a Congressman. That only means that he is highly trainable. But so is my Parakeet."

I had my last regularly scheduled appearance with Kruiser on WVLK on September 18, then settled in for the last 6 weeks of the Campaign.

We ripped and roared and I campaigned right up to the last hour the polls were open. We drove that big shiny bus all over hell's half-acre (which, by the way, is located in the 6th Congressional District in Central Kentucky).

I thought we might have a chance right up until the votes were all counted. Then the reality set in. The Democrats turned out to be as cowardly when they didn't have anything to lose as when they did. They had a free shot at Ernie and they stayed at home. The final count turned out to be Fletcher 71%, Galbraith 27% and Gailey 2%. I was both crushed and elated.

Naturally I was very disappointed to lose the race. As I said before, I never have gotten into a race where I didn't think I could win. Of course, I'm an optimist. As I have said before, " I had the jury in the palm of my hands right up until they returned the Guilty Verdict."

On the other hand, upon reflection and some research, I discovered that my 27% was the highest percentage that an Independent Candidate had received for a major office, in the entire USA, for at least 50 years. There have been some 3d Party winners like Socialist Party Bernie Schwartz, Representative from New Hampshire and the Reform Party's Jesse Ventura, Governor of Minnesota, but they had a Party.

I had absolutely no Party affiliation and I've never been more proud than to have received such an honor from so many Central Kentucky voters. Many of them told me afterwards that they had seen me standing on corners, at all hours and in all kinds of weather, and decided that if I wanted it that bad, I had their vote. In this age of media blitzes and incessant advertising, I believe the personal touch is greatly missed by the average voter and that they will respond to the truly personal appeal. Let me put it this way. If I had a million dollars to run on next time, you would still see me standing on the corners with a smile and a wave for everyone.

❖ *Goodbye, Jerry*

While the Campaign itself didn't hold any surprises, there was huge one that came at me right out of the blue. That was the unexpected and sudden death of my best friend and fellow warrior, Jerry Hammond.

Next to my own family, I don't think I ever held a person in more respect and admiration than Jerry. As far as my heroes go, he is right there with Willie Nelson, Jack Herer, Dennis Peron and Marc Emery. They have all laid everything they have on the line, on behalf of the people, and have done so with class and courage.

Jerry and his wife, Mary Lou, were sitting on their boat on the Ohio River when Jerry suffered a massive heart attack. He seemed to fight their efforts to revive him and that wouldn't surprise me with Jerry. He had often told me, and others, that he wanted a quick death and would not countenance a slow death, hooked up to tubes and medical machines. He got his wish and it was over quickly.

Jerry Hammond was buried on October 25 of 2002. He was 59 years old. I believe he has joined that band of guardian angels watching over me today. Say hello to Teddy for me, Jerry.

❖ The Hempsters: Plant the Seed

It generally takes me 3 to 6 months to recover from a campaign and this was no exception. Yes, I know that I swore never to run again for about the umpteenth time and this time I meant it. God knows I had other things to do.

Who knows? I might become a movie star.

Beginning around 1995, I was made aware that a film crew from Dallas had been to Central Kentucky to make a film about hemp activism. They had accompanied Woody Harrelson when he traveled to Eastern Kentucky to plant 4 hemp seeds to challenge the state law, which failed to legally distinguish between "hemp" and "marijuana." They stayed for several days, interviewing Woody, Craig Lee (of the Hemp Museum), Jake Graves (a banker and a 6th generation hemp grower during WW II) and his son Andy, who was now a criminal if he tried to continue his family's heritage. Then they interviewed me and we hit it off.

Over the next several years they also interviewed Willie Nelson, Merle Haggard, Julia "Butterfly" Hill and a host of other activists about the cannabis plant and their efforts to regain it as a cash crop. Each person has their own reasons and perspective and the overall effect is to introduce the audience to aspects of the issue that no one person can cover.

The name of the film is HEMPSTERS: Plant the Seed. It's 83 minutes long and should be required viewing by every voter in America. The laws against Cannabis would be changed overnight.

It has received swell reviews when it played, by invitation, at the Santa Monica Film Festival in February and the Dallas Film Festival in April of '03.

And on May 1st, 2003, we held the Kentucky Premier of the movie in Lexington at one of my very favorite places, the Kentucky Theater. Some 400 people attended, long hairs and crew cuts, young and older. They all seemed to enjoy themselves and found out information about this plant that they never imagined. They also found out that it was being shown in conjunction with the first annual Cannabis Liberation Rally, held at Phoenix Park, next to the Library in downtown Lexington on the following Saturday.

❖ *Cannabis Liberation Rallies*

On the first Saturday of every May, more than 300 cities around the world hold demonstrations to call for the decriminalization of cannabis. This was begun in New York in the '90s by my friend Dana Beal and he has managed to institute a Global network where it is being debated in at least 30 languages.

While I had been a guest speaker at these demonstrations in New York, Chicago, Atlanta and Paducah, I had intentionally stayed away from hosting one in Lexington. I wanted someone else to take the lead, to pick up the firebrand. I was happy to see some youngsters try to get it started in May of 2002, but it didn't take off, so I decided in 2003 to get involved.

On Saturday, May 3, 2003, we held a morning rally for Cannabis Liberation from 10:00 until Noon, in Phoenix Park in downtown Lexington. More than 70 people showed up and we all had our say on the matter. We then marched around the block where the new Courthouses now stand, went to the front of the City Office Building and returned down Main Street to the Park. No Police. No Nonsense. No Hassles. Pure Americana.

From here on out, I plan to hold a similar rally at Phoenix Park each and every First Saturday in May. I know it's Derby Day in Kentucky but it's also Cannabis Liberation Day worldwide and, by God, Lexington, Kentucky is going to participate. Of course it will be in the morning each year because, like millions of others, I want to see the Derby too.

❖ *Me & State Politics*

For the several months following my '02 Congressional race, I was determined not to run for another office. The Gubernatorial Primaries were being held in May of '03 and many folks wondered aloud if I had an interest in that race. My response was, absolutely not. I already had a friend in the race.

It was obvious to a great many people that Ernie Fletcher would be the Republican nominee for Governor, even though he had opposition in the May Primary. And it was only a little less obvious that the Attorney General, Ben Chandler, would defeat his challengers to secure the Democrat's nomination.

I was for Ben Chandler.

I certainly wasn't for him because he was a Democrat. No, I was for him despite his being a Democrat.

At this point in my life, I wouldn't piss on either Party if it was on fire. They are both mouthpieces for the special interests, to the great detriment of the people. However, I admire anyone who has actually held office and had any part of maintaining common principles in the face of offers to sell out in the name of the Party.

While he was Attorney General, Ben Chandler was presented with a dilemma. Nominated for the AG position by the Democrats in the same May 1995 Primary where Jerry and I had been defeated for Governor by Paul Patton, Ben went on to win the position in the Fall of '95. So he was Attorney General when Patton and two of his cronies were charged with violating the state's Campaign Financing laws. It was Ben's duty to initiate the investigation and pursue the charges if they proved to be true.

The pressure must have been intense. It is dicey business to prosecute a sitting Governor or his "bagmen", especially when they are of your own Party. I know for a fact that several of the biggest political operators in the state tried to get Ben to drop the prosecution but he did not. He pursued it with style, vigor and a tenacity that did justice to his Office and his personal and professional Integrity.

Simply put. Ben Chandler could not be bought.

For that reason alone, I wanted him to be Governor. For that reason alone, I had made up my mind early that I would stay out of the 2003 Governor's race and support Ben all the way. For that reason alone, the corrupt core of the Democrat Party mounted a challenge to him in the Primary. They ran the Speaker of the House, Jodie Richards, against him, along with a neophyte office- seeker, named Bruce Lunsford, who spent 8 million dollars of his own money trying to disparage Ben.

Lunsford's diatribes and incessant advertising against Ben were a mystery to me at first. Then I discovered that he had been in the health care business, the running of nursing homes, before relieving his company of 80 Million dollars, then leaving the scene. Just before the company went defunct some months later and put elderly nursing home folks into the street.

Ben had looked to prosecute him but Lunsford ducked it and now he was looking for revenge.

As it turned out, he was probably a "ringer" anyway. There was no hope in hell that he would win the nomination, but he was put into the race by someone, to bang on Ben with his own money, so they wouldn't have to. I believe that was why he dropped out of the Primary a week before the election and endorsed Richards for the job. I think he was buying his way out of an Indictment.

But it didn't work in the Primary. As expected, Ben and Ernie won their respective Party's nomination and began the political ads right away. The Republicans had enough money to set a wet mule on fire in a thunderstorm, (for you city folks, that's a hell of a lot of money) and they spent as much of it as they could. The Democrats had about half as much and were a little more judicious in spending it.

Ernie and the Republicans went negative right away, trying to color Ben with Paul Patton's sins. They had plenty of material to work with when it came to finding fault with Patton and the Democrat Party.

Even if the Democrat's 32 year stranglehold on the Capitol had not resulted in the institutional corruption, ignorance, theft, mismanagement and malfeasance that followed, Paul Patton's reign as Governor would succeed in sounding the death knell for the Democrat Party because he brought his own personal brand of arrogance and yahooism to what once-Governor Happy Chandler called "the best job in the world."

In addition to fleecing the state treasury to pay off his cronies and political contributors, it was revealed in the latter part of 2002 that Patton also used the Governor's Office itself to secure certain "personal" favors from a woman looking for reciprocal favors.

Tina Conner, a Western Kentucky "businesswoman" who owned a nursing home subject to state regulation, went public that she and the Governor had been having an affair and that he had interceded on her behalf with some state regulators. She and another unnamed party had even had a "threesome" in the Governor's Office. (I wonder if Bruce Lunsford was the third party, along with Paul and Tina, which constituted the threesome. Getting it on in the Governor's office. Maybe there's just something about screwing the elderly in nursing homes that makes you want to screw the Governor in his Office. Who knows with assholes like that?)

Now that Paul had dumped her, he was using the state against her by siccing those same regulators on her operation.

Damn. The fur and the printer's ink literally flew all over the state. Charges and counter-charges, lies, fibs and rumors emerged from everywhere. At first Patton categorically denied having an affair with the woman, and his wife Judy stood behind him. The he went on TV two days later and admitted that he had lied and begged for forgiveness. You've never seen so much snot and so many boogers expended by a politician in your life. He made Jimmy Swaggart and Jim and Tammy Faye Baker look like amateurs when it came to cryin' and confessin' sins.

Old Paul should have resigned his office, right then and there, and gotten himself a television ministry. Anybody who believed his performance that night would have been a very easy mark for sending him money.

Overnight, Paul Patton had taken the Office of Governor of Kentucky to an all-time new low. He was a cheat and a liar, but his debacle did serve to offer some hope. When various Party members and officials came forward in his defense, they proved beyond a doubt that they were a part of the problem themselves and should be removed. That they were all Democrats just made the Republican's effort to replace them all that much easier.

So the Democrats were on the ropes from the beginning and Ben Chandler had to bear the burden despite having fought tooth-and-nail against the corruption within his own Party. It remained to be seen whether honesty and principal had a place in Kentucky's politics. I reckon only a few of us hoped that it would.

❖ *Me and the Water Company*

Meanwhile, my focus was on a most important issue unfolding before the public, the local control of the Kentucky American Water Company.

This issue was huge during the Mayor's race of 2002 and her support of local control probably won Teresa the office. However, that certainly wasn't dispositive of the matter. There were still many steps to be taken before the city could take ownership of the utility, and the huge foreign corporation, which had purchased the company, was willing to do whatever it could to maintain ownership.

A company, known as the American Water Company had purchased the Kentucky Water Company in years past and was now known as the Kentucky American Water Company. In turn, in 2002, they sold themselves to RWE, a giant German conglomerate with unknown owners. When the Public Service Commission approved the sale, concerned citizens became alarmed and began organizing to support the city's acquisition of the company through the process known as eminent domain.

Eminent domain is a concept whereby a government may acquire private property for public use through a process known as condemnation. This is the method whereby we get the land to build public highways and expand airports, among other things. The 5th Amendment to the United States Constitution guarantees that the owner receive "just compensation" for the property and, if a price cannot be agreed upon between the owner and the government, a jury of citizens is convened to set the price.

A citizen's group called FLOW (For Local Ownership of Water) emerged, led by former Governor Ned Breathitt and several other notables including W.T.Young, a highly successful businessman and philanthropist.

These folks publicly encouraged the city to proceed with the acquisition of the company and volunteered to furnish $750,000 to defray the legal costs. They agreed that they would forego repayment if the city lost its fight to acquire the company. Only if the city was successful would they look to get repaid without interest.

RWE immediately began a campaign to disparage the city and everyone who stood in their way of adding this Water Company to their worldwide collection of dozens more. They committed hundreds of thousands of dollars to sway public opinion on the matter including the dissemination of lies and half-truths to obscure the facts of the matter such as the real cost of acquiring the company and how the city would pay for it.

They tried to implant the idea that it would be the taxpayer's dollars spent on the acquisition, which isn't true, (The water users would pay for it through their water bills, which would not be raised by the purchase) and that said taxpayer's dollars should be spent on other city business.

They worked hard to hijack the support of other, unrelated, groups such as the Fraternal Order of Police and the Firefighters by saying that the reason their pay was not sufficient was that the city was "wasting" the taxpayer's money in pursuit of the Water Company. Then they exploited the fringe element's of our society, who generally hate all things to do with government, by saying that our City government was incapable of owning the company and that same was sure to be mismanaged and politically exploited.

By the time they got rolling, RWE had also paid several local mouthpieces to advance their cause in front of the Lexington Fayette Urban County Council, including the infamous local corporate bagman Bill Lear. (The same guy who had rewritten the state laws to prohibit the return of hemp as a cash crop.)

At the Council meeting where the vote was to be taken on whether the City was to proceed with the condemnation, RWE had several parties speak to defeat the measure. The FOP tried to say that it would harm their ability to get a pay raise and that the city had no business in the water business.

Then Lear took the podium and, I swear, if you shut your eyes and listened to him, you would think you were listening to Al Capone threatening all those who would oppose his wishes. He threatened that RWE would cost the City so much money by fighting their effort that the city couldn't afford to pursue the matter. He said that RWE was going to construct as many obstacles as possible, and at as high a cost as possible, over as long a period as possible. Then he forecast that any of the Council members who dared opposed him and his client RWE would pay the highest political price in their bid for re-election. The only thing he left out was a baseball bat upside the head of a Council member.

I couldn't stand it any longer. When it came time for the public to speak, I was the first to respond to RWE's bullying tactics and I addressed it in terms that no one else had broached at that time.

"One of the first things I want to ask everyone here is Who owns RWE?" No one responded. I asked again and no one offered an answer.

"I understand that Osama Bin Laden owns it!" "And the crowd went wild."

"That's right," I continued amid the uproar. "Who here can tell me that he doesn't?" And no one answered. Even RWE didn't know what to say.

"Doesn't that tell you something," I asked the Council? "Even the company can't, or won't, answer that question."

"Then let me ask you this," I continued. " How many of you'all believe that Homeland Security is a joke?" They all looked at me askance. "You all understand the necessity of protecting our homeland, don't you?" They all nodded cautiously.

"Then how can it serve Homeland Security by placing the ownership of our basic public utilities onto the sea of international commerce, where any bloc of money can obtain ownership once it leaves our control?" Nobody answered but several Council members nodded.

"And I've certainly had enough of Mr. Lear's threats and bullying tactics. He reminds me of a fellow from down home who would piss down your leg while trying to convince you it's raining. He's totally untrustworthy and you should not fall victim to his tirade. I encourage you to vote for acquisition of this basic public utility for benefit of the city and its citizens." And they did by a vote of 9 to 6.

But the battle was/is far from over. Immediately thereafter, RWE began recruiting political wannabes to run against those Council members who voted for acquisition. The first elections to occur will be in May and November of 2004 and then we will see if their big bucks will carry the day against the interests of the people. I have pledged to kick the butt of this international corporate behemoth because there is no way they have the best interests of the people at heart. Their only goal is a larger corporate profit and that can only come at the expense of We the People.

And I am perfectly sure that the owners of RWE have never said the Pledge of Allegiance to the United States of America or to the Republic for which it stands. And they are not warm and fuzzy about us, or our children, or our grandchildren. They see the Constitution and the Bill of Rights as impediments to the implementation of their New World Order and their global economy. People will always come in second to their corporate bottom line. We would be fools to let them own our basic public utilities.

With these sentiments in mind, I wrote the following letter to the editor:

Dear Editor,

It has come to my attention that various persons are being recruited by the Water Company to run against incumbent counsel members who support the purchase of the utility by the city of Lexington.

Let me get right to the point. I personally and specifically question the common sense and the patriotism of anyone, and especially the politicians, who support the sale of our basic public utility to foreign entities where we lose all local control over who may own it from then on.

I have investigated the ownership of RWE and it is a mystery. Allegedly a group of German Mayors own about 35%. The identity of the owners of the remaining 65% is clouded in corporate legalese. They could be Saudi Arabia, North Korea or even a terrorist group. And if it is not now, it could be once we place the ownership of the company on the international sea of commerce.

If I was a terrorist with cash (Hussein had over One Billion in cash in one of his vaults) and had a long-term plan to destroy the United States, I would certainly have figured that ownership of their basic public utilities would prove to be a great advantage, especially ironic too, if the American water users were guaranteed to give me a 9% return on my money.

Is this too far-fetched? Am I being xenophobic? I think not.

We have been attacked on our own soil by committed, life-long terrorists. We are at war in Afghanistan and Iraq with daily attacks on our military and civilians. We have troops in 122 different countries and plenty of enemies everywhere.

Especially in this day and time, common sense dictates that we maintain local control of our source of water delivery, and reap its guaranteed return on our investment with which we can fund public safety and sanitation.

As W.T. Young once said of the deal, "It's a slam-dunk business decision." To which I might add, "and a patriotic one too."

So I guess it's clear where I stand on that issue. It might not be settled for several years but I live by a simple principle: America first and screw the international financiers who look to feed off of us.

❖ *Me and the Attorney General's Office*

As we moved up to and through the May Primaries of 2003, I had no intention of running for another office. I wanted Ben to win the Democrat's nomination and he did. But the results of another race caught my eye and apparently the interest of many other Kentuckians.

In the primary for Attorney General, both Parties had a tight three-way race which ended with the nominations in the hands of a couple of scalawags whose track record qualified them for jail time more than their Party's nomination.

The Dems chose their Majority Floor Leader in the House, a fellow named Greg Stumbo. This man was responsible for deciding which legislation would make it to the House floor for a vote, a very powerful position that he held for 19 years. As such, he was a recognized Party operative during the very most corrupt times in the Legislature.

His two opponents were Chris Gorman, who had been Attorney General from 1987 to 1991 and Ed Hatchett, who was finishing his second term as Auditor. Both of these men were certainly qualified, but they spent most of their time and money picking on each other, and Stumbo squeezed past them with 37% of the vote.

The Republicans also fielded three men, all of them political unknowns. As with the Democrats, it was expected that this race would be between two Party regulars. The odd man out was Jack Woods, who had distinguished himself by having been officially sanctioned by the authorities in the only two positions of responsibility he had ever held.

An attorney, Jack was charged and tried for arson sometime in the early '80s but found not guilty. After being elected District Court Judge in Southern Kentucky, Jack was found in violation of judicial ethics by the Judicial Retirement and Removal Committee and had his pay discontinued for 6 months. He went back to his family business of laying carpet.

No one expected jack from him but Mr. Wood had a plan. He teamed up with Dr. Paul Simon, the most active anti-abortionist in Kentucky, who, without any public fanfare, sent 40,000 letters to his mailing list, endorsing Jack. When the election results were tabulated, Jack was the upset winner with 37% of the vote.

The Republican Party was really upset. They immediately tried to distance themselves from their own nominee, excluding him from their Party functions and omitting his name from their list of candidates.

Hey, while I could empathize with that, having experienced the same treatment from the Democrats years ago, I couldn't sympathize with him. He had been a tyrant on the bench, treating those who appeared before him with contempt and ill-temper. I just don't like tyrants.

As a politico I was amused and, as a Kentuckian, I was dismayed at the choices in that race. Next to Governor, the Attorney General occupies the most powerful Office in the Commonwealth. Among other duties, they are responsible for representing the Commonwealth in criminal appeals from the Circuit Courts, consumer protection, representing ratepayers when utilities seek rate hikes, administering Kentucky's "no-call" list for tele-marketers and investigating and prosecuting public corruption.

Since I believed that both of these nominees represented what public corruption was all about, I feared that the election of either of them would block that office from exercising its duties. I especially believed that Paul Patton and the Democrats who had committed crimes during the last 8 years would get a free pass from their fellow Democrat Stumbo.

These were general personal considerations of mine and included the fact that neither of the nominees was the first of choice of more than 60% of their own Party. But they weren't enough to compel me to run for the office. That would take the input of other opinions.

And those opinions were not long in coming.

Within two weeks after the Primary, and within two days of each other, I received calls from officials in both Parties, who asked to remain anonymous, and who encouraged me to consider a run for Attorney General as an Independent.

Shortly after that, I was approached by an elected Democrat and later, a Republican officeholder, who begged me to run. I was wavering. Then, when I was telling a friend about it, he told me that 500 people could tell me not to run but if three folks said, "Okay", I would consider it a Draft. That guy knows me really well. I succumbed to the Draft.

I don't know if too many people were surprised by my announcement. I think a lot of them were happy to hear it.

I immediately set about to acquire the 5,000 signatures necessary to put my name on the ballot. Beginning on July 1st, my friends and I averaged over 240 signatures a day for the next 31 days. 7,500 in all. The public response was overwhelming. Folks would cross the street and wait for the chance to sign the Petition. I was mighty pleased and certainly humbled.

As in past races, I learned from the people what the real issues were in the race. Disgust at the "Corruption" was rampant and a majority seemed to advance the views that it was time to "Clean House" and "Throw the Rascals Out!"

Hey, that was a view I had advanced for more than a few years and, now, it was the mantra of the Republican Party and a sizable slice of the Democrats. The only problem I had with it was that Ben would lose if that became a reality.

Personally I thought Ben was the only real honest one up there but now I couldn't endorse him because I thought it would be unseemly for an Independent candidate for Attorney General to have a party favorite for Governor. I would have to prosecute either one of them if they stepped out of line.

Qualifying in August for a November 4th election left me to pull a ninety-day wonder. It would take everything I didn't have; money and a statewide organization. What I did have was commitment, energy and a small group of dedicated people willing to make a personal statement by their efforts. Thanks David and Sue, Ralph, Fred and Norman.

That group thankfully contained folks who knew computers and their role in campaigning. It was our most effective tool for taking our message beyond Central Kentucky.

Utilizing various methods, we compiled about 300,000 email addresses in Kentucky and sent them each three messages throughout the race. We got a total of twenty complaints about this "spam" and I tried to be sympathetic. But there are very few affordable opportunities for a political Independent to spread the word widely and the Internet is one of them. I predict that its use as a political channel will mushroom wildly, especially given its success in Howard Dean's campaign for the Democrats' nomination for President.

As for me, it was my best shot at establishing a statewide presence, which it did, but it was confined to computer owners. It was no match for the media exposure purchased by the Parties' nominees and the compulsion for lifelong Party members to pull the straight Party ticket, no matter who they might elect.

The straight Party button/lever on the voting machine is pure evil. It's what keeps Kentucky in chronic straits because it removes the necessity for the individual voter to have to think about whom they are electing. They don't have to examine the individual candidates or their credentials. They don't have to consider the issues confronting the office. They only have to have their egos stroked at being a die-hard Party stalwart who will support the straight ticket. And they fall for it every time.

(I believe that there was legislation introduced in the 2004 session to remove the straight Party button from the ballot, but it didn't get far. Neither did much else in that session.)

I hit the road as often as I could and tried to concentrate on the major media markets. Open-mike radio talk shows, where the host or hostess allows the expression of all viewpoints, represent the best opportunities to spread a candidate's message, along with community access programs on local cable systems.

These must be a particularly American phenomenon, these airways available to the average person to express their opinions. Think about it. In what other country can a farmer, or plumber, or shoeshine boy or homeless person or anyone else, get a minute or two to express their opinion on a matter to tens of thousands of listeners at a time. Maybe hundreds of thousands.

It's easy for a lot of us to take this avenue of expression and free speech for granted but we can't afford that. Like every other freedom, we must exercise it to give it life. That's another reason why campaigns such as mine are so important. They exist because of our Constitutional guarantees, including freedom of expression.

You can bet that there are a lot of people who would like to see me shut up, voluntarily or otherwise. The enemies of the Constitution and the American way of life. The pharmaceutical and petrochemical companies. The transnational, fascist corporations. The synthetic monopolists and all those who put corporate profits before human life. They would love to control these airways even more than they do already. And they are working on it, trying to centralize the ownership of the media in the hands of fewer people all the time. As that happens, the avenues of expression will diminish accordingly.

When I wasn't traveling, I was standing on street corners. Again. Holding a big yellow sign. Again. Waving at folks who waved and honked at me. Again. It's like a drive-through mental handshake. I love it.

Meanwhile, the opportunities for face-to-face debates with my opponents were few and far between. Stumbo believed his lead was large enough that he could afford to ignore me, while Wood was counting on the Republican Party's momentum to carry him into office. I appeared at several events billed as a debate when neither of the others showed up. I thought that was cowardly, and certainly rude to the event organizers. That attitude lasted until the annual Lexington Community College Poll came out and showed we three candidates in a virtual tie for the lead. This poll was mostly conducted in the 16 counties of the 6th Congressional District and it blew Stumbo and his supporters away.

Stumbo and his union-based entourage showed up at the next three events. In two of those, his lead "hit man" tried to shout me down by calling me marijuana man and such, but when I acknowledged it, I got a round of applause and that cut short their planned attack. They shut up.

❖ *I declare Marijuana Legal in Kentucky*

My affiliation with the marijuana issue was the subject of discussion at two other forums; the KET debate, televised state-wide, and a debate held at the University of Louisville's Law School, with an audience of Judges, Law Professors and Students. In both cases, the first question asked me by a reporter was the same.

"Mr. Galbraith, do you smoke marijuana?"

"Yes I do," I responded without hesitation.

"Then Sir," they continued, "how can you expect to be the top law enforcement official in the state when you break the law every day."

"Well," I replied, "that's because it is not against the law to smoke marijuana in the state of Kentucky."

By their expressions you would have thought I had lapsed into tongues and madness. They assumed the look of total incomprehension and didn't know what to say next.

"Look", I began my explanation with an academic tone, "let me lead you through this."

"In 1909, the Kentucky Legislature passed a law which prohibited the possession of all alcohol in the Commonwealth. This was challenged, of course.

And in a 1909 case, Commonwealth v. Campbell, the Kentucky Supreme Court held that an ordinance, prohibiting even for private use, the possession of intoxicating liquor, was unconstitutional state action because it intruded upon 'inalienable rights possessed by the citizens.'

In that case, the Court interpreted a right to privacy from the Kentucky Bill of Rights and enumerated a standard for evaluation which remains intact today: '... it is not within the competency of a free government to invade the sanctity of the absolute rights of the citizen any further than the direct protection of society requires...' (emphasis mine) ***and further, 'It is not within the competency of government to invade the***

privacy of a citizen's life and to regulate his conduct in matters in which he alone is concerned or to prohibit him any liberty the exercise of which will not directly injure society.' Id. (emphasis mine)

Later cases cite this standard, as in *Commonwealth v. Smith*, (1915). 'The power of the state to regulate the conduct of a private individual is confined to those cases where his conduct injuriously affects others.' Finally, Smith holds that 'the police power may be called into play [only] when it is reasonably necessary to protect the public health, or public morals, or public safety.'

They did not say that we have a Constitutional right to possess alcohol. They said we have a Constitutional right to privacy in our homes, under which fits the possession of an extremely poisonous substance called alcohol.

Now this is the law in Kentucky today. In fact, it is these rulings which keep the Kentucky State Police from kicking down the doors of people possessing alcohol in Kentucky's 77 'dry' counties right now and hauling their butts off to jail.

Now, marijuana is a demonstrably less harmful substance than alcohol and presents far less of threat to the public's welfare. So it also fits into a person's right to privacy in their home. It's beyond the police power of the state as long as I don't sell it and it's for my own personal use.

Since our rights under the Constitution apply equally to us all, then I demand the same rights to privacy in my home as those people who possess alcohol in dry counties. They are not breaking the law and neither am I. Any questions?"

And there were none.

But apparently I didn't get to explain myself in enough venues and I didn't get the support I had hoped for. Greg Stumbo won Attorney General with 47.7% of the vote. Jack Wood got 41.8% and I got 10.5% or 109,085 votes. That's a hell of a lot of votes considering that I only went to 12 of Kentucky's 120 counties and spent less than $20,000. God Bless you one and all.

Stumbo however, was livid. He obviously thought he could hang me over the marijuana issue, and here I was explaining Constitutional law to him which, I still don't think he comprehends. I guess I'll find out. He said that when he became Attorney General that he would show me how wrong I was about the law.

Well, Greg. You won Attorney General. And I'm still waiting.

❖ *Me & Some Early Reflections*

So here I sit. 57 years old. Practicing Law in Lexington, Kentucky. 57. Hell. That ain't old. The way I see it, I'm at that age where the girl, her mother and her grandmother all look good to me.

But what to do with myself?

Obviously I have to practice law. I'm broke and have to earn a living. Losing races for statewide offices doesn't pay worth a damn.

(By way of note, I practice three kinds of law. Criminal defense, serious injury accidents and Lottery Winners.)

I am absolutely going to continue my crusade to educate people about God's most wonderful medicine. I am absolutely going to call out the tyrants and ghouls who profiteer from keeping this medicine away from the people who need it.

What's the Last Free Man in America going to do with himself?

As I see it, I've accomplished three of the four resolutions I made to myself, standing in the middle of that road in 1971.

I did go to college. (check)

I did become an attorney. (check)

I did run for Governor. (oops) (oops) and (oops)

I did change the laws on marijuana in Kentucky. Well, let's be fair here. The laws have been the same since 1909 and 1915. All I did was subject them to an analysis benefiting the people. (Oliver Wendell Holmes once said, "Dragons are far more fierce in the darks of their caves then when they are dragged out and examined in the sunlight.")

In the sunlight of Constitutional law, we find a right to privacy in our homes which extends beyond the power to state to regulate us, as long as we are not harming the health, safety, welfare of the public.

Most people didn't know that until I came along. Even now, most of them don't understand it. They don't understand that they are free if only they insist on it. And live like it.

They are like the slaves who were set free and didn't know what to do with it. Everyone is so conditioned to accept whatever the officials tell them. They can't handle thinking on their own.

So let me tell you here and now. You are free to smoke cannabis in your home. It is not against the law!

You don't need a medical excuse to have this right. It is yours, by Law!

Now I want you to tell everyone you know about this. Gatewood Galbraith says Cannabis is legal. I especially want you to tell all of your friends and family who are sick, in chronic pain or dying, what I just said.

Then tell them I promise that cannabis is the most wonderful medicine on earth. And that thousands of Doctors agree with me.

Then I want you to tell your state Representatives and Senators that you and Gatewood think they have their heads up their asses for keeping this medicine out of the hands of the people who need it. Don't let them snicker or shrug their shoulders and walk away. They are good at that but they aren't very good at helping us solve our problems.

Tell them that you have a good idea for solving the State's Budget crisis and the Health Care crisis. Medical cannabis could save Kentucky as much as $500 Million Dollars a year in healthcare and related cost. It would cut the number of emergency runs to the hospitals and increase the number of folks who choose to die at home instead of in high priced hospital settings.

It has been shown to stop a full-blown asthma attack immediately. It will shrink the size of certain cancer growths. It will dissipate anxieties, help you sleep and stop the pain. USE IT PEOPLE

It would cut the cost of medications consumed by patients by at least 25% and avoid those emergencies caused by overuse or misuse of synthetic substances. And you can grow it in your own garden or flower box.

But remember now. The Government does have the right to prosecute you if you are dealing the herb. They have the right to regulate commerce but not possession for personal use in the home.

I do not believe that a Judge in Kentucky will sign a search warrant for a home based on an allegation that someone in that home smokes marijuana or possesses a small amount for personal use.

Even if the police are in your home for another reason, and find marijuana, I do not believe they have the right to confiscate it unless they have reason to believe you are trafficking in it. Unless they can prove trafficking, I believe they must return the seized cannabis to you. Just like alcohol in "dry" counties.

Ain't the Constitutional form of government Grand!!?

Meanwhile, I've got to figure out what I'm going to do with myself.

I've got between 10 and 20 years left to get something done for the People. I don't think I'm going to last much longer than that.

And I've got to consider what I want my ending to be.

Do I want to wait around until I finally suffocate from my condition of emphysema, hooked to an oxygen tank and gasping for air after a simple walk?

What are my options?

As I borrowed from Jean Paul Sartre earlier, man's ability to consider suicide, intellectually, is what sets him apart from the rest of the animals. But I think that man's real choice goes beyond that. The true choice is, "Should I make the world a better place by taking some really worthless son-of-a-bitch with me when I go?"

And does this kind of figuring run counter to the type of Karma that my guardian angels are encouraging me to manifest?

There's where the real figuring comes in.

But I know it's too early to be figuring that. I've got some good years left in me and I need to educate a lot more people about their freedom. Their freedom is my freedom. And my children's freedom. And their children's freedom.

And I can't win their freedom for them tomorrow. But I can win their freedom for them today. And that is exactly what I intend to do with my actions and words.

The Last Free Man in America will stand as a role model for personal freedom as long as he can draw his breath. And he challenges you to be more free than him. Live it People! Dance when you get the Chance!

And By The Way.

For all you Petrochemical-Pharmaceutical-Military-Industrial-Transnational-Corporate-Fascist-Elite-Bastards, I've Got Your Karma Right Here.

❖ Snitch and the Columns on Addiction

DRUG ADDICTION

I guess you thought I was through preachin' but there's one last thing I think I should tell you about because it might be of great use to many of you.

Beginning in March of 2005, I was asked to become a columnist for a weekly newspaper called Snitch. This was a sporty little publication that covered the local courts and reported on who got charged with what and how the the matter was resolved.

The paper became defunct at the end of 2005 but during that year I wrote several columns concerning drug addiction which generated a great deal of feedback. I have condensed them here in hopes of helping those millions of Americans who need help with a drug problem.

I have written many times about my experiences with drugs and the lessons I learned from those experiences. Marijuana, LSD, mescaline and mushrooms constituted my spectrum of choice and I purposefully avoided the powders, pills, serums and needles because I could see, even in the early 70s, that they were addictive and self-destructive. When a drug led people to steal, or sell themselves, to feed its habitual use, then even I was sufficiently forewarned to avoid experimenting with it.

That pretty much meant I didn't do "uppers", "downers", pain pills, coke or opiates, so I didn't fashion a classical physical "addiction" to any of the synthetic products patented by our Pharmaceutical "friends." (I did manage to prove my personal addictive propensities by hooking up with tobacco, but that's another story).

Lots of other people were not so lucky. Since the 70s, rates of addiction to legally-produced pharmaceutical products have skyrocketed, fed by incessant advertising on TV, a generation of doctors who over-prescribe these addictive pellets at the drop of some pharmaceutical payola, and the public's blindly accepted medical model that a pill will cure everything.

In my profession, I deal with many individual human beings who bear the consequences of that corporate, profit-driven, wholesale distribution of dangerous and highly addictive drugs.. I deal with the "addicts", people who have entered the criminal justice system, as defendants, because they have become physically dependent on these patented medicines and can no longer procure them from "legitimate" sources, their doctors. The M.D.s have given them enough to develop a habit, then refused to refill the prescription, cutting the patient off from the original source. Since many of these physical addictions can take hold in less than 30 days, these patients are put into a very sticky situation, especially if they are faced with a chronic-pain injury that they must learn to deal with.

At first, lots of these folks try to tough it out but, too often, their dependence on, and craving for, the substance is so overwhelming that they will resort to stealing, or giving themselves sexually to the dealer, to feed an oxycontin habit or forging a prescription for Lortab and try to get it past the pharmacist. These are a majority of the unfortunate souls you see in the Court system charged with drug offenses. The "users", and small time dealers who are only trying to make enough to feed their own habit. The higher ups rarely get brought to justice and most of them remain in business because they don't consume the product they are dispersing so freely.

And it is my distinct impression that these people, the user defendants, are continuing to increase in number, filling our Court dockets, creating a Black Market economy that has made criminals rich and corrupting our medical-delivery system by erecting barriers to effective pain management for legitimate patients. Among other woes.

For the individual user, this is a living hell. Lots of them were injured on the job, or in an automobile wreck, and their lives were disrupted enough as it was. They may have lost their job, and job identity, because of their disability, which affected their self-respect They may have limited mobility and they most certainly have chronic pain. And we're not talking about a toothache or a severely sprained ankle which, while it hurts like hell, will eventually get treated and go away. We are talking about pain 24/7, where it ain't going away and there is no position that you can put your body in that will bring relief.

Other addictions to the pills are started much more insidiously. 30 to 60 Lortabs for a housewife's painful periods. 30 days hydrocodone for a broken bone. For some people, it simply doesn't take much exposure to addictive substances to establish not only the physical craving for its continued use, but also a willingness to deal with an "illegitimate" source to continue its uninterrupted availability to feed their habit. No matter what the cost in self-denial, elaborate deception, shattered families, bankruptcy, loss of credibility and the danger of dealing with a career criminal element that is the backbone of a Black Market.

Many of these people go through this downward spiral because they are driven by an actual physical craving for the drug they have been using. What has happened is that a molecule(s) of that drug has attached itself to certain receptor sites in the brain and its presence there produces the desire to continue its use. When that demand is not fed, the addict's body reacts by going into withdrawal, the results of which include increasing aches and pain, nausea and flu-like symptoms, paranoia and depression. When this begins to occur, the user will go to any lengths to satisfy their body's demand for the drug.

Many people simply try to stop taking the drug. They tell themselves "never again" and don't renew their prescription. Then they wake up at 4 in the morning with aches and pains and an overwhelming anxiety over lack of the drug. They are driven to find it either through another doctor or a "friend" who might keep some on hand for their "friends." They are "hooked"

Young, old, rich, poor, housewives, students, doctors, cops and professionals of all sorts. These drugs will nail anyone who takes them long enough. And nobody really wants to stay on them. They all want to get the monkey off their back.

But it is very rare for an individual to complete a successful withdrawal on willpower alone. I have friends who have done it but they tell me that today, 25 years later, they still have a craving for the substance. Their receptor sites still have a memory of the desire.

The necessity of assistance is recognized by those corporations who have created the Charter Ridges of the world, "drug-treatment" centers that specialize in treating patients referred to them by families and sometimes the Court system for the purpose of helping them through withdrawal. They may offer 30, 60 or 90 day "in-patient" treatment programs and provide a hospital-like setting with counseling but they can't erase the craving itself and it is that physical drive which compels so many folks to return to the habit once the insurance runs out and they are put back on the street. That is why there are so many repeat offenders in "Drug Court."

But it is apparent that laws will not solve the problem. That is because the nature of addiction is complex and varied, depending on the substance or activity to which one is addicted. The classical addiction is thought of as substance-based, meaning a person craves the ingestion or introduction of a substance into the body which brings it relief from the craving. However, the definition of addiction has been changed dramatically in modern times, given the present understanding of addiction and how it works.

It is now understood that the drugs of addiction that are introduced into the body do not, within themselves, contain the "high." What they do have is the power to stimulate the body to flood its central nervous with its own "peptides", i.e. naturally produced chemicals which bring pleasure and pain relief. That is generally a pretty graphic physical experience for drug users but more subtle releases of lesser amounts of pleasure chemicals that become habitual may be triggered by such diverse activities as gambling, sex and athletic exertion. (A famous long distance runner once said that he hurt all the time because he had "a twenty mile a day habit and a ten mile a day body.")

The brain contains 6 sets of receptor sites which are shaped to allow the attachment of certain molecules of certain substances. 4 of these receptor sites each attract opiates, cocaine, methamphetamine, alcohol and nicotine. When any of these drugs are consumed, their molecule activates that receptor site to release the body's own pleasure hormones into the central nervous system thereby bringing the "rush" to the user. Notice that the substance itself does not bring the feeling of pleasure, it simply "mines" the body's own chemical reservoir of pleasurable substances such as serotonin, dopamine and other endorphins.

As the use of an addictive substance becomes more frequent, the body finds it harder to replenish this reservoir's supply to a full level between the sessions of drug use and therefore it takes increasing amounts of the ingested drug to "mine" enough hormones to achieve the expected "high".

Essentially, the body seems to lose its ability to release these "pleasure chemicals" in natural amounts and activated by natural means such as simple emotions or activities. Their release seems to become dependent on the sponsoring drug and therefore the addict's body craves that drug. It is unnatural and painful for the body to cease its natural access to these necessary chemicals and the addict must seek relief. But it's a downhill slide all the way.

(Incidentally, recent bio-thermal imaging of the brain shows that people who believe that are being furnished with their drug of addiction can activate a release of their endorphins even though they have been fed a placebo, i.e. a non-drug. I guess that proves that very few people can consciously heal themselves and that we all believe that we need the help of something else besides our own natural resources). I reckon that describes the nature and character of the addictive personality.

When people seek treatment for addiction and face withdrawal from the addictive substance, it takes a while for the reservoir to replenish itself. A rule of thumb is generally one month for every year of addiction. If you've been addicted for 6 years, it will take about 6 months for your body to respond naturally with pleasure hormones to natural activities.

However, the body will always have a memory of the drug even with years of abstinence. That pesky little molecule is still on that receptor site to remind the user for the rest of their life. That craving may never go away.

It seems pretty damn bleak doesn't it. Especially if you are one of the folks caught up in this merciless, never-ending cycle of trying to satisfy a habit.

But there may, indeed, be an answer to the cycle. A natural substance contained within the root bark scrapings of a shrub grown in Africa named Tabernanthe Iboga, called Ibogaine, has the unique ability to dissuade the body from going through many of the symptoms of withdrawal and at the same time, cleansing the brain's receptor cells of the drug's molecules, thereby removing the effect of craving the drug. And, miraculously, the body has no memory of ever craving the drug so there is no physical compulsion of any sort to return to its use.

In essence,a one-time treatment with this substance will "cleanse" the receptor cell of the addicting molecule and relieve the immediate craving and the body's memory of that craving. It also immediately replenishes the body's reservoir of its pleasure hormones so that they may be accessed by natural processes, which eliminates the symptoms of withdrawal and may avoid the necessity of tapering a user off a long term habit.

This does not rule out relapses based on psychological disturbances and lifestyle choices. Lots of folks have other problems which are masked by their addictions. Their ability to stay clean from drugs might depend on how they get a handle on those troubles. (BTW, in the movie Ray, when Ray Charles is withdrawing from heroin and the doctor says, "We have something to help you with the withdrawal," he is speaking of Ibogaine).

The natives use it as a sacrament and they consume enough of it to hallucinate, which may or may not be the experience of those using it to interrupt addiction. I do know this. I have seen a one-time treatment, lasting 24 hours, completely remove the cravings of a 3 year oxycontin habit. Other reports from trusted sources report great success in treating heroin, crack, cocaine and opium addictions. The hardest habit to interrupt is a methadone habit. It generally takes two treatments. Many treatments are priced to fit the ability to pay. They go for as little as $1000.

Ibogaine is illegal in the U.S., Belgium and Switzerland. It may be found in Holland, Britain, Canada and Mexico if you are lucky. Learn lots more on the internet at ibeginagain.com or simply searching Iboga. You may also call Cures not Wars at (212) 677-7180 or a Canadian number (416) 603-4737.

I hope you heed these warnings never to develop a habit to this stuff. If you already have one, I hope this information is beneficial to you. Good Luck!

❖ Snitch and the Sparrow Column

It is part and partial of the human condition that we often find we have painted ourselves into unimaginable corners of unintended consequences. Looking up at the mess we have created we wonder, "What in the world was I thinking?"

Of the folks who find themselves in trouble and come to me for help, most of them generally know that it is trouble of their own making. They took advantage of someone or tried to. They stole something or bought or sold something they shouldn't have. And when these guys or gals get arrested for it, most of them know the routine and how to respond to questions from the police. "I want my attorney."

But even the experienced arrestees often talk too damn much and a significant part of my practice is spent trying to overcome the damage done by statements made by my client to everyone from the police to "friends" and bystanders.

And those who are brought into the "system" for the first time all seem to want to explain or justify their actions to anyone who will listen, including unsympathetic police officers who are looking for any statement, erroneous or otherwise, to use against them.

So, for many years I have tried to come up with core advice on how to respond to being arrested that would fit any scenario and I have gotten it down to three things to remember. The first is, Do not resist! They outnumber you so don't give them a reason to rough you up.

The second thing to remember is to ask for your attorney immediately.

The third bit of advice comes in the form of a parable. This is the best way to educate folks so I hope you will bear with me until the end. And I hope it imprints indelibly upon your consciousness.

There was a little Kentucky sparrow who decided to spend his summer in Canada. He went up and had a heck of a good time for several months. Then, one day, he noticed that the morning air had a little chill to it and he thought of going home, but he decided to stay a little longer.

Which he did.

About a month later, the morning air was just plain cold and he decided to head back to Kentucky. As he crossed the Canadian border, he ran head first into an ice storm and it was brutal right from the start. High winds, cold rain, sleet and snow. The little bird fought valiantly with all his might.

Ice formed on his wings and obstructed his breathing but still he flew on. He simply refused to give up. But even he was just a little bird and he couldn't overcome such a ferocious act of God.

His breathing got more labored and his flight more erratic. He tried and he tried but finally he could go on no longer and he plummeted to the ground. KERPLOP! Right into the middle of a Kentucky cow pasture where he lay exhausted and near-frozen.

The sound of his fall was considerable and it attracted the attention of a big, yellow cat in a nearby barn who looked up, saw the ice-covered sparrow and decided it was too cold to bother with. He went back to sunning himself.

Then Fate itself walked in. And as Fate would have it, as the little bird lay there, up walked a big cow who delivered a big, hot, green pile of s_ _t which covered the sparrow completely. And it was stinky and it was nasty but it was also warm and soon it began to revive our heroic feathered friend.

His wings de-iced and his heart began to resume a normal beat. He was alive. He had made it. He couldn't hardly believe it. He literally swam to the top of the cow pie which covered him, broke through the surface with his head and lifted his voice to the sky. Chirp! Chirp! Chirp! It was the sound of life!

And the big cat over in the barn heard it too and he sauntered over to the excited bird and SLURP!, he ate him right up!

Now there are three morals to this story which I want you never to forget. You will experience them all before your life is through.

The first moral is that it is not always bad to get s_ _t on.

The second moral is that it is not always your enemies who s_ _t on you.

The third moral is: When you find yourself up to your neck in a pile of s_ _ t, Keep Your Mouth S_ _T!

❖ *So You Want to do Something About it, Eh?*

Are you as tired of it as I am? Got any good ideas about changing things around? You can share them with me at gatewood@gatewood.com. You can also visit me on my web site at www.//gatewood.com.

You can order more books by emailing me or writing me at P.O. Box 1438, Lexington, Ky. 40588. $29.95 for the hardcover or $15.95 for the paperback plus $3.50 shipping and handling. I'll pay the sales tax.

Finally, if you are a Lottery winner and want to put some of that money to good use, get in touch. I might not be through with politics yet.

Handguns are a Woman's Best Friend. They are the Great Equalizer with one overwhelming Asset. They Keep the Big Guy off the Little Guy.

If Cavegirls Had Handguns!!!!

"Lay Off Me You Big Neanderthal Before I Make You Extinct Faster Than You Can Spell Evolution!"

Gatewood 1/19/03

❖ Acknowledgements

There are many people to whom I owe much and it is impossible to name them all, especially those who have been so generous anonymously. But I couldn't tell my story without thanking Gene and Susan, Bobby and Harriett, Paul Cornwell, and all of the lieutenants, partners, right-hand men and women, clerks, volunteers and true believers out there who make it all happen while the folks I speak of in this book tend to get the attention. You are not forgotten. You are what makes the stir actually happen around us swizzle sticks. Without you, we would just be one voice.

Finally, I wish to thank my family, all of whom have stood by me through everything, and two other heroes whose spirit I try to emulate every day. Lech Walesa and the Chinese gentleman who stopped the tank in Tienaman Square…